TRIAL
— by —
ICE

W9-AYJ-510

BY RICHARD PARRY

The Winter Wolf

The Wolf's Pack

The Wolf's Cub

That Fateful Lightning: A Novel of Ulysses S. Grant

TRIAL
— *by* —
ICE

*The True Story of Murder
and Survival on the
1871 Polaris Expedition*

RICHARD
PARRY

BALLANTINE BOOKS • NEW YORK

A Ballantine Book
Published by The Ballantine Publishing Group
Copyright © 2001 by Richard Parry

All rights reserved under International
and Pan-American Copyright Conventions. Published
in the United States by The Ballantine Publishing Group, a division
of Random House, Inc., New York, and simultaneously in
Canada by Random House of Canada Limited, Toronto.

Ballantine is a registered trademark and the Ballantine colophon is a trademark of
Random House, Inc.

www.ballantinebooks.com

LIBRARY OF CONGRESS CONTROL NUMBER: 2001119473

ISBN: 0-345-43926-0

Manufactured in the United States of America

Cover design by David Stevenson
Cover engraving from *The Arctic World*, 1877, T. Nelson and Sons.

First Edition: March 2001
First Trade Paperback Edition: February 2002

10 9 8 7 6 5 4 3 2 1

To my wife, Kathie,
Just keep reminding me that
over the next hill lies a new adventure.

And to my sons, David and Matthew,
For making me proud of them . . .

CONTENTS

Acknowledgments   ix
Author's Note   xi
Corrected Muster Roll of the *Polaris* Expedition   xiii
Introduction: Tragedy   1
 1. A Grand Beginning   6
 2. A Hearty Crew   28
 3. Flags and Fanfare   44
 4. First Ice   63
 5. Nipped   79
 6. Death   96
 7. Disorder   120
 8. Calamity   153
 9. Retreat   170
10. A Dreadful Night   186
11. Marooned   204
12. Adrift   213
13. On the Beach   230
14. Slow Starvation   246
15. The Inquest   262
16. The Whitewash   282
17. 1968   296
Aftermath   306
Select Bibliography   311
Index   312

ACKNOWLEDGMENTS

Unlike the ill-fated vessel *Polaris*, this manuscript had many loyal hands, which skillfully guided it from inception to its final state. I feel fortunate in having had two editors direct my efforts. I would like to thank Gary Brozek for his insightful comments during the early stages of the manuscript. I am especially grateful to Tracy Brown and his assistant, Abby Durden, for grasping the reins in midstream and carefully guiding this project to solid ground. Their attention to detail and commitment to excellence are reflected throughout the finished product.

David Stevenson's artistic rendering of the book's jacket unerringly depicts the danger and uncertainty that must have terrorized the ship's crew. Jie Yang as production manager and Nancy Delia as production editor deserve special recognition for transforming the manuscript into print.

As always, my thanks to my agent, David Hale Smith of DHS Literary, Inc., for his unwavering faith and support.

I would also like to thank Robin Benway, Marie Coolman, and Kim Hovey of the Ballantine Publishing Group for their help in publicizing my work. Last but not least, a special thanks to Joanne Miller, my Arizona publicist, for beating the desert on my behalf.

AUTHOR'S NOTE

Truth is stranger than fiction. Nowhere is that statement more true than in the facts surrounding the first American expedition to the North Pole in 1871. No fiction writer could invent a more convoluted plot. No one would believe what transpired aboard the *Polaris*. Yet what follows is true.

The events that led to the death of the expedition's leader, Charles Francis Hall, the disaster that left half the crew adrift on an ice floe in the dead of the Arctic winter, the folly that eventually sank the *Polaris* might read like a fantastic murder mystery or a Greek tragedy; nonetheless, what transpired is well documented. The plot contains all the elements of an epic novel: a glorious purpose; a journey led by a noble and dedicated man; a mission destroyed by treachery and the darker sides of human nature; a battle of man against the heartless elements, where unimaginable conditions degrade the best ideals humanity has to offer until those trapped sank to the level of considering cannibalism; embarrassed people in positions of power moving hastily to protect their own interests at the expense of the truth.

Even the dialogue is true, taken from the men's testimony at the inquiries following their return to the United States, their written journals and diaries, and their published accounts of the ordeal they endured. What these men had to say reveals the exciting truth of an expedition gone fatally wrong. Throughout the series of mistakes and misdeeds that plagued the *Polaris*, one fascinating truth emerges: miraculously, not all the men were lost. Despite the volume of material available that recorded these exploits, several puzzling questions remain. How could these men have such widely divergent perceptions of the events that took place? Who or what was ultimately responsible for Charles Francis Hall's death? And

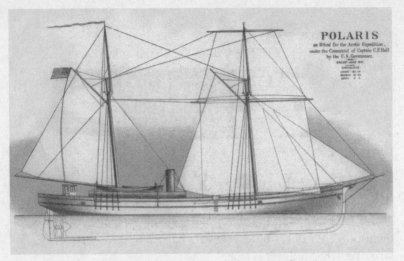

Polaris *as fitted for the Arctic expedition (Culver Pictures)*

perhaps most troubling of all, how much did the extremity of the conditions they endured and the imperfections in their troubled souls contribute to their collective and individual failure?

The select bibliography in the back of this book lists only the books from which direct quotations were used. An effort was made to use material published close to the time of the disaster so as to avoid the subtle variations in meaning that result over the passage of time. The list is by no means a complete record of all the resources consulted. In regard to the scientific, nautical, medical, and polar explanations, I drew upon my personal reading, my experience sailing in the Arctic, thirty years of medical practice, and the twenty years I lived in Alaska.

The astute reader will note the variation in spelling of places and persons in this work. This is due to the different spellings used in the historical references of the time. Within the body of the text all effort has been made to use the modern spelling, such as Disko for Disco, but the quotations retain the exact spelling used in those works.

CORRECTED MUSTER ROLL
OF THE *POLARIS* EXPEDITION

Corrected muster roll of the *Polaris* expedition as made out by Captain Hall on July 2, 1871, and forwarded by him to the secretary of the navy. (Nationalities added by the author.)

C. F. Hall . . . . Commander
Sidney O. Buddington . . Sailing and Ice Master
George Tyson . . . . Assistant Navigator
H. C. Chester . . . . First Mate
William Morton . . . . . . Second Mate
Emil Schuman . . . . Chief Engineer (German)
Alvin A. Odell . . . . Assistant Engineer
Walter F. Campbell . . . . Fireman
John W. Booth . . . . Fireman
John Herron . . . . Steward (former British citizen)
William Jackson . . . . . . Cook
Nathan J. Coffin . . . . . . Carpenter

SEAMEN

Herman Sieman (German)   Joseph B. Mauch (German)
Frederick Anthing (Russian/German) G. W. Lindquist (Swedish)
J.W.C. Kruger (German)   Peter Johnson (Danish)
Henry Hobby   Frederick Jamka (German)
William Lindermann (German)   Noah Hayes

SCIENTIFIC CORPS

Emil Bessel . . . . Surgeon and Chief of Scientific Corps (German)
R.W.D. Bryan . . . . Astronomer and Chaplain
Frederick Meyer . . . . . . Meteorologist (German)

TRAGEDY

I believe that no man can retain the use of his faculties during one long night to such a degree as to be morally responsible. . . .
—NOAH HAYES, SEAMAN, POLARIS EXPEDITION, 1871

November 10, 1871. The black sky leaned heavily upon the land. So dark was the air that the earth glowed brightly by contrast—a pale, ethereal light radiated from the ground itself. Faint blue and violet shapes of snow-covered earth blended with wildly strewn blocks of ice littered the landscape. Without distinction solid land and frozen water, sky and earth floated together into one shimmering, surreal dream.

But this was no dream. This was the Arctic winter, and a nightmare for the weary procession that wended its way over the ice. Led by a single figure holding a lantern, which cast a feeble light and flickering glow that the cold air quickly swallowed, the party moved slowly across the snow in a broken column. Behind them rose the dark hulk of their ice-locked ship, the *Polaris*, their only sanctuary in this hostile world. Slowly, reluctantly, the procession trudged on, separating themselves from their lifeline. Even as they shuffled in a single line, the party was sharply divided. While all ventured forth to bury their fallen commander, half feared his death might have been a result of deliberate acts.

Trapped in the grip of ice, the *Polaris* no longer resembled the sleek ship she was. A fish out of water, a vessel "nipped" in the Arctic ice provided neither speed nor security for its crew. Without open water to which to run for safety, their vessel was potentially a pile of scrap wood.

The black needles of the steam schooner's masts jabbed futilely at the sky to protest their captivity. Canvas tenting cloaked the decks while slabs of ice and snow were banked about the ship's sides to insulate it and to keep it from rolling as the implacable ice squeezed the hull out of its frozen cradle like a pip from a rotten apple.

Ahead, barely visible in the gloom, two tiny figures waited near a shack. Beside them an American flag drooped from a spindly flag-pole. The fur-covered men pulled a rope that dragged a sled. Draped across the sled, a second American flag trailed its corners in the grooves left by the runners. Under the flag rested a hastily built coffin. Beneath the pine lid lay their captain, Charles Francis Hall, dressed in a simple blue uniform and wrapped in another American flag. The crew of the *Polaris* was burying their leader with as much ceremony as they could muster. No funeral dirge sounded. Only the scrape of the sled's runners and the crunch of their boots on the fresh snow broke the silence. Here in the Arctic, men replaced horses; a simple sledge replaced a funeral carriage.

This far above the Arctic Circle, no sun would rise in November, even though it was one hour before noon. Since October the sun had no longer battled with the growing Arctic night, no longer struggled to rise above the horizon, and simply fled south, abandoning the land to the perpetual blackness of the Arctic winter.

The party trudged along in silence, dwarfed by the immense presence of the sky, the unending whiteness, and the threatening rise of a shale bluff that towered before them like a crouching beast. Observatory Bluff, the sweeping rise of wind-scoured rock was called. Today it rose over them like a granite wave, waiting to roll down and crush them. Panting from exertion, the party drew to a halt beside the waiting individuals.

A wisp of wind riffled the flag and sent snow devils spinning across the ice. The men looked about uneasily. A burst of wind could easily fill the air with snow, blinding them and causing their ship to vanish. Men had frozen to death mere feet from safety in such whiteouts.

The wind ceased. The snow settled, and the sky cleared into an inky blanket pierced by innumerable diamond-hard chips of star-

Funeral of Capt. C. F. Hall, November 10, 1871 (Culver Pictures)

light. The men's fears abated, and they turned back to the business at hand.

Before them lay a shallow depression scarcely two feet in depth. The hole looked like a sullied refuse pit where the snow and ice had been scraped from the hard earth and the frozen gravel attacked with pickaxes and shovels. From there the diggers had encountered permafrost, the eternal slab of ironlike ice that dwells beneath the Arctic ground. Since the last Ice Age, this permafrost possessed what ground the water renounced, and a mere mortal's grave was no cause to relinquish its hold.

Two days of backbreaking work with pick and crowbar had yielded only this rudimentary grave. Like every attempt by man on its sovereignty and secrets, the Arctic resisted. The coffin would lie in the meager depression, half-exposed. The only thing left to do was to cover the exposed box with shale and gravel from the diggings and hope a bear would not rip the lid off. The thought of their captain's corpse dragged over the hills by a playful polar bear, then left for the foxes and lemmings to shred, bore heavily on the crew's minds.

But this was the best they could do. Captain Hall's grave would be like his quest to reach the North Pole—a work unfinished.

The coffin was lowered into the ground, and Mr. R.W.D. Bryan, the ship's astronomer and chaplain, stepped forward to read the service. On board the *Polaris* were copies of four prayers written especially for the expedition by the famous Reverend John Philip Newman, the leading evangelist of the time. Cleric to kings, presidents, and magnates, Newman was the one who would baptize the dying President Ulysses S. Grant in 1885, then claim his prayers had done the trick when Grant miraculously recovered from a massive hemorrhage.

But Newman's prayers dealt with success, not death. One was to be read on reaching the North Pole. So Bryan read the simple seaman's burial service from the captain's Bible. Even this was difficult. In the gloom, George Tyson, the ship's navigator, thrust forward his lantern so that Bryan could read the words.

As he spoke, a serpentine coil of light burst forth overhead and snaked, hissing, across the sky. Undulating in bands of violet, blue, and red, the aurora severed the blackness from horizon to horizon and cast an unworldly glow upon the party. Suddenly the men could see their faces and hands shimmering in the light like apparitions from another world. Amazed and startled by this show of fireworks, they shoveled the scarce spadefuls of dirt over the coffin and hurried back to the security of their ship.

Emil Schuman, the ship's engineer, readied a wooden headboard with a hastily penciled inscription: "C. F. Hall, Late Commander of the North Polar Expedition, died Nov. 8, 1871. Aged 50 years." Noah Hayes, an Indiana farm boy far from home, struggled to drive it into the frozen ground. The board splintered and fell facedown across the mound. Cold, frightened, and depressed, Hayes drove his crowbar into the earth in frustration. In his journal he wrote of the iron bar. "A fit type of his will. An iron monument marks his tomb."

There it stood jutting crookedly from the mound like a melted cross, marking the grave.

Hayes and Schuman hurried after the rest of the crew, heads bent, unmindful of the sinuous lights dancing over their heads. To them it was a coincidence, a scientific demonstration of the magnetism and electricity they had come north to study.

Behind Schuman and Hayes came the Eskimo guides of the *Po-*

laris. Shuffling away from the grave of their longtime friend, the Inuit purposefully kept their backs to the northern lights. Unseen by the white men, each Inuit held a drawn knife behind his back, between him and the lights, for protection. For to the Inuit the hissing lights overhead were the spirits of the restless dead, those who had died violent deaths or had been murdered.

Not one of them doubted that their friend Captain Hall's spirit was overhead. Hall's spirit was calling out. Was he calling for vengeance? Bad things lay ahead for all of them. Their trial on the ice was just beginning.

Chapter One

A GRAND BEGINNING

Under a general appropriations act "for the year ending the thirteenth of June, eighteen hundred and seventy-one," we find the Congressional authority for the outfit of the "UNITED STATES NORTH POLAR EXPEDITION."

Be it enacted, That the President of the United States be authorized to organize and send out one or more expeditions toward the North Pole, and to appoint such person or persons as he may deem most fitted to the command thereof; to detail any officer of the public service to take part in the same, and to use any public vessel that may be suitable for the purpose; the scientific operations of the expeditions to be prescribed in accordance with the advice of the National Academy of Sciences.

—CONGRESS, JULY 9, 1870

Executive Mansion, Washington, D.C., July 20, 1870
Captain C. F. Hall:

Dear Sir: You are hereby appointed to command the expedition toward the North Pole, to be organized and sent pursuant to an Act of Congress approved July 12, 1870, and will report to the Secretary of the Navy and the Secretary of the Interior for detailed instructions.

—U.S. GRANT

Sixteen months before, things were quite different.

By 1870 the United States was ready for something new. To be the first to reach the North Pole fit the bill. Doing so would meld national pride with hard-nosed business. Such an expedition transcended politics and touched Southern and Northern hearts alike. Here was something to raise the spirits of everyone: an American expedition. With eyes fixed northward, those on both sides of the Mason-Dixon Line could forget the slaughter of five years before, the carpetbaggers plundering their property, and the legions of shattered bodies that had littered their hometowns. Grasping the unknown land to their bosom once more gave Rebel and Yankee a noble ideal, a worthy one that fit them both.

Here was an especially worthwhile endeavor, especially since the British had failed so miserably at attaining the same goal. There was little love for England in either Dixie or the North at this time. After all, John Bull had failed to enter the war on the side of the South yet had managed to extract an embarrassing apology from President Abraham Lincoln over the *Trent* affair. If the Americans were to succeed where England had failed, it was only just.

Besides, there was money to be made. Whaling was a million-dollar industry. Before the advent of petroleum mining, whale oil lit the lamps of the world. Baleen supplied the stays for ladies' corsets, and precious ambergris and spermaceti from the sperm whales made perfumes and cosmetics. And north was where the whales were.

Driven by this lucrative trade, whaling ships from New Bedford already braved the Davis Strait in the east and the Bering Sea in the west. A Northwest Passage would eliminate the need to sail round Cape Horn and cut months off the trip. Trade with the Far East would also benefit. Glory was all well and good, but a profit was even better.

The United States was going north to plant the Stars and Stripes at the North Pole. No matter that Danes, Britons, French, and Norwegians had tried and failed; the United States of America, fresh from a divisive civil war, was flexing its muscle. With Yankee ingenuity and American resolve, the first American polar expedition would succeed. No question about it.

America was ready.

And with typical Yankee stinginess, the Navy Department selected an unused steam tug named the *Periwinkle* for the honors. Why spend extra money to lay a fresh keel when this scow lay gathering barnacles? Weighing 387 tons, the screw-propeller *Periwinkle* had never been farther north than Gloucester. But to her went the honors of being the one to carry the flag farther north than anyone had previously gone. Planting the flag at the top of the world was the ultimate goal. Nothing less would do.

But a complete refitting was needed. In her present condition, the *Periwinkle* would not make Greenland, let alone the North Pole. Money being tight, a bill, called the Arctic Resolution, introduced in the Senate requested $100,000 to fund the expedition. Immediately the bloc of southern senators protested. Spending money to find the North Pole that could better go toward Reconstruction galled them.

Attached to a general appropriations bill, the resolution barely passed the Senate. Only the vote of Vice President Schuyler Colfax broke the tie. The bill was passed on to the House, where the Appropriations Committee, with its own share of southerners, compromised and promptly whittled the sum in half. Fifty thousand dollars might see the *Periwinkle* properly refitted, but nothing would be left over for supplies, equipment, and wages. The expedition appeared doomed.

Then behind-the-scenes jawboning by Sen. John Sherman from Ohio, the powerful brother of Gen. William Tecumseh Sherman, brought a reprieve. Having a hero of the Civil War as your brother and commander in chief of the army as well carried some weight. In the House Representative Stevenson (also from Ohio) lobbied heavily for the extra money the committee had cut. Each man had introduced the bill in his respective chamber. And President Grant added his cigar smoke to the smoke-filled rooms. Sullenly and discreetly the Committee on Appropriations guaranteed an additional fifty thousand dollars for refitting the ship alone.

It was no coincidence Sherman and Stevenson had pushed so hard for full funding. To them and most other Americans, only one man had the necessary credentials to reach the North Pole, Charles Francis Hall, a fellow Ohioan.

While the country had just fought a war to preserve the Union, states' rights and regionalism were by no means dead. Ohio would bask in the reflected glory of one of her sons planting the Stars and Stripes at the top of the world. Besides, both President Grant and the congressmen relished the idea of a western man leading a scientific exploration. It tweaked the noses of those in the East who thought all learned knowledge stopped short of the Allegheny Mountains.

It made no difference that Hall had actually been born in New Hampshire in 1821. As a young man, he had the good sense to move west to Cincinnati. That made him a western man to his supporters. Filled with the spirit of adventure, the young Hall headed for what he thought was the frontier. But the frontier was rapidly moving west, far faster than Hall had imagined.

Working as a blacksmith before drifting into journalism, Hall craved more adventure than the rapidly civilizing Cincinnati could provide. The mild success of patenting "Hall's Improved Percussion Press" for making seals, owning an engraving business, and opening a newspaper did little for him. Soon he was languishing in the same dull existence he had sought to escape. Marriage and children failed to provide him what he craved—adventure. With little formal schooling, Hall still had a voracious appetite for knowledge. Night after night he expanded his grasp of mathematics, science, astronomy, and geography, devouring book after book on the subjects. In time he became expert in those areas. Yet he lacked the scrap of paper that would certify his breadth of knowledge. That missing diploma would haunt him.

Then on July 26, 1845, something happened that would direct Hall's focus to the Arctic and change his life forever. The aging Sir John Franklin, commanding an expedition to discover the fabled Northwest Passage across the frozen Arctic Sea to the Orient, vanished from the sight of civilized man. One hundred and twenty-nine men aboard the Royal Navy ships *Erebus* and *Terror* waved farewell to the *Prince of Wales*, a nearby whaling ship, slipped their moorings from an iceberg in Baffin Bay, and simply disappeared into the Arctic fog.

The world was shocked. The sixty-year-old Franklin, arguably too old for Arctic exploration, still had considerable experience in the region. As a young midshipman, Franklin had fought with Horatio Nelson at the Battle of Trafalgar before going on to complete a distinguished career exploring the far North. Many believed him the best qualified in the entire world to lead such a quest. William Edward Parry, Franklin's peer among the British Arctic explorers, endorsed him enthusiastically to the British Admiralty. "He is a fitter man to go than anyone I know." Then, with typical bonhomie, Parry added, "And if you don't let him go, the man will die of disappointment." And Franklin's crew loved him. A common seaman wrote, "Sir John is such a good old fellow—we all have perfect confidence in him!"

None of that mattered. The silent, waiting Arctic swallowed up the best-prepared expedition that any nation had ever mounted. Two naval vessels carrying 136,656 pounds of flour, 64,224 pounds of salted pork and beef, 7,088 pounds of tobacco, 3,600 pounds of soap, two musical organs, and one hundred Bibles evaporated into the cold, thin Arctic air. The North apparently cared little for cleanliness or godliness.

Like the ill-fated Scott expedition to the Antarctic in the next century, Franklin's party carried fatal but hidden flaws that the region would exploit. South or north, the extremes of the globe are extreme in all things. There is never room for mistakes. The slightest error can be fatal.

British naval tradition required Sir John's men to wear woolen uniforms and leather boots rather than adopt the sealskin parkas and mukluks the Inuit had refined through centuries of trial and error. Arctic wind penetrates canvas and wool, where it will not pass sealskin. Sealskin boots, oiled with blubber and soled in the thick hide of *oogrik*, the walrus, repel water and grip ice better than any leather or India rubber boot can.

Wet feet in the Arctic meant frozen feet, with frostbite and gangrene the end result. Unlike the dog, whose legs will not develop frostbite unless a tourniquet is tightened enough to cut off the blood supply, man's extremities succumb to freezing fairly easily. In an attempt to preserve the body's core temperature, blood is shunted away from the fingers and toes whenever necessary. Only recently has modern medicine discovered the exact mechanism of damage due to frostbite. The cause is both simple and devastating: ice crystals.

Over a certain span of temperature during the freezing process, ice crystals form inside the body's cells as the water inside each one freezes. The needle-sharp ice crystals cause all the damage. Like a thousand tiny knives, these crystals puncture and spear the membranes of the important organelles inside the cell. If the solidly frozen part is *slowly* rewarmed, the crystals will reform and do their worst while the body's temperature rises through that critical period. Freezing, slowly rewarming, and then refreezing and thawing are the worst of all possible scenarios—almost guaranteeing gangrene and the resulting amputation of the affected part.

A solidly frozen limb is best left frozen until proper treatment can be initiated. Then *rapid* rewarming affords the best hope of saving the part. Of course, the early explorers of the Arctic knew nothing of this.

A subtler but equally deadly factor played another part. At Beechey Island, a windswept piece of hardscrabble rising from the water near the junctions of Lancaster Sound, Barrow Strait, and Wellington Channel, lies Franklin's first winter camp. Here rest the rectangular rock outlines and piled embankments of workshops, a house, and three untended graves. Preserved in the permafrost and perpetual cold are the bodies of three men from the *Erebus* and *Terror* who lie as mute signposts to the Franklin disaster. Scattered about the campsite are empty meat tins.

Recent studies of these tinned cans used to preserve the party's food reveal a startling finding. Since 1810 storing food in tinned cans had enabled far-flung voyages. Lead-based solder was used to seal the cans. But the toxicity of lead was not discovered until the 1880s. Unknown to Franklin and his followers, the lead solder was turning their food poisonous. A modern autopsy of two of the men who died early on in the expedition revealed toxic levels of lead. Franklin and his men may have fallen victim to lead poisoning.

But with two to three years of provisions, the Franklin expedition was labeled "lost." No one could imagine them all dead, merely lost. Surely the men were trapped somewhere in that vast white expanse, gamely waiting to be saved. Rescue hysteria engulfed Great Britain. The government, prodded by the press, offered twenty thousand pounds' reward to the first intrepid adventurer to find and relieve the "Lost Franklin Expedition."

Adding to this fervor was Lady Jane Franklin herself. Aided by her considerable wealth and the help of clairvoyants and astrologers, she funded ships and relief parties on her own. Not to be outdone by a grieving wife, the government mounted three relief parties. The first searched the Bering Sea in hopes Franklin had successfully completed the passage from east to west and was waiting for them. They found nothing. The second party, starting in the middle of northern Canada, descended the Mackenzie River to its braided terminal of twisted channels into the Beaufort Sea. Expert trackers and fur traders on loan from the Hudson Bay Company could discover no clues of Franklin or his men. A third search, led by Sir John Ross, breached the ice-choked Lancaster Sound with two ships, the *Enterprise* and the *Investigator*, to search the maze of frozen inlets and bays of Somerset Island. Overland parties fanned out in all directions. Again not a trace of the missing men was found.

Brokenhearted, Ross returned to Lady Franklin the worn letter she had asked him to deliver to her missing husband. "May it be the will of God if you are not restored to us earlier that you should open this letter & that it may give you comfort in all your trials . . . ," it read.

Failure of the search parties only fanned the flames of speculation and sold more papers. Books, lectures, and pamphlets extolled the mysteries and dangers of the uncharted North. To a world choked in industrial smoke and blinded by the drab monotony of factory towns, the pristine Arctic, deadly yet enthralling, offered escape.

Far away in Cincinnati, Charles Francis Hall read every word published about the lost Franklin expedition. While running his newspaper, the *Daily Press*, he filled its pages with facts about Franklin and the missing men. Secretly he dreamed of finding them. Here was a cause that fired his imagination. Finding them would fulfill all his dreams in a single stroke. Wealth, fame, and recognition would be his. He set out to learn everything he could about the Arctic. Nothing else mattered now. His family moved to the background; his business withered. Finding Sir John Franklin and exploring the Arctic became his raison d'être.

By 1859 Hall's fascination with Franklin and the Arctic spilled over onto his editorial page. Editorials headed DOES SIR JOHN FRANKLIN STILL LIVE? and LADY FRANKLIN appeared in his paper. In

Charles Francis Hall (Culver Pictures)

an editorial he volunteered to join an expedition led by Dr. Isaac Hayes that planned to reach the North Pole.

Hayes never responded. But at thirty-eight Hall cast his die, and the roll changed his life. Two weeks after printing his article, he sold his newspaper. He would form his own expedition and rescue the Franklin survivors. Despite having a wife, a young daughter, and a son on the way, Hall abandoned everything and directed all his energies toward reaching the Arctic.

Without money to outfit an expedition, Hall's dream languished while he planned and stuffed his mind with facts about the far North. He wrote, petitioned, and visited every influential person he could in Ohio, impressing Gov. Salmon P. Chase and Sen. George Pugh. While Hall was traveling to the East Coast, fortune linked him to Henry Grinnell, founder and first president of the

American Geographical Society. A millionaire shipping and whaling magnate, Grinnell had retired to pursue his humanitarian interests, of which polar exploration ranked highest. Grinnell had privately funded a rescue expedition to find Franklin in 1849 after the United States refused to spend the money. In 1852 Grinnell funded a second exploration under Dr. Elisha Kent Kane.

When Capt. Francis McClintock of HMS *Fox* returned with evidence that Sir John Franklin had died and the *Erebus* and *Terror* had been lost, official enthusiasm for a rescue attempt ended. But Hall was undeterred. Many unanswered questions remained. Later he would write: "I felt convinced that survivors might yet be found."

However, securing passage to the Arctic did not go smoothly for the would-be explorer. While Hall negotiated with Capt. John Quayle for a ride, his nemesis, Dr. Isaac Hayes, stole his captain. With funding to expand on Dr. Kane's discoveries, Hayes no doubt hoped to find Franklin as well. Hall fumed for days over Hayes's action. "I spurn his TRICKERY—his DEVILTRY!!" he scratched venomously in his diary.

Finally, after fits and starts, opportunity struck. Hall wrangled a berth on the *George Henry*, a whaling bark heading north from New London, Connecticut. Using funds raised by his friends in Cincinnati, New York, and New London, Hall paid his passage and outfitted a small sailboat to explore the region in search of Franklin's lost men on a modest budget of $980. Grinnell donated $343, but most of the others gave only a few dollars. Pitifully, even Hall's wife donated $27 from her pinched household budget. The "New Franklin Research Expedition," an exalted name for Hall's one-man show, was on its way to the Arctic.

While little prospect existed that the Franklin party remained intact, persistent rumors still fanned hopes that survivors were living among the Eskimos. A fierce gale on the twenty-seventh of September 1860 changed Hall's plans. Whipping through the region, it sank and scattered the fleet with which Hall traveled. His own small craft wrecked, Hall was now on his own. Undaunted he commandeered a dogsled and headed inland.

Two and one half years later, he reappeared. Now a seasoned Arctic traveler, he had proved himself capable of surviving in the far

North. His bundle of sketches, charts, and detailed notes also confirmed him as a capable explorer. The self-taught cartographer and explorer showed he had learned his skills well. Exploiting leads gleaned from the Inuit, he returned with solid evidence that he had found Sir Martin Frobisher's lost colony on Kodlunarn Island in Countess of Warwick Sound. Mining activity there proved to be the site of Frobisher's gold scraped from the frozen earth some 285 years before. Maps that Hall made during his travels proved highly accurate—so exact, in fact, that the world would have to wait until aerial photography to improve upon them.

Most important, Hall had made valuable contacts among the Inuit. Living among them, he adopted their methods with notable success, something other white men had failed to do. In turn, he had gained the trust and respect of several Inuit. Two gems in the rough returned with him, Ebierbing and Tookoolito. Called Joe and Hannah by white men, whose tongues stumbled over their Inuit names, the husband-and-wife team had already proved invaluable. Both spoke English, the result of a voyage to England in 1853. Tookoolito spoke fluently and could read some, making her useful as an interpreter. Ebierbing was a skilled pilot, well versed in the treacherous ways of the Arctic pack ice. Additionally both had "acquired many of the habits of civilization," Hall acknowledged. In fact, the two were celebrities in their own right. Both husband and wife had taken tea with Queen Victoria, and Tookoolito often wore European-style dresses.

Now incurably infected with the Arctic bug, Hall raised more money and lectured throughout the winter. Now that he was a proven success, funds and support flowed to him wherever he went. Come spring he raced back to the Arctic to take up where he had left off. While the country plunged into its bloody civil war, Hall fought his own battles with the cold, the darkness, and the isolation of the Arctic. In the following years both the United States and Hall emerged changed, hardened and focused by their trials yet resolved to move on.

On his second trip Hall found artifacts from the lost expedition. With the help of his Inuit friends, he gathered cups, spoons, and boxes abandoned by the doomed men. The engraved arrow of the Royal Navy on the items left no doubt about their ownership.

On King William Island, he stumbled upon a skeleton partially hidden in the blowing snow. One of the teeth remaining in the bleached skull contained a curious metal plug. After some hand-wringing, Hall gathered up the bones and brought them back with him. Study of that dental work in England identified the remains as belonging to Lt. H. T. D. Le Vesconte of the *Erebus*.

That convinced Hall that all the men of the Franklin expedition were dead. He could no longer help them. But now a fresh passion drove him. Wandering among the desolate peaks, he saw his new destiny. *He would be first to plant the American flag at the North Pole.*

He now called himself an explorer.

Craftily Hall wrote the Senate of a gigantic whale struck in the Arctic Ocean by Captain Winslow of the whaling bark *Tamerlane* that yielded 310 barrels of oil. The profit from that whale alone reached twenty thousand dollars. Seven such whales would more than pay for the five years of exploration. Knowledge gained from an expedition led by him, he implied, could only improve America's whaling profits.

Lobbying, lecturing, pressing the flesh, Charles Francis Hall moved about the country preaching his quest for the Arctic grail. Wealth, fame, adventure, scientific exploration—he offered it all to anyone who would listen. He prowled the halls of Congress to advance his cause. Hall sought the ear of anyone with influence. Many listened carefully.

His burning desire and single-mindedness of purpose poured forth in all his speeches, moving his listeners. Hall was on a mission, and his passion to claim the North Pole for the United States rang with the same zeal as that of the long-dead abolitionist John Brown. In everything he did, Charles Francis Hall left no doubt in the minds of his listeners that reaching the North Pole meant more to him than his life.

Though not everyone was willing to pay such a price, the shimmering, shifting cap of ice covering the very top of the world has captured explorers' attentions from the first moment they realized the world was round. Between 1496 and 1857 no less than 134 voyages and expeditions probed the Arctic. During that time 257 volumes were published dealing with Arctic research. But that implacable white expanse would swallow many lives and fortunes before relinquishing its secrets.

After the philosophers' stone of the Middle Ages failed to materialize, the quest for the fabled Northwest Passage began. If it wasn't possible to transmute lead into gold, a shorter path to the precious metal was the next best option. Finding the quickest trade route from Europe to China and India promised untold riches to the lucky explorer who unlocked that door. For this reason incursions north, probing along the coast of North America, found ready backers. Merchants were always willing to risk their money rather than their lives for greater profit. Since Spain and Portugal regulated the southern routes to the East, occupying strategic stopping places and discouraging ships of other nations with a vengeance, many thought to venture north, presumably unfettered. If the Orient could be reached going south, surely a way through northern waters also existed.

Henry VIII gave letters of patent ordering John and Sebastian Cabot "to discover and conquer unknown lands" on their way sailing north to Cathay. Sir Hugh Willoughby, under the papers of the Muscovy Company of London, closely followed. While mistaking Newfoundland for the mainland of China, John Cabot sailed as far north as the Arctic Circle. The treacherous ice pack, however, seized Sir Hugh's ship and carried it southwest with the ocean's current. Eventually the vessel, its entire ship's company frozen to death, fetched up off the coast of Lapland.

From 1576 to 1578 Martin Frobisher explored for Henry's daughter, Elizabeth. He returned to England with piles of black ore, termed "witches' gold," that he found while exploring along the coast. Speculation that the material would yield gold ran rampant in the court, and Elizabeth herself funded Frobisher's other trips.

In 1610 Henry Hudson sailed into the expanse of water that now bears his name. Tricked by the sheer size of Hudson Bay, he believed it to be the Pacific Ocean and sailed south in search of China. The rapid onset of winter forced the expedition to lie near Southampton Island until spring. Nearly starving, his men mutinied. Henry Hudson, his son, one loyal ship's carpenter named John King, and a handful of scurvy-struck seamen were set adrift in an open boat. Perhaps the greatest navigator of his time then vanished forever in the gray waters. Those of his mutinous crew whom the Indians did not kill returned home. To save their necks from the hangman's rope, they diverted attention to their discovery of the "true route" to the Orient.

A flurry of activity followed. William Baffin sailed north in 1616 through the ice of Davis Strait to discover Baffin Bay. Turning west along the bay, he encountered Lancaster Sound. Rising in the distance, the mass of Somerset Island convinced him that the sound was merely another of the endless bays that befuddled him. Sailing away, Baffin never realized he had found the true opening to the Beaufort Sea and the Arctic Ocean. Two hundred years later, Sir James Ross would make the same mistake. Enthusiasm for a Northwest Passage to Asia waned as each explorer returned empty-handed.

But a new treasure emerged—one unrelated to the Far East. Furs—the soft gold of lynx, seal, and sea otter hides—commanded lofty prices as fashions changed. In fact, at that time the Asians started buying. Yet only the bitterest winters cultivated the finest furs. That meant going north. In Alaska the Russian Trading Company decimated the sea otter population, along with the Aleut nation, in its ruthless quest for the animals' buttery skins. In the Northwest the Hudson Bay Trading Company chose the more humane method of trade to amass its piles of furs. Wool blankets, metal knives, and cooking pots exchanged well for furs, and the natives remained friendly. British trading methods proved far more cost-effective than Russian subjugation. With peaceful commerce, much less money had to be spent on forts and soldiers, thus ensuring greater profit.

What took the most prodigious bite out of the profits was the arduous voyage around the tip of South America. Notorious for its stormy passage, the Horn claimed countless ships and thousands of tons of cargo. Sailing around Cape Horn was possible only during certain times of the year. A winter voyage was suicidal.

Once again pressure rose for a shorter route to bring the goods to market. A passage across the top of Canada would be ideal. In 1743 Parliament offered twenty thousand pounds as an incentive. The race resumed. But Captain George Vancouver's meticulous surveying along the northwest coast proved conclusively that no major waterway led from the Pacific side of the continent. If any way could be found to traverse the top of Canada to approach the West Coast, the Atlantic side held the key. Even if a ship could sail close enough to the Pacific to link with overland or river routes, it would be a great improvement. Thousands of sea miles would be eliminated.

Despite the cost of fighting the rebellious American colonies, the British Admiralty still could find money in its purse to offer prizes for Arctic exploration. Besides the reward for discovery of the passage, an additional twenty thousand pounds would go to the first to reach the North Pole and five thousand pounds to anyone who came within one degree of the magnetic pole. What once was a matter of commercial interest now evolved into one of national pride, involving the honor of the Royal Navy.

Enter one William Scoresby. While an enterprising and imaginative sailor, Scoresby did not have the privilege of naval rank. He made his living hunting whales. In the summer of 1806, he found himself facing a strange occurrence. The preceding winter had been unusually dry and warm. So had the spring. As a result the Greenland ice pack, which stands like a silent guardian, impeding all northern progress and preventing passage up both sides of Greenland, receded north instead of advancing across the open waters as it usually did.

Suddenly Scoresby found himself facing open water. Instead of lying to to await the southern migration of their quarry like the others in the whaling fleet, Scoresby loosed his canvas and sailed north. Soon he encountered the deadly ice, but due to the warm weather and light snow, areas of the pack ice proved thin enough to navigate. With consummate skill, Scoresby threaded his fragile ship through the icy eye of the needle. Using only the power of wind, battling currents reaching three knots, and fighting his doubts, the whaler slipped between icebergs that could easily have crushed his vessel. To his amazement and his crew's relief, Scoresby broke past the barrier and emerged into "a great openness or sea of water." On he sailed, making careful notes, measuring the seawater's temperature, and filling in the blank portions of his charts.

Miraculously the whaler pressed onward to the latitude of 81°30' N, farther north than anyone save Henry Hudson had ever sailed. As the apogee of the earth, the North Pole is at 90° N;

consequently Scoresby rested less than six hundred nautical miles from the top of the world.

Undaunted by the physical and fiscal dangers of the enterprise, Scoresby indulged his scientific bent as he sailed, mapping the coast of Greenland, studying the effects on his compass as the magnetic core of the earth pulled the instrument's needle farther and farther to the west the farther he traveled north, and documenting the varied animals he encountered. One lowly whaler performed the work of an entire scientific expedition.

Ten years later similar changes in the ice pack recurred. Scoresby, now a veteran of fifteen voyages to that cold region and author of numerous papers on his findings, called this favorable event to the attention of the Admiralty. Now was the time to mount an attack on the North Pole, he urged. He offered his services, and if a few whales were struck along the way, he added, it might help to defray his expenses.

The navy was outraged. To the lords of the Admiralty, Scoresby's prodding only rubbed salt in their wounds. Here this commercial sailor had achieved success where the Royal Navy had not. The greatest sea power in the world, fresh from defeating the combined Spanish and French fleets, rankled at its failure. Now this whaler presumed to tell the navy its business—and suggest pulling a profit as well. Scoresby's scientific achievements also alienated the Royal Society, whose chair-bound members resented his careful work. Without letters behind his name, the whaler's work simply could not be taken seriously, they protested.

This division between academics and lay scientists laid the foundation for trouble for every future expedition into the Arctic. The rugged demands of Arctic travel required a robust, hardy, and adventurous nature—one not usually found in the scholarly men who frequented universities. An ever-widening gulf would develop between those with formal education and those with knowledge gained from enthusiastic, on-site experience. On the one hand, you had the academics with impeccable credentials who were ill suited for the rigors and stress of Arctic travel. On the other hand, you had the explorers, able to withstand the extremes of cold, hunger, and darkness the North held, men whose findings were not accepted in the centers of learning because they lacked formal education. The gap was never resolved in the nineteenth century.

This same chasm would plague Charles Francis Hall to his dying day.

The Admiralty did mount an expedition, but it was to be wholly a naval operation, commanded, crewed, and run like a military operation. Scoresby was snubbed. Even though he was best qualified to lead, Scoresby was refused command of the expedition; however, their lords did offer him a minor position. Of course, the proud captain refused. Academe went along to complete his humiliation, refusing to acknowledge him by name, referring to Captain Scoresby only as "this whaler" or one of the "Greenland captains."

The Admiralty foray, led by Capt. James Ross, fell afoul of the same optical illusions that had baffled Baffin as he explored Lancaster Sound. The shimmering peaks of Somerset Island merged with the haze from the frigid waters to convince him that the sound was a bay. Turning back, he missed his golden opportunity to discover the passage into the Arctic Ocean. Once again the Arctic had conspired to mask its inner secrets. Men had not yet paid a high enough price for that knowledge. More lives and tears in tribute would be needed. And more would come.

Standing on the deck beside Captain Ross was William Edward Parry, a young lieutenant. Unlike Ross, Parry believed that Lancaster Sound was indeed a sound and not a bay. Being a sound meant that the body of water was open on more than one side and not just a vast, blind-ended indentation in the gray land. That promised exciting possibilities.

Returning in 1819 with two ships, the *Hecla* and the *Griper*, Parry breached Lancaster Sound and sailed northwest into Barrow Strait. The route to the Arctic Ocean lay open. His ship *Hecla* sailed within the vaunted one degree of the magnetic pole on September 4, and Parry claimed the five thousand pounds' reward.

Forced to winter over near Melville Island when the ice trapped his ships, Parry added another facet to Arctic exploration. Putting the delay to good use, he mounted overland forays using sleds. Returning a second time, Parry continued his combined sea-land operations with increased success. From then on exploration into the Arctic would consist of driving as far north as possible by sea before the ice seized the ship and then using the trapped vessel as a springboard for mounting sled trips into the unexplored territory. The tools to pick the lock of Arctic secrets lay at hand.

Anxious to unlock the door, Parry returned in 1824 with *Hecla* and *Fury*. The wreck of *Fury* halted that trip.

The year 1827 found Parry mounting an amphibious assault of sorts on the Pole. Departing from Spitzbergen with two covered boats that could be fitted with sled runners, his party sailed away, expecting to slide their boats over solid ice and sail whenever they could. This well-planned expedition soon became a living hell.

Snow blindness forced the men to travel at night. But in the summer, even the nights are not dark. Old wounds opened and scars separated as scurvy struck the sailors. Parry and his men learned through painful experience why the Eskimo language has more than fifty words to describe ice. Not all Arctic ice is the same. Some forms are helpful, whereas others are deadly.

Sikurluk is the Inuit name for a rotting ice floe, one that will give way and plunge the unwary into freezing water, just as *aakkarniq* is the same rotten ice forming into melting streams. *Maniillat* is the saw-toothed pressure ridge forced into the pack ice by wave action. *Imarnirsaq* is the opening in sea ice, but only *quppaq* is the lead in the pack ice that is suitable to navigate. Each subtle differentiation came of necessity, learned through bitter experience by the Inuit. All Arctic ice is far from smooth and slick as the British presupposed.

Rough ice blocks, sharp as razors and tough as flint, shattered and split Parry's wooden sled runners. With little wind, ice crystals form in the frigid Arctic air to settle out as fine diamond dust. Snowfall combines with this hoarfrost and rime to layer the pack ice and exposed ground with a powdery cover. But strong winds can shape the snow into dunes and pack the loose crystals into rock-hard mounds. Erosion of these hillocks produces rugged, sharp-faced *sastrugi*. These steep, sharp rows, often three to six feet high, cut into the sled runners like teeth on a saw.

Pancake ice, floating in the seawater, trapped his boats and impeded their progress. To the Natives, being caught in their kayaks by the floating disks meant certain death. Too thin to stand upon, pancake ice will surround a boat and hold it immobile. Paddling is futile, for the round disks spin off each other like the smoothed sides of grains of quicksand. With the ice whirling about without moving aside, no passage for the boat can be forged. The unwary seal hunter entrapped in pancake ice could only prepare himself for an agonizing death by starvation and freezing.

Then something unexpected happened. No matter how far they traveled north on the ice floe, each day their noon sextant shots placed them *farther south*. To their dismay, Parry and his men discovered that the endless field of ice over which they struggled was moving south. The ice floe was drifting relentlessly south with the ocean's currents. Like the White Queen in Lewis Carroll's *Alice in Wonderland*, they had to run as fast as they could to stay in one place. Battling north almost 300 miles, they now found themselves less than 175 miles from their starting point, the *Hecla*. Brokenhearted, the expedition packed it in.

By 1829 steam entered the equation. Now a ship could forge onward during windless days. HMS *Victory*, a side-paddle steamer, sailed and steamed its way to "Parry's farthest" latitude. A cross between a sailing vessel and a Mississippi paddle wheeler, the *Victory* pressed valiantly northward—only to be trapped in the ice just as all the others had been.

Discouraged by the lack of progress, the British Admiralty withdrew its support and set about licking its sea wounds. Attention turned to land routes, backed by the Hudson Bay Company. Following the Mackenzie, Coppermine, and Great Fish rivers, which flowed north into the sea, men crept north with one foot on the land for security.

Then came 1845 and Sir John Franklin. Suddenly the Arctic once more filled the headlines. The name of Charles Francis Hall would become similarly well known when the American expedition was launched a little more than twenty-five years later.

It was no coincidence that in 1870 Vice President Colfax cast his vote to break the tie in the Senate and pass the Arctic Resolution. The day before the bill was introduced, Colfax had sat in the front row of the Lincoln Hall in Washington beside President Grant while Hall preached his gospel. Hall pointed to the president and shouted that for $100,000 he could outfit an expedition to explore the Arctic. In an impassioned address, he called upon Congress to place the monies directly into President Grant's hands for disbursement. The house came to its feet amid cheers. Basking in the glory, Grant and Colfax smiled and nodded their heads repeatedly. After that outburst and show of enthusiasm from the crowd, there was no doubt about the funding. There was also no doubt about the expedition's leader. Charles Francis Hall's dream was becoming reality. At last he could head a full-fledged expedition to explore the top of the world.

Work began in earnest on the *Periwinkle* once the additional money arrived. As winter winds stripped the last colored leaves from the maples, hammers rang throughout the Washington Navy Yard. Mixing with the rasp of saws, the flat thud of caulking hammers reverberated in the cool light, driving oakum into any seam that might leak. Red-hot rivets glowed atop coal-fed fires, waiting their turn to be pounded into iron plate. The tang of hot pitch and burning charcoal filled the air. All around a small ship in the dry dock, an army of workers swarmed like ants infesting a honey bun.

The hull was stripped down to the keel, and then the ship's bare ribs were planked with six-inch solid oak. New caulk filled the seams before the oak beneath the waterline vanished under fresh copper sheathing. To batter through ice, the bows were layered with more oak until almost solid, then iron plate secured to a sharp prow. As an added precaution, a watertight compartment was built behind the bows for those who had doubts that heavy sea ice might not respect modern engineering.

Hall moved about the Navy Yard with growing enthusiasm, making suggestions, approving modifications, and adding his knowledge to the refitting. His years spent on the ice gave him a good grasp of what it could do. Rocked, tossed, and driven by capricious winds as well as the currents, the nature of the pack ice could change without warning. In minutes a stolid ice field, placidly encasing the ship and the sea around it, could turn into an attacking wall of frozen water. Offshore winds could drive slabs of ice the size of buildings onto each other like scattered dominoes. Grinding

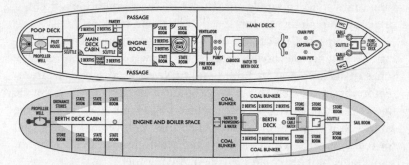

Floor plan of the Polaris *(Courtesy of Richard Parry)*

and slithering tons of advancing ice would crush anything in their path. Scores of flattened campsites littering the shoreline attested to the dwellings of unwary Inuit demolished by sudden attacks of shore ice. Camping beneath the shelter of bluffs provided protection from the biting wind but always carried a risk. It was the action of the ice along with the wind that had hollowed out those dunes. Without warning the ice could return and claim more lives.

Wisely, masts were fitted to the vessel, adding the rigging of a fore-topsail schooner to the steamer. Why waste coal in the boilers? Whenever the wind could be used to power the vessel, that was the preferred method of locomotion, Hall argued. Bitter experience learned from whaling ships that ventured into those frozen lands showed that what coal a vessel needed for its engines must be carried along. More than one whaler had limped home by burning its own timbers in its boilers, cannibalizing the ship to its waterline. In the high Arctic, ice, water, and rock prevailed. Firewood and coal were nonexistent, and little else could be burned for warmth or fuel.

To guard against heavy ice's snapping the propeller blades, a slot was cut in the stern so that the drive shaft to the screw could be unfastened and the propeller raised out of harm's way. A powerful, compact engine, made especially in Philadelphia by Neafles & Levy, drove the propeller. The engine was a masterpiece, incorporating the latest advances in steam engine design. Being small meant that more space could be allocated to carrying precious coal. For all its advanced design, the engine packed less horsepower than that found in a modern family car. Under the best conditions, it could drive the ship along at a top speed of less than ten knots.

The ship's boilers carried out dual responsibilities. Besides driving the engine, the boilers heated the crew's quarters through a series of steam pipes. Sir John Franklin's vessels also had steam radiators fitted to their ships. What good it did them will never be known. At Hall's suggestion, engineers even modified one of the boilers so it could burn whale or seal oil. With limited space, coal for fuel competed with foodstuffs and scientific gear. In the event of a shortage, blubber could provide lifesaving fuel.

Other innovations abounded. From the stern hung a life buoy sporting an electric lamp with wires reaching the ship's electric generator. A spring-loaded device allowed the life preserver to be released from the pilothouse. If a man fell overboard or became stranded on the ice, the light and cable attached to the buoy would aid his rescue. In the perpetual winter night and swirling snow, men separated by mere yards vanished from sight. In a storm the howling wind swallowed all sound. Only such a lighted beacon would help.

For exploration the ship carried four whaleboats and a flat-bottomed scow that could be dragged over the ice from one open lee to another. Roughly twenty feet long with a width of four feet, whaleboats carried oars and a collapsible mast and sail and normally held six to eight men. Designed for speed and durability, they were slim, sharply keeled, and built of heavy wood. A standard but inefficient practice was to use the whaleboats as makeshift sleds for exploring the ice pack. At Hall's urging a special collapsible boat patented by a man named Heggleman was added. Constructed of folding frames of hickory and ash, the twenty-foot-long boat could be packed aboard a sled for easy transportation. Once the frame was assembled, a waterproof canvas covering fitted over it. Theoretically, the folding boat could carry twenty men.

While in the Arctic, Hall had greatly admired the *oomiak* used by the Inuit to hunt whales and walrus. Similarly designed of a wooden frame, the *oomiak* was covered with walrus skin. Had Hall inquired, he might have discovered that the Inuit took special pains to cover their boat in the lighter-weight hides of the female walrus instead of the thick skin of the male. Weight was an inherent prob-

lem in a boat that size and shape, especially one intended for hauling on and off ice floes. At 250 pounds, the Americans' folding boat
would prove next to useless.

Extra spare parts that could not be fabricated crammed into
whatever space food and coal did not occupy. Spars, line, kegs of
nails, a spare rudder were stowed away. At the navy's insistence,
the hold held a small mountain howitzer with sufficient powder
and shot to intimidate any unfriendly Natives they might encounter.
After all, this was a naval expedition. Anyone giving it much
thought would have realized that the cannon was a useless and
heavy item. If the howitzer were fired on the slick ice, the first shot
would either upend it or send it speeding across the ice into the
closest patch of open water.

In the captain's cabin, Hall packed books on Arctic exploration, including a copy of Luke Fox's *Arctic Voyage of 1635*. In
one corner the workers loaded a cabinet organ donated by the
Smith Organ Company. No one drew the parallel that Sir John's ill-
fated party had carried two organs.

One thing seriously flawed the newly refitted *Periwinkle*. The
ribs and keel of the old *Periwinkle* were kept and used for the ship's
back. To do otherwise would have been too costly. But the *Periwinkle*'s keel was not designed to deal with ice. It was too narrow
and too sharp-bowed. With a wide, thick-waisted beam, a ship
"nipped" in the ice would lie level. As pressure from the floe increased, the wide keel would not allow the hull to be easily gripped
by the ice. Instead, the broad hull would be squeezed literally out of
the ice like a seed from a grape to lie comfortably atop the frozen
water. The *Periwinkle*'s narrower design doomed it to be seized by
the ice. The ice's grip would tilt the ship precariously, while mounting pressure would spring the planking, opening the seams to seawater. The ship's slender hull would plague the expedition and
eventually lead to the vessel's death.

Hall, the landlubber, transformed from an intrepid explorer
into an *explorer and a sea captain*, now unknowingly did something that no sailor would ever do. He renamed his vessel, a sure
sign of bad luck to come. Inspired by the lofty aim of the expedition, he changed the name of the *Periwinkle* to *Polaris*.

Chapter Two

A HEARTY CREW

There being attached to the expedition a scientific department, its operations are prescribed in accordance with the advice of the National Academy of Science. . . .
—GEO. M. ROBESON, SECRETARY OF THE NAVY

Work on the newly named *Polaris* progressed feverishly throughout the winter and spring of 1871. Any delay extending into the summer months might doom the ship to miss its narrow window for sailing. Then the uncaring pack ice would close its open lees, icebergs calved from the pack and glaciers would choke the seas with deadly, white battering rams, and the fearful nor'easters would whip the seas. By October, when most people were celebrating their harvest, the Arctic sun slipped below the horizon, not to be seen again for months. Timing is critical in the high North, a land of extremes in which success often wobbled on the thin knife's edge of picking the best moment to proceed.

The refitting scheduled at the Washington Navy Yard progressed rapidly. Once completed, the ship would steam up to the Brooklyn Navy Yard for its final fittings. Time for departure was drawing close.

Hall now faced another problem. President Grant had appointed him in overall command of the expedition, and Congressman Stevenson, on reading the joint resolution, had referred to him as *Captain* Hall.

But Hall was no captain. The title was at best honorary. Still, it stuck. After that he was Captain Hall. At best Hall was a self-taught man with valuable Arctic experience—*experience on land.*

With the stroke of a pen, the explorer gained a title he was ill suited to carry.

Wisely, though, Hall realized he needed a stouthearted crew to man the ship. In an interesting departure from the British, Hall and the American navy turned to those sailors with the most experience in the Arctic. To them whaling men were the most obvious choice. Where the Admiralty placed its faith in the traditions and training of its officers and men, the first official American exploration into the Arctic turned to civilians to man the ship, which was still a registered Navy vessel. Perhaps those in the Navy Department with an instinct for self-preservation sniffed a fiasco and were hedging their bets. If so, their waffling would come back to haunt them.

To a man like Hall, knowledge and experience were everything, so he picked sailors who had served on whaling ships and faced the ice. But such men hold a loose allegiance to their officers, signing on whichever ship pays the best wages. Moreover, military vessels sail under strict, ironclad rules, grounded in years of harsh, swift punishment for disobedience. Such respect for order would hold a crew together in the face of adversity. Nothing but adversity would flow from the far North.

In the end lack of discipline would drive a knife deep into the heart of the *Polaris* expedition.

No expedition would succeed without a good ship's master. Fortunately Hall knew just the man. The fierce storm that had shattered Hall's small sailboat during his first visit to the Arctic also struck the nearby whaling ships. Many were sunk, including the *Rescue*, which accompanied the *George Henry*. Another brig, the *Georgiana*, was driven hard onto the rocks. Commanding this ship was George Tyson, a man with twenty years' experience whaling the Arctic waters. Only Tyson's ingenuity saved his crew and eventually the vessel. As the wind and waves battered his ship, the angle of the stricken vessel prevented launching the whaleboats. Attempting to swim in the frothing waves meant certain death. Tyson, keeping a cool head, ordered his men to secure what they could before floating them ashore using extra spars as life rafts. In the end his ship withstood twenty-four hours of pounding and was kedged free. Here was a captain who was lucky as well as good.

It also helped that both men were remarkably similar in background and appearance. Tyson had struggled in an iron foundry, dreaming of the Arctic, before escaping to sea. Both lacked formal education and were self-taught, self-made men. While Hall read about the North and gained experience on the land, Tyson followed the humpback whales and learned about the sea. In appearance the two men looked alike. Hall, the larger and more bearlike, could easily have passed for Tyson's older brother. With thick, dark hair and full, curly beards, heavy brows, and dark eyes, the two appeared robust and vigorous. Hall wore his hair parted on the left side and brushed across his forehead, while Tyson pushed his hair straight back, ignoring his receding hairline.

Unfortunately, when Hall approached Tyson to be the sailing master and ice pilot for the expedition, Tyson told Hall he had other plans. He was scheduled to hunt sperm whales.

Discouraged, Hall turned to his second choice: Capt. Sidney O. Buddington. Buddington, connected to a long line of New England whaling captains, had skippered the *George Henry*, the ship that first brought Hall to the North. During their voyage the men became friends, and Buddington introduced the novice Hall to the Eskimo pilots and hunters he knew. In his subsequent sorties Hall sailed often aboard Buddington's vessels. Certainly Buddington's expertise, with twenty years' whaling in the Arctic, equaled that of Captain Tyson. Buddington's trade wore more heavily on him than on Tyson, giving him a much older, careworn visage. He resembled a tired version of James Garfield. Tracts of gray streaked his thinning hair and grizzled his beard. Lines furrowed his high brow and encircled his eyes. He looked like a troubled and beaten man.

And Hall had a problem with his second choice. On one occasion the two men had quarreled bitterly over the two Inuit interpreters, Ebierbing and Tookoolito. The trouble arose during the summer of 1863 as Hall struggled to finance another trip to his beloved northland. But the bloody battles at Vicksburg and Gettysburg held the country's attention that summer, not the Arctic. Without resources Hall simmered in New York.

Buddington did have a whaling cruise scheduled. Whether he offered passage to Hall is unknown, but the point is moot. Lacking funds for food and supplies, Hall still could not go. Then, without asking Hall's permission, Buddington offered the two Inuit a ride back to their homeland. At the time Ebierbing and Tookoolito were living with Hall in New York and showing signs of homesickness.

On discovering Buddington's plans, Hall exploded in rage. Vitriolic letters flew back and forth. "I trust neither I nor the Esquimaux will ever trouble your house again," Hall wrote spitefully. Buddington sailed away without Joe and Hannah.

Hall's tirade highlights two curious things. The first was the possessive attitude of these men toward "their Inuit," as they referred to the Eskimo. At the very time their countrymen were fighting and dying to free the black slaves in the South, northern whalers and explorers like Hall regarded the Inuit as something subhuman. The Inuit's customs undoubtedly contributed to this impression. Their demonstrations of shamanism, cruel treatment of the elderly with ritual murder, and habits of eating fish and blubber raw seemed barbaric and inhuman to the whalers. However, the Inuit traditions masked a culture highly evolved to survive in a hostile setting. But white men stumbling around in an alien world where one misstep meant disaster often missed these subtleties.

While they would have vigorously denied ownership in the legal sense, the white men felt that their Native acquaintances in some way belonged to them. Not unlike the Southern slave owner, men like Hall assumed total responsibility for the care and feeding of Inuit who, for one reason or another, attached themselves to the whites. In doing so, they robbed their charges of all freedom of action. The Eskimo responded by becoming passive followers when in the "civilized" world. Back in the Arctic, the Natives reverted to their proven ways of surviving and ignored the whites whenever it suited their purposes.

The second thing was that Hall showed himself to be remarkably thin-skinned for an Arctic explorer, especially when events beyond his control blocked his drive. Although he was inured to the cold, darkness, loneliness, hunger, and fear, his feelings could be easily hurt. Buddington's offer highlighted Hall's impotence: not being a whaling captain himself and without a ship or money to charter one, the explorer's return to the North remained uncertain. Perhaps Hall also feared that the whaling captain meant to steal his two Inuit just as Dr. Hayes had stolen Captain Quayle. Ebierbing and Tookoolito were precious commodities and essential to exploring the North.

Eventually the two men reconciled. But scars from the rift festered below the surface. Still, good sea captains with knowledge of the Arctic were scarce, so Hall offered the job to Buddington, and the captain did accept the position. Slots for captains sailing north were limited. Normally the skipper of a whaler received a share of the profits, sometimes as much as 10 percent. But striking sufficient whales to turn a profit was no sure thing. Bad weather and a bad season meant no money at all. Unlike a whaling venture, this trip guaranteed his salary, a handsome one at that.

Besides, Hall grew desperate to put the pieces of the expedition together as fast as possible. He showered presents on Buddington, promised a pension for his wife should he die, and dangled the carrot of fame before the captain. Had Buddington the ability to look into the future, he would have turned down the offer. When Buddington accepted the position as skipper, ignoring the remnants of hard feelings that existed between the two men, one more piece fell unnoticed into place, one more link added to the chain of events that would drag the expedition to its doom.

Ironically, events linked the three men after all. Tyson's position with the New London whaling fleet fell through, and he moved his family to Brooklyn just as the refurbished *Polaris* sailed into the Brooklyn Navy Yard for its final additions. Hall found him and this time would not accept no for an answer. Again twisting arms, Hall secured a position for Tyson as assistant navigator and master of the sledges, a curious title but one somehow carrying the rank of captain.

Unknown to Hall, dating back many years, Tyson harbored ill feelings for anyone with the name of Buddington. In 1854 Sir Edward Belcher abandoned the *Resolute*, a British Admiralty vessel. One year later, while serving under Capt. James Buddington (Sidney's uncle), Tyson spotted the *Resolute* frozen in the ice miles from where their ship lay. Following a harrowing trek over the ice to the frozen vessel, Tyson found it intact, preserved down to the decanters of wine in the officers' mess. Although Tyson risked his life to reach the *Resolute*, Buddington claimed possession of the ship, cheating the man out of thousands of dollars in salvage money. On the young Tyson's very first cruise to the Arctic whaling grounds, none other than Sidney O. Buddington had served as first mate. Neither man talked much about their first meeting, and that cannot be construed as a sign of a positive and warm acquaintanceship.

Now the *Polaris* had three captains aboard—two too many by any count. Like the first ice crystals shifting on a mountainside leading to an avalanche, circumstances, insignificant in isolation, were accumulating that would later imperil the expedition. One after another, undetected yet fatal flaws were being woven into the fabric of the *Polaris* expedition. Facing the harsh cold and darkness of the North, the fabric would start to unravel.

Fate now struck another blow, one far more serious than personality disputes among three captains. Nationality raised its divisive head.

Congress, always wanting the most for its money, had saddled the expedition with two tasks. Not satisfied merely to reach the North Pole, something no one had yet accomplished, the legislators decided the polar expedition would also be the premier scientific exploration of its time. The armchair adventurers under the Capitol dome ordered the undertaking to follow the directives of the Smithsonian Institution and the National Academy of Sciences. Perhaps goaded on by Congress, a committee of these august scientists essentially ordered the expedition to study everything conceivable: biology, geology, hydrology, climatic changes, atmosphere, magnetism—the list was endless. Sealed copper cylinders carrying notes on the expedition's progress were to be thrown over the side and buried in caches ashore as the journey progressed. Ever mindful of the Franklin expedition's mysterious disappearance, the committee wanted a paper trail of this expedition. To fully comply with the scientific requirements, a task force would have been needed instead of a converted tug. Both the National Academy of Sciences and the Smithsonian shared the task of appointing a chief scientist.

Immediately Hall grew uneasy—and with good reason. His lack of formal education returned to haunt him. The old division between academics and explorers, first evident with the whaler Captain Scoresby, lived on.

Even before Congress had finalized the bill, an old nemesis of Hall's, smelling blood in the water like a shark, had emerged from obscurity to strike at Hall's appointment. Just as details of the polar expedition were being finalized, Dr. Isaac Hayes materialized in Washington and testified before the Committee on Foreign Relations that he had an expedition of his own in the works and deserved the allocated government funding far more than Hall did.

Hayes and Hall had crossed ice axes at various lectures as the two jousted for the unofficial title of the American most knowledgeable about the Arctic. Notwithstanding the fact that Hayes had not set foot in the Arctic for ten years, he almost wrested command of the party away from Hall. Hayes's doctorate and his book, *The Open Polar Sea,* gathering dust in the Library of Congress, nearly capsized the self-made explorer's dream. Here, after all, was an explorer with letters after his name—just what the academics wanted.

Hall fought for his life. He scoured Hayes's book, looking for errors and evidence of intellectual dishonesty. He stressed that he had also written a book, *Arctic Research and Life among the Esquimaux,* published in 1865. In the end he even tried humility. He stood before the Committee on Foreign Relations to refute Hayes's claim. "I confess I am not a scientific man," he admitted. It must have hurt him deeply to say that. All his life he had struggled to be just that, a Renaissance man, versed in the natural sciences. All his adult life he had been weighing, measuring, and sketching. His self-worth was bound up in his view of himself as a scientist. "No, I am not a scientific man," he argued. Then he hit the nail on the head. "Discoverers seldom have been."

Congress agreed. Those who pressed past their fears to disappear into the ice fog—men like Frobisher, Hudson, Franklin, and Parry—needed a special madness. Reaching the Pole demanded someone like Hall, someone with fire in his belly.

Hall's argument saved his job as head of the exploration, but it cost him the role of chief scientist. Congress hedged its bets. Only someone with letters after his name would do for that. Despite Hall's love for science, another would oversee that task, someone with the necessary credentials. Hall's place was to discover the North Pole; it would be left to someone else to subject to scientific analysis what was found there.

With animal cunning, Hall moved to block the appointment of

Dr. Hayes as chief scientist. Having his adversary within the ranks would be intolerable. He suggested Dr. David Walker for the post. Walker, young and well conditioned, had served aboard the *Fox* on its trip to the Arctic in 1857 and gained considerable expertise during the voyage. A combination of surgeon and naturalist, Walker served in the medical corps of the army with experience fighting Indians as well as the Arctic ice pack. Still on active duty in the army, Walker could be reassigned by order of President Grant, Hall suggested, and his salary still paid out of army funds. To sweeten the deal, Hall slyly hinted at donating the trove of relics and artifacts he had amassed on his Arctic tours if Walker were selected.

Spencer Baird, secretary of the Smithsonian, liked the idea. As he was always battling with Congress for funds, not having to pay for Walker appealed to the tightfisted Baird. Besides, an exhibition of the last fragments of Franklin's doomed party would draw packed crowds. Morbid curiosity was as strong then as it is today.

George Robeson, secretary of the navy, and Joseph Henry, president of the National Academy of Sciences, agreed. So did the surgeon general of the army. Walker was the right man to go.

Elated, Hall directed his attention back to the *Polaris* itself, basking in his newfound glory. While in Washington, his spirits soared when President Grant recognized him in a crowd and made it a special point to shake his hand and inquire about the progress of the expedition. Hall should have watched his back during this tranquil period.

Unknown to Captain Hall, the fates were conspiring against him. A letter arrived from August Petermann, a highly noted geographer residing in Gotha, Germany. During the summer of 1868, Petermann had completed a successful scientific expedition north of Spitsbergen aboard the vessel *Albert*, which belonged to a walrus hunter named Rosenthal. Petermann's assistant during that trip was a young man named Emil Bessel. In his letter Petermann extolled the virtues of Bessel and urged that he be appointed as chief scientist instead of Walker.

Emil Bessel's credentials were impressive. From the wealthy upper class, Bessel obtained his doctorate of medicine from Heidelberg and then went on to study zoology and entomology at Stuttgart and Jena. Letters attesting to Bessel's skill as a surgeon flowed

Emil Bessel (Courtesy of National Portrait Gallery/Smithsonian)

to the selection committee, but it was the fact that he was primarily
a scientist that impressed Spencer Baird and Joseph Henry. Dr.
Walker was essentially a physician with a scientific bent. And Bessel
had all those credentials after his name that everyone loved.

The committee did an about-face. Emil Bessel replaced Walker.

At twenty-four, Emil Bessel would have been called handsome
by his contemporaries. Thick, wavy brown hair rose to an extrava-
gant pompadour that added inches to his short stature and framed
a broad, flat forehead and low-set ears. His sideburns blended with
a trim, square-cut beard. Dark, deep-set eyes stared imperiously
from beneath straight, even brows. A small hump marred the
bridge of his otherwise straight nose. Slightly flaring nostrils overrode a trim mustache. On close inspection the downward curl of
the right side of his lower lip hinted of cruelty.

Size was Bessel's main problem. A contemporary description of him states that he "would pass for a handsome man, built on rather too small a scale." Strange praise, indeed. Quick, nervous in temperament, or high-strung, Bessel moved about in short, twitching steps, while his eyes darted and flashed. If Charles Francis Hall might be described as a bear of a man, Bessel was a bantam rooster. Definitely not a "people person," Bessel loved to study insects.

To further complicate matters, Bessel was not even in the United States at the time. *He was serving as a surgeon in the German army.*

The impulsive shift from Walker to a German to head the first *American* polar exploration might seem strange until one considers the times. Germany was regarded as the foremost home of modern scientific knowledge. Anyone who wished to establish his credentials went to Germany to study. With Theodor Bilroth and Emil Theodor Kocher advancing the field of surgery, the Allemagnkrankenhaus was deemed the finest hospital in the world. America's dean of modern surgery, William Stewart Halsted, studied in Germany before establishing the department of surgery at Johns Hopkins. Scientific degrees from a Teutonic university inspired awe.

Besides, the flood of thousands of Germans to the United States had changed the mix of the American people from one of mainly Scots-English descent to one with many German and Irish additions. Arriving in the early sixties, both Irish and Germans had earned their rights by shedding their blood in the Civil War. More than two hundred thousand Germans had fought for the North, mainly due to the recruiting genius of Lincoln's friend Carl Schurz. Whole regiments of blue-coated Germans marched into battle with no one speaking English.

A major difference separated those German emigrants from Dr. Emil Bessel. They came to America to escape the tyranny of Otto von Bismarck and to make America their new home. Bessel came for other reasons.

Germany had a spidery relationship with Greenland and possibly with the undiscovered lands to the north. Greenland belonged to Denmark, and Prussia had just defeated the Danes in 1864 in a war over the troublesome areas of Schleswig and Holstein. In another year Bismarck would complete his unification of Prussia and the German States into a single country. The Danes still seethed over the loss of North Schleswig, an area where the population was predominantly composed of Danes. Anything to keep Denmark off balance suited Bismarck's purpose.

Already Germany was shifting from a rural nation to one whose industrial growth threatened Great Britain. The United States, too, had just emerged from its own war of unification. Rapidly industrializing as well, Germany and the United States progressed along remarkably parallel courses. Did the wily Bismarck worry about rising alliances between Denmark and the United States? Certainly Germany had an interest in the North Sea and the North regions. Its ships and commerce flowed through that area, and its fishing fleet worked the Greenland coast.

In 1869 Germany had mounted another polar exploration on the heels of the Petermann trip. A screw-fitted steamer named the *Germania* and a supply brig, the *Hansa*, departed Bremen on June 15, 1869, to the sounds of a brass band. No less a personage than Kaiser Wilhelm himself saw the ships off. Captain Koldewey, who piloted Petermann's ship, led the expedition. The *Hansa* soon lost sight of its sister ship, got caught in the ice, and was crushed. The unfortunate crew spent the winter drifting south on an ice floe. Eleven hundred miles later they were rescued by a Moravian mission station close to Cape Farewell in Greenland. The *Germania* fared better, with its crew wintering over, mounting land explorations, and naming their farthest point north, a barren cape, after Bismarck.

Even as late as the Second World War, German influence in that region was evident. Iceland, although commandeered by the Allies, still maintained a pro-German attitude.

Petermann's letter was all it took to convince the selection committee. Its members should have looked more closely at their choice. The *Germania* and *Hansa* expedition shipped with "several eminent men of science, provided with every requisite necessary for the successful performance of their duties." Obviously the Germans were still interested in examining the nature of the Arctic region. Why, then, was Emil Bessel not included in their list of "eminent men of science"? He would seem the ideal choice. He had just been there. He knew the land, the material, and had the scientific tools.

If his bona fides were so stellar as to woo the Americans, why weren't they good enough for his own country? It cannot be assumed that Bessel wanted a break from Arctic studies, for the *Polaris* expedition followed close behind the German one. Was there something that the Germans knew about Bessel that made him undesirable to them? Or was there an entirely different reason Petermann placed Emil Bessel among the Americans?

Like any large bureaucracy, the German army, although known for its efficiency on the battlefield, had its own paper-trail nightmares. Yet Bessel's release from the German army came remarkably quickly, possibly with the army's encouragement. President Grant had to approve Dr. Walker's transfer. Did Bismarck himself give his blessing to Bessel's assignment? To add to the mystery, another interesting thing happened. Oelrichs & Company, a German steamship firm, transported Emil Bessel to New York free of charge.

So Emil Bessel arrived as surgeon and chief of the scientific corps, barely speaking any English. He was arriving, not as an immigrant with dreams of a new home, but as an expert from afar, casting his pearls among the swine. He arrived as a German, and he remained a German. Despite the fact that he received a salary as chief scientific officer and served aboard a commissioned United States naval vessel, he took no oath of loyalty to either the United States or the U.S. Navy. Mystery still shrouds this man. Upon his arrival, the composition of the crew began to change.

Hall personally had asked for Hubbard Chester as first mate. A native of Noank, Connecticut, Chester was a longtime whaler with years of cold-water experience. The two men had met aboard the *Monticello*. With large, wide-set eyes, arrow-straight nose, and an exuberant mustache that ran from the corner of one cheek to the next, Chester bore a passing resemblance to the writer Robert Louis Stevenson. The other man Hall requested was William Morton. With more than thirty years in the navy, Morton was trustworthy, solid, and ever-enduring, like the oak planks that now covered the hull of the *Polaris*. Morton had accompanied Hall's idol Dr. Elisha Kent Kane on both of his Arctic explorations more than twenty years before. Gray-haired and bearded, Morton would prove a rock.

R.W.D. Bryan, an enthusiastic graduate of Lafayette College in

Pennsylvania, was appointed to the dual position of chaplain and astronomer for the scientific corps. To the ever practical and penny-wise navy, both positions dealt with heavenly subjects and so could wisely be combined.

But Frederick Meyer, a native of Prussia, secured the position of meteorologist. In fact, Meyer had graduated from the Prussian military academy and served in the Prussian army as a lieutenant. Crossing the Atlantic with an appointment to Maximilian's army in Mexico, he found himself unemployed when the emperor was overthrown. He then enlisted in the United States Army, eventually ending up in the signal corps. Suddenly Germans dominated the scientific staff, holding two of the three positions.

Emil Schuman, another German with drafting skills, was appointed chief engineer. Schuman, sporting full muttonchops and a waxed mustache, looked the proper burgher. To the day the ship sailed, Schuman spoke less than a handful of words in English.

Herman Sieman, Frederick Anthing, J. W. Kruger, Joseph Mauch, Frederick Jamka—one after another, Germans signed aboard the *Polaris*. After the roster of ten ordinary seamen was filled, only one man, Noah Hayes, was born in the United States.

Other than asking for Buddington, Tyson, Chester, and Morton, Captain Hall appears to have had little input as to the rest of the crew. The army may have pushed Meyer in order to have a hand in any glory, and the academics picked Bessel and Bryan.

The first American polar expedition would have difficulty calling upon Yankee patriotism to advance the flag, because half the crew were Germans. As problems later developed, trouble mounted when the crew divided along lines of nationality.

It is easy to suggest that rapid migration to the newly opened West occupied the minds of most Americans at the time and that it seriously reduced the pool of mariners from which to choose. But the preponderance of Germans is truly puzzling. Why were there so many? Only one Dane and one Swede signed aboard. And where were those hardy seafaring souls of other seagoing nations? Where were the Norwegians? Where were the Portuguese?

Another equally serious division grew as the time to sail approached. Was the primary goal of the expedition to reach the North Pole or to study every conceivable aspect of the far North?

Joseph Henry appointed a committee to detail the scientific instructions. Besides himself, he selected Spencer Baird and other prominent scientists like Louis Agassiz. In their exuberance they produced a list of instructions almost impossible to complete. Every known field of study filled their catalog.

Scientific study threatened to sink the exploratory aspect. Even at first glance, the two goals were diverse and conflicting. Reaching the North Pole meant dashing northward through a narrow window of opportunity before weather, sea conditions, and the Arctic winter slammed that window shut. To study all that the committee requested meant careful, time-consuming measurements and observations, the kind best done from a static observatory. One goal demanded risk and gambling; the other required restrained contemplation. To accomplish both tasks meant dangerously dividing the thinking and actions of the party in half.

To Hall, reaching the North Pole was paramount. Quickly he wrote to Henry stressing that. But Henry remained adamant: science first. Hall resisted. "Science must be subordinate," he underlined that phrase in his orders. "The primary object of our Expedition is Geographical discovery," the captain wrote, "and to this, as the main end, our energies will be bent."

Then Henry, fearing conflict, appealed to Hall's kindness. "I doubt not that you will give every facility and render every assistance in your power to Dr. Bessel, who, though a sensitive man, is of a very kind heart." How could Henry make this pronouncement about Bessel? He hardly knew the man. Still, he persisted. "As I have said, Dr. Bessel is a sensitive man; I beg, therefore, you will deal gently with him."

The last thing any dangerous mission needs is a thin-skinned chief scientist.

Misgivings flooded over Hall. To an old friend in Cincinnati, Judge Joseph Cox, he expressed fears his mission would fail, primarily because of insubordination among the officers and crew. He complained bitterly about the makeup of the scientific side of his party to Dr. Robert Newton. Darkly he hinted that strong-arm tactics compelled him to accept the scientists. Refuse the present arrangements and you will not command this expedition, he was told. To Hall this was his best chance to reach the Pole, perhaps his only chance. At fifty he was already old for such rigorous pursuits. For him this truly was a once-in-a-lifetime opportunity. Another command might never come his way. Besides, he could never face the humiliation of being replaced, and he was too proud to accept a subordinate role.

Once before he had refused when Lady Franklin suggested that Hall share command of an expedition in search of her husband with Francis McClintock. He might be marginal in the civilized world, but in that harsh, white world he loved so dearly, command was his strong point. There he had the will, the strength, and the flexibility to succeed. He could endure the mind-numbing boredom of sitting cross-legged for days in a darkened igloo while waiting for a whiteout to blow through. He could stand the gnawing hunger that forced him to chew on blackened strips of sealskin, and he could press on while his vision burned from the thousand tiny flashes of sunlight-fired ice crystals suspended in the air.

Command he could, but he forgot that prior to this he had commanded only himself and a few Inuit, mainly Tookoolito and Ebierbing. Captain Hall had no experience leading larger parties.

In the end he bowed to the bureaucrats. Unknown to him, he was right in one respect. This was to be his final passage to the North.

> All persons attached to the expedition are under your command, and shall, under every circumstance and condition, be subject to the rules, regulations, and laws governing the discipline of the Navy, to be modified, but not increased, by you as the circumstances may in your judgement require.
>
> GEO. M. ROBESON, SECRETARY OF THE NAVY,
> INSTRUCTIONS TO CAPT. C. F. HALL, JUNE 9, 1871

In theory, Congress had passed a bill authorizing funding for the expedition and the use of a naval vessel and "public service" officers where available. In theory, those military men were ultimately under the command of President Grant, the commander in chief. In reality, only Morton and Meyer were in service. The rest of the crew and officers were civilians to be paid at the end of the journey. Hall was ordered to assume command of mainly foreign whalers and a haughty duo of German scientists who themselves had separate instructions from the American scientific community. Never having held a naval commission, Charles Francis Hall had no idea what the "rules, regulations, and laws governing the discipline of the Navy" were. Neither did the scientists and seamen he was expected to command. No better recipe for a confused command could be devised.

Even the mission's top priority remained unresolved. What was the primary goal to be: exploration or science? On the day it sailed, the *Polaris* carried a divided crew on a divided mission.

Chapter Three

FLAGS AND FANFARE

*Wishing you and your brave comrades health, happiness,
and success in your daring enterprise, and commending you
and them to the protecting care of the God who rules the
universe.*
—GEO. M. ROBESON, SECRETARY OF THE NAVY

On June 10, 1871, the *Polaris*, sporting a fresh coat of paint and
festive bunting, slipped its moorings, steamed out of the Washington Navy Yard, and made its way down the Potomac River.
Crowds of women in bright crinolines and men sporting top hats
and broadcloth coats lined the banks, cheering and waving American flags while the navy band played "The Star-Spangled Banner."
The smell of fresh grass and magnolias mingled with the tang of
pitch and coal smoke blown back upon the foredeck by the following wind.

Captain Hall leaned against the railing by the pilothouse and
waved, while Captain Buddington shouted orders to the helmsman.
Below decks Chief Engineer Schuman stalked among the bright
brass cylinders of his new steam engine, oiling fittings and valves,
cursing in German under his breath at his two firemen.

Only weeks before, Hall had hosted a reception aboard the *Polaris* for President Grant, Navy Secretary Robeson, and the Reverend Dr. Newman. Now the ship headed up to the Brooklyn Navy
Yard for finishing touches under the careful eye of Mr. Delano, the
navy constructor at that yard. George Tyson was not aboard, however, an absence that worried Hall. Tyson's commission languished
on some bureaucrat's desk. Hall made a note to appeal directly to

U.S.S. Polaris *(Culver Pictures)*

Robeson the minute the ship docked in New York. In their numerous prior meetings, the navy secretary had proved an enthusiastic and helpful friend.

Even Hall's official orders scarcely reached him before the ship sailed. "Having been appointed by the President of the United States, commander of the expedition toward the North Pole," the orders read. Thoughtfully, Hall had underlined those words with his pen. The orders gave him two and one half years, but they left the actual length up to Hall. He could stay longer if he had enough supplies or cut it short if disaster struck. Like the directions from the scientists, his naval orders showed an obsession with documentation. Hall and anyone who could write were to keep journals. He was to collect them at the end of the expedition and collate them into his final report. With the bureaucrats ever mindful of the vanished Franklin expedition, Hall was instructed to seal progress reports in bottles and throw them overboard as the sea journey progressed. On land similar notes enclosed in copper cylinders were to be placed in stone cairns as the party moved north. Who came up with the idea of the floating bottles is unknown, but it demonstrates the naïveté that pervaded the planning; a divided crew with conflicting goals expected someone in the government to find message bottles floating in the vast ocean.

Delano put the finishing touches on the *Polaris* in three days. During the layover the American Geographical Society held a reception. If the primary reason for going north eluded the government, the members of the society had no such misgivings. They were geographers and explorers like Hall, and they supported his lust for the North Pole. What could be placed on a map excited them. Bugs, fish, and shooting stars were secondary.

Speaking before the members of the society, Tookoolito charmed the members with her soft, accented English, and old Bill Morton brought tears to their eyes as he reminisced about his Arctic travels with Elisha Kent Kane. The good doctor had died in Havana in 1857 but still remained warm in the members' hearts. Even now there is an active Elisha Kent Kane Society.

Emil Bessel, perhaps recognizing he was among an unsympathetic crowd, muttered a few words of faint praise for Captain Hall's "enthusiasm," calling that a "stimulus," and expressed regrets over his limited English. These listeners' hearts were lost to exploration like Hall's rather than minute measurements. "If anything could be an additional stimulus to us during our trip, I think it will arise from the fact that such eminent men of science, such as compose this Society, are watching with interest the actions of our expedition," he said. For someone who claimed to possess limited proficiency with the language, Bessel managed to come across as articulate.

There it was again—the reference to "science" as opposed to "exploration."

The two men were well on their way to forming a dislike for each other. Hall's exchange of letters with Professor Henry and his complaint to Dr. Newton suggest he worried about Bessel and had even at that point stepped on the "sensitive" man's toes. And already whispers were circulating about Bessel's increasing rudeness to Captain Hall. It was becoming clear that Bessel regarded his commander as an unlettered oaf far beneath him in intellectual matters. His discussions with Hall wavered between condescension and outright insubordination. Bessel, in turn, embodied the threat to reaching the North Pole that Hall feared from the committee's massive scientific requirements, and served as a constant reminder of Hall's lack of formal education.

Hall rose last, and it was he, their explorer, who brought them to their feet when he spoke. Wisely, he thanked the government, especially mentioning his near worship of Secretary Robeson. Hall was learning to be politic. Uncharacteristically, he bared his soul to them.

"The Arctic Region is my home," he confessed. "I love it dearly, its storms, its winds, its glaciers, its icebergs. When I am there among them, it seems as if I were in an earthly heaven or a heavenly earth."

At the reception Henry Grinnell, whose two personally funded expeditions had done so much to foster polar exploration, presented Hall with a flag to be carried by the expedition. The banner was the same one that had been carried to Antarctica by Charles Wilkes on his ill-fated expedition in 1840.

"This is quite a noted flag," Grinnell began, "and has seen peril by ice and sea. In 1838 it went with Wilkes' expedition to a higher latitude toward the Southern Pole than any American flag ever went before."

Grinnell went on to enumerate the list of explorers who had carried the flag to the far ends of the earth. "Dr. Kane took it, with another expedition, to a still higher northern latitude."

Hall idolized the dead Kane, as did everybody assembled. Then Grinnell carelessly mentioned Hall's nemesis, Dr. Hayes, the man who had nearly wrested the expedition from his hands. "When Dr. Hayes went on his expedition I loaned it again to him, and he carried it about thirty-seven miles higher than an American flag had ever been before." Grinnell held out the standard. "Now, I give it to you, sir. Take it to the North Pole, and bring it back a year from next October."

Hall must have seethed inwardly at the name of his enemy. Here was a challenge he would meet. He would beat Hayes's mark or die in the process.

Hall stepped forward and grasped the weathered banner. "I really feel from the bottom of my soul that this flag, in the spring of 1872, will float over a new world; a new world, in which the North Pole star is its crowning jewel."

While members of the Geographical Society warmly applauded what they saw as a heroic link between both ice caps, seasoned salts viewed the presentation as something far different. Insubordination and strife had riddled the Wilkes expedition, leading eventually to Wilkes's court-martial. Bad luck hampered the Wilkes party, and to the superstitious sailors, anything associated with that trip carried the same stigma. Both Kane and Hayes had carried the flag, and they, too, had had problems.

Deepwater sailors are a highly superstitious lot. Facing the raw power of a storm at sea, a force able to make even the largest vessel seem insignificant, many a mariner has found religion. As Herman Melville wrote: "He who would learn to pray, let him go to sea." Over hundreds of years of losing to the oceans, seamen learned to grasp at anything that might improve their odds. Traditions and superstitions abound, enough to fill a book. Don't start a voyage on Friday, never ship aboard with a black seabag, fresh-cut flowers brought aboard mean an impending death—the litany goes on and on. Always stepping on board with your right foot first led to the common phrase, used even by landlubbers, of putting your right foot forward. First the *Periwinkle*'s name had been changed to *Polaris*, and now it would fly the colors of an ill-fated predecessor. It did not bode well.

Without thinking, Grinnell had laid another Jonah upon the *Polaris*.

Whether due to that or not, cracks opened in the *Polaris*'s organization. As the *Polaris* readied herself to sail, the cook, one of the common seamen, and one of the firemen jumped ship and deserted. Wilson, the assistant engineer, also vanished. Apparently Wilson and the fireman found working under Emil Schuman too loathsome to bear even for three days. The steward turned out to be consistently drunk and was set on the beach. Last, the ship's carpenter, Nathan Coffin, fell ill with an inflammation of the lungs and was hospitalized when the ship sailed. But at the eleventh hour Tyson's special orders arrived, and he clambered aboard. At this time he simply accompanied Captain Hall at the captain's pleasure. He would have to wait for the arrival of the coal tender *Congress* to receive his appointment as assistant navigator.

Below strength, the *Polaris* still steamed out of the Brooklyn Navy Yard on June 29 as the sun set over the land. The slanting rays of the sun flickering over the western landscape of buildings, trees, and squat hills fired the low-hanging clouds to the east. Tongues of crimson and orange licked along the underbellies of the nimbus and altocumulus clouds covering the harbor. So far, so good, many of the sailors sighed: Red sky at night, sailors' delight.

Seventeen hours later the *Polaris* anchored at New London, Connecticut. The special stop was made to pick up Alvin Odell. A veteran of naval action during the Civil War, Odell came highly recommended to fill the slot of assistant engineer. John Herron and William Jackson signed aboard as steward and cook, respectively. Adding another fireman and common seaman brought the crew to full complement.

Word also reached Hall that the carpenter, Nathan Coffin, had recovered from his illness and survived the navy doctors as well, no mean feat given the state of medical knowledge at that time. Coffin would join them in Greenland when the *Polaris* rendezvoused with the *Congress*. The newly graduated chaplain, Bryan, also would arrive on the *Congress*. The Reverend Dr. Newman, never missing a chance to save souls, would ride along to administer his final blessing on the ship and crew when it left that last vestige of civilization. Now a full complement had signed on, twenty-five brave souls. Loyally following Hall on board the *Polaris* were "his Eskimo," Ebierbing, Tookoolito, and their young adopted daughter, Puney. During his stay in New York, Ebierbing had drunk heavily, as have too many Inuit under similar circumstances. Both Hall and Ebierbing's wife, Tookoolito, hoped the return to his homeland would effect his cure.

In regard to his own wife, Mary Hall, and his two children, young Charles and Anna, Charles Francis Hall essentially abandoned them in Cincinnati. Business and family were a closed chapter to him now. His burning desire to reach the North Pole left little room for anything else. They lived on the meager remnants of his liquidated business. For all her quiet suffering, Mary Hall retained her pride. When Lady Franklin learned from Henry Grinnell that Hall's wife was in financial need while Hall was missing in the Arctic in 1869, the lady sent Mrs. Hall a gift of fifteen pounds. Mary Hall refused to accept the money. Just before Hall's crucial lecture at Lincoln Hall, his wife traveled from Cincinnati to Washington to visit him. She brought along his son, whom Captain Hall had only seen for a total of three months of the boy's ten years.

One day before Independence Day, July 3, the *Polaris* weighed anchor and left New London. Departing at four P.M. to take advantage of the tide, the ship headed north. As night fell, a sudden squall struck the vessel, tested the strength of the new refitting, and shook out those men without sea legs.

Summer storms occur when low-pressure cells crossing the Atlantic from Africa warm along the Gulf Stream and pick up moisture before colliding with colder air from Canada and the Arctic. Strong winds and sheets of rain drive the seawater before them. When that block of water, rolling along like the world's largest and heaviest freight train, hits the continental shelf, especially the shallow underwater table called the Grand Banks of Newfoundland, steep, short breaking waves form. Such waves are unsettling and damaging.

The *Polaris* proved a sound ship. No seams sprang, and no hands were lost overboard. Some poorly stowed supplies broke loose and battered several storage holds, but that was all. Lightning flashes lit the night sky and claps of thunder smote the air, yet nothing struck the ship. Undamaged, it sailed on to its first port of destination, St. John's, Newfoundland. For all its Jonahs, the little tug turned Arctic explorer would deal kindly with all of its crew except one.

In 1870 St. John's existed for one reason only. It was the finest natural harbor on the eastern side of the island of Newfoundland. Ever since Europeans came to the New World, the thick schools of cod drew fishermen to the waters of the Grand Banks, and those men needed a protected shelter. The natural topography surrounding St. John's fit the bill nicely. Completely encircled by hills and mountains tall enough to deflect the raging winds, the harbor can be entered only through a narrow channel that blocks most entering waves. A mile long and half a mile wide, the calm waters within this rocky circle are ideal for anchorage. At that time commerce and community roughly divided the town in half. Oil storage tanks, ships' chandlers, and red-painted warehouses dotted the east, while the hills to the west sprouted fashionable clapboard houses and shingled-roof cottages.

Trouble reared its ugly head amid the placid waters and wildflower-covered slopes. Several seals on the boilers needed replacement, and the engine required readjustment. Also, the skills of their carpenter, now aboard the *Congress*, were sorely missed. Hall and Buddington tried unsuccessfully to hire a carpenter from the town to fix the battered storage compartments. Summer was the busy season for the fishing fleet, and everyone with the needed skills was either at sea or inundated with repairs on the local vessels. The carpentry work would have to wait until Coffin caught up with them.

The seeds of dissension sowed by the unresolved questions of priority and command now sprouted roots. Bessel forcefully rejected any idea that Hall commanded him or members of his scientific corps, even though Captain Hall's orders specifically gave him *overall* command of the expedition. With his Prussian heritage, the meteorologist Meyer sided with Bessel, as might be expected. Their actions bordered on insubordination. While the two carefully avoided a direct confrontation, they seemed to be waiting, biding their time for the right moment to strike. That moment would not be far off.

Here again the foglike nature of the command structure created problems. If *Polaris* had been a full-fledged military vessel crewed and commanded by naval personnel, Bessel and Meyer would have been clapped in irons and sent home for court-martial when the *Congress* arrived. But they were not commissioned officers. Even Captain Buddington was without commission.

Hall found himself backed by Tyson and Morton, while Buddington and Chester waffled. Worse, the officers' quarrel spread below decks to the men. Soon they, too, divided—and along national lines. Not surprisingly, the Germans sided with Bessel. Reverting to their native tongue, knots of German-speaking crew members congregated in the fo'c'sle, more concerned that their fellow countrymen won the argument than with the goals of their mission.

George Tyson later related to E. Blake Vale:

A point of discussion arose as to the authority of the commander over the Scientific Corps. Strong feelings were mutually exhibited, which extended to the officers, and even the crew, among whom was developed an unmistakable feeling of special affinity on the score of national affiliation.

Here Hall should have acted decisively. But he didn't. Instead, he chose to bow to the wishes of Bessel. He backed down. "However, matters were smoothed over," Tyson advised. "The Scientific Corps were left free to follow their own course, and the threatened disruption of the party avoided." Members of the scientific corps were given a free hand to do what they wished. But the weed of dissension remained alive.

Charles Hall's lack of command experience obviously played a part in his abdication, as did his feelings of inferiority when dealing with the cultured Bessel. In the back of his mind hung the threat detailed to him by the shadowy parties in Washington. In addition, he had a tendency to overreact, and he knew it. On his first trip to the Arctic aboard the *George Henry*, he became convinced the crew thought he was eating their rations and meant him ill. Officially not a member of the crew, Hall had brought his own provisions. Food is a precious commodity in the Arctic and remained constantly in the back of the sailors' minds. Unable to convince the crew members that he ate only his own food, Hall took to his cabin and began a hunger strike. It took the intervention of Captain Buddington to resolve that crisis. Maybe Buddington reminded Hall of that episode.

But another, far darker incident weighed more heavily on his mind and caused him to back off. In the summer of 1869, Hall had killed a sailor named Patrick Coleman. At that time he had contracted with five whalers to aid him in his search for Franklin. An argument broke out on July 31 over whether the men were working hard enough. Presumably Hall was paying their wages and felt he was not getting his money's worth. Hot words flew back and forth, the sailors besting Hall with their experience in swearing. One man in particular, Coleman, fanned the flames and stood out as the leader. Hall implored him to cease his "mutinous talk and conduct" and laid his hand on Coleman's shoulder. The seaman took greater offense, doubling his fists, and prepared to launch himself at Hall. Normally Hall might have been a match for Coleman, but he feared the other four whalers would join the fray. And one of the rebellious men, Peter Bayne, held Hall's rifle. Sensibly, Hall demanded it back, and Bayne sensibly handed it over. The beleaguered explorer rushed out of the whaler's tent to his own tent with the rifle in hand. That should have ended the affair, but Hall next did something that is hard to excuse.

Seizing his Baylie pistol (a six-shot revolver) from his tent, Hall rushed back to confront Coleman. Again, he demanded to know whether Coleman still felt mutinous. The results were predictable. Coleman's blood was up, and he would not back down. The man's response grew more threatening, and Hall shot him.

Most seamen carry a knife for utility work aboard ship, so Coleman and the others might not have been completely unarmed. When faced with an unruly crew, a prudent sea captain would collect the men's blades and have the blacksmith strike off the pointed tips. Thus "tipped," the knives could not be used to stab the officers yet still retained their function to cut line. A sailor carrying a tipped knife bore the stigma that he might be trouble. But no mention is made of any knife drawn during the argument. In a modern court of law, Hall's actions would constitute manslaughter, possibly even murder.

Hall then turned on his heel, walked out of the tent, and handed his pistol to one of the startled Inuit who crowded outside. Returning to the fallen Coleman, Hall dragged the wounded man over to his own tent, half expecting the sailor to gasp an apology with his last breath. But Coleman refused to die, much less repent.

Stricken now with guilt or remorse, Hall resolved to nurse the critically wounded Coleman back to health. Only moments before, he had aimed directly at this same man's heart, resolved to kill him. The avenging angel had instantly transformed into Florence Nightingale. Days passed as Hall tried everything he knew to save Coleman. Coleman died two weeks later, on August 14, having endured a slow and painful demise from infection and probably peritonitis and pneumonia. Two days after Coleman's death, the whaling ships returned to Repulse Bay. On the day the ships left to hunt whales, Hall awoke to find himself alone. His remaining whalers had deserted. Again, he was alone with the Inuit.

Killing a man quickly is bad enough. Killing one of your own companions is even worse. Watching someone's protracted demise from your bullet, hearing his labored, gurgling breath, changing his fetid dressings in the close confines of a small tent, and watching his skin pale and mottle as his life slowly drains away must be horrendous. No doubt it seared deeply into Charles Francis Hall's mind.

No official action came of the shooting. Judge Roy Bean might have been the only law west of the Pecos, but that far north there was no law at all. What authority visited this desolate notch along the western edge of Foxe Channel came and went with the whaling ships that wintered there. And that authority related only to the captain's law aboard his own vessel. That summer the whalers had long since sailed in search of the humpback.

On his return to New York, Hall dutifully confessed his actions to his patron Henry Grinnell, who found that no one wanted authority for that desolate region. Repulse Bay, where the shooting had taken place, lay beyond the territorial borders of the Dominion of Canada. Years later Peter Bayne claimed that Coleman and he had discovered evidence as to the whereabouts of Sir John Franklin's grave from Eskimo and thus earned the enmity of Hall for their meddling, possibly adding revenge to the cause of the shooting.

One thing is certain: The cold, isolation, alien landscape, and unforgiving ice make even the smallest slight grow out of proportion. In a place where the endless sky and boundless white land merge into one colossal landscape that assaults and overwhelms the senses, the value of a single human life diminishes to nothing. A person's very soul is threatened, so the mind turns inward in self-defense. Imagination and fear go hand in hand. Since everything is in short supply—food, firewood, shelter, and warmth—survival becomes the main preoccupation. The land dispenses with cockeyed optimists quickly. A hidden crevasse, fragile ice, a sudden storm and the unwary vanish forever. No doubt Hall reacted as he did because he knew that in the Arctic the glass is always half-empty, never half-full.

Stepping back from this confrontation only weakened Hall's command. The Germans aboard now saw their fellow countryman

Bessel as stronger than Hall, and the science projects vaulted to equal importance with the quest for the North Pole.

Up to this time, Hall had regarded Bessel as lower in the command structure than the man's title of chief scientific officer implied. As late as June 20 Hall referred to Bessel's role as "naturalist and photographer" and "most likely . . . the surgeon" in a letter he wrote to astronomer Henry Gannett of the Harvard College observatory. Now Bessel had challenged his command, and Buddington had refused to support Hall.

In a quandary, Hall spent his days away from the ship, climbing the hills while the engine was repaired.

With the rift widening, the *Polaris* steamed north into the Labrador Sea and headed for the western coast of Greenland. Proceeding along that serrated coast, it took advantage of the northerly flowing West Greenland Current, which hugs the coastline. The usual banks of fog and walls of mist and drizzle greeted the ship, while the air grew cold and heavy with the reek of salt and rotting sea grass.

Reaching Holsteinsborg (now called Sisimiut after the modern tendency to restore the Inuit names to Greenland), the *Polaris* anchored. Here Hall hoped to purchase additional coal for his boilers and reindeer hides to clothe his crew. During his visits with the Inuit, Hall had recognized the value of using reindeer hides for outer clothing. The waterproof, hollow shafts of each reindeer hair provide natural buoyancy that aid the animals in crossing rivers and furnish superior insulation against the cold. At a time before synthetic fibers, no finer winter clothing could be found. The pullover style of the Eskimo parka with matching pants retained body heat much better than European dress, with its buttonholes and loose flaps. Wool loses its insulating property when it becomes wet. Hypothermia, frostbite, and death rapidly follow. Hall did not plan to repeat Franklin's mistake of requiring his men to wear wool and canvas coats.

Unfortunately he was thwarted on both accounts. The remote settlement of Holsteinsborg had little coal to spare, and reindeer skins were scarce. The warming trend that favored thin ice for his expedition had also altered the annual migration of the reindeer.

Warmer weather meant less need to wander south in search of the lichens and moss the herbivores ate.

Meeting an old friend, Frederick Von Otto, who headed a returning Swedish exploration, Hall did receive good news. Von Otto's crew had sailed as far north as Upernavik. *Baffin Bay was open*. The ice field had receded. Only an occasional iceberg dotted the leaden water between Disko and Upernavik. Hall was elated.

In an instant he changed his route of attack. Originally he had planned to sail as far west as he could into Jones Sound, the gap between the saw-toothed fingers lining the bottom of Ellesmere Island and the top of Devon Island. Once the *Polaris* encountered ice too thick to drive past, the expedition would take off overland for the elusive Pole. That was the plan he'd presented to the academy and to the government.

But Von Otto's report changed everything. Smith Sound, directly north of Baffin Bay, might be breached. With skill and luck Hall could sail the *Polaris* through that narrow gap into Kane Basin and on into the Kennedy Channel. Only sixteen miles of water separated Greenland from Ellesmere Island at that spot. The Humboldt Glacier, with its towering columns of ice, flanked the eastern shores of Kane Basin. He would slip north of that devilish ellipse on the charts marking the eightieth parallel. Within six hundred miles of the North Pole!

He must act swiftly, he realized. The ice could re-form at any minute. He could not wait for his supply ship, the *Congress*, to arrive. Putting aside his feelings, Hall left word of his change of plans and ordered the *Polaris* to make for the island of Disko, the sharp-edged lump of rock jutting into Baffin Bay roughly halfway between Holsteinsborg and their final jumping-off port, Upernavik. Driving the engines full-out, the ship made the village of Godhavn on Disko in twenty-four hours.

For six anxious days, Hall and his crew fretted over the absence of the *Congress*. Every day they waited meant a missed opportunity. The captain used the time to purchase the precious furs and extra sled dogs the party would need. Disko had no reindeer hides either, so sealskins and dog skins were substituted. He also secured the services from the Danes of another Inuit named Hans Christian, whose renown as a dog handler and hunter were without equal. With Hans and Ebierbing, the dog teams now had expert handlers.

But Hans Christian was at Prøven, 60 miles south of Upernavik. To the first mate fell the yeoman's duty of taxi driver. First, Chester searched among the fjords in an open whaleboat for Karrup Smith, the district inspector of Disko and ranking Danish official. Paddling more than 175 miles up and down the coast, the mate returned with the inspector only to be sent off to fetch Hans Christian, the new Inuit addition.

On August 10, cheers rang across the deck of the *Polaris* as the black smoke and funnels of the *Congress* hove into sight. Larger than the *Polaris*, the supply ship carried much-needed coal and extra stores. Karrup Smith, delighted to be furthering diplomatic ties with the United States, readily allowed the extra coal and food to be stored in the government warehouse.

With the *Congress* came Tyson's written commission, and he officially became an officer. Up until that time he had served only at Captain Hall's pleasure, an extra cog not integrated into the machinery of command. More than a month had passed while the crew sorted out their tasks and tested the mettle of their officers. Like seamen since the beginning of history, *Polaris*'s sailors used that time to see what they could get away with, subtly probing their leaders for weakness and testing to find how slipshod their actions could be before they were called to task. Sailors can be either experts at efficiency or strict minimalists if not properly motivated. Regrettably Tyson's inaction during this time critically undermined his leadership. Lasting impressions were formed while he did nothing. Thus, his authority over them never fully matured. This weak link would make its results felt in the months to come.

Waving heartily back from the *Congress* was the theologian the Reverend Dr. John Philip Newman. By Newman's side stood the newly appointed astronomer and ship's chaplain, Mr. Bryan. Tucked inside Newman's coat pocket were special prayers for the expedition. One, to be opened and read only on reaching the North Pole, would never be used.

While the *Congress* came placidly on, insurrection seethed below decks on the *Polaris*. From Hall's cabin came the heated voices of the captain, Frederick Meyer, and Emil Bessel. Both men had picked their ground to openly defy their captain's orders. As he would later report, beyond the bulkhead the black steward, John Herron, listened in amazement. Two against one, he mused, both against the captain. Peering through a crack in the boards, the steward watched the drama unfold.

"I am the commanding officer of this vessel," Hall fumed. "I ordered you to keep my journal. You are to write what I dictate."

Meyer must have glanced furtively at the chief scientist. Seeing support in Bessel's dark eyes, he squared his shoulders. "I cannot, Captain. It interferes with my primary duties as meteorologist." Meyer had considered adding the word *regret* but decided against it. From the corner of his eye, he saw Bessel nod his head.

"What?" Hall's face flushed.

From his hiding place, Herron held his breath.

"Captain, I must go ashore to take readings. I cannot remain on the ship to do your writing if I am to take those measurements. My orders from headquarters require me to do that scientific work."

"Orders? What orders?" Hall towered over the smaller man, opening his meaty hands and closing them into fists. "Produce these orders!"

Meyer blanched. He had no such orders. He was only parroting what Bessel had told him to say. And unlike the newly arrived Bessel, Meyer's six years in the United States Signal Corps gave him much more to lose. His head dropped. On the verge of backing down, he opened his mouth.

But before Meyer could capitulate, Dr. Bessel stepped out of the shadows of the cramped cabin. To exacerbate their obvious dislike of each other, Hall had the odious habit of standing over him while talking, as if to emphasize their size difference. And Bessel hated looking up to him.

"Mr. Meyer is under my orders," Bessel interceded smoothly. "He's a member of *my* scientific corps." He emphasized the pronoun. "If he desires to go ashore to take readings, he is free to do so *whenever he wishes.*"

Bessel watched smugly as Hall's face contorted in rage. "He will not!" Hall shouted. "If he disobeys my direct order, I'll send him back with the *Congress*. He can answer to his superiors in Washington."

Visions of iron manacles flashed before Frederick Meyer's eyes. His career was ruined.

But Bessel appeared unaffected. "Mr. Meyer is under my authority, Captain. You cannot do that."

"I can, and I will! I'm in overall command of this expedition. And I do have that in writing."

Bessel shook his head slowly. He released a long-drawn sigh. "Very well, if you insist. But, if Mr. Meyer leaves, *so will I*." Bessel paused to gauge the effect of his words. "I will go in support of him." With satisfaction, the doctor watched his sentence strike the captain like a blast of icy sleet.

Now it was Hall's turn to blanch. Color drained from his face. The shadowy faces and whispered threats of those in Washington returned to haunt him. If Bessel left, Hall knew he would be replaced.

Bessel delivered his final blow with perfect timing. "And, Captain, I have the assurances of the German crew that they will leave with us. . . ."

Seven days later Captain Davenport, commanding officer of the United States tender *Congress*, leaned against the binnacle of his ship and watched the *Polaris* steam away. The cheering from both ships no longer rang in his ears. His tars had long since turned back to their tasks as the shouting voices of the bos'ns urged them to achieve perfection. On a brave ship departing on a noble mission, it should have been a moment to savor. Unhappily the dirty tail of black smoke that dragged behind the *Polaris* sent a feeling of foreboding running through the skipper. Beside him stood the Reverend E. D. Bryan, who had come along to bid farewell to his oldest son, R.W.D. Bryan, the *Polaris*'s new chaplain and astronomer. Next to the minister stood Capt. James Buddington, also a passenger aboard the *Congress* to see his nephew Capt. Sidney O. Buddington off. Davenport must have sensed their depression. He shook his head. A ship heading for trouble.

The open defiance of some members of the *Polaris*'s crew

toward their captain sent a shiver through the seasoned sailor. Hall had confided in Davenport, offering him a glimpse of the troubles that beset the *Polaris*. Davenport knew that nothing of this sort could be tolerated on a navy vessel. In all his years in the navy, Davenport had never faced such a thing. He offered to clap the offenders in irons and drag them back to the navy yard for trial.

Strangely Hall declined. While Meyer was on loan from the army, Bessel was a civilian, the *Polaris*'s commander admitted. So were his entire crew, save for old Morton and a few others. And Hall himself did not strictly hold a naval commission. Neither he nor Tyson nor Buddington did. Trust Washington to splice a civilian crew onto a naval vessel, Davenport mused.

The old captain probably smelled the rot of politics in all this. Bessel was anointed by those nabobs in Washington, the Smithsonian, and the National Academy of Sciences. Bessel was their pick. If he came up lacking, it reflected poorly on their judgment. The waves would spread to the secretary of the navy until the waters of this mess lapped at the feet of President Grant himself. No wonder Hall was cautious.

To make matters worse, Hall was not a sea captain, and it showed. His crew sensed it, too.

But Hall should have been able to rely on Buddington. At least that man had his sea legs, even though they had been gotten on whaling vessels and not in the navy. Buddington should have known how to man a ship. Then Hall admitted to Davenport that Buddington liked the demon rum. When both ships transferred cargo, the sailing master got drunk. He had his little supply stashed away. Buddington also raided the pantry for milk and sugar like a three-year-old. Well, clap him in irons, too, the navy man suggested.

After deliberation, Hall realized his trip was doomed if Davenport sailed away with half his crew in the brig, and so he asked Davenport to make an appearance to strengthen his sagging command. The old commander cut an intimidating figure when he came over. Boarding the *Polaris* with two marines as honor guard, he insisted on being piped aboard. The men snapped to smartly when they saw his sword and all his gold braid.

When Davenport left the *Polaris*, order appeared restored. Captain Buddington repented his ways, and Meyer had signed a statement in the margin of Hall's official orders. "As a member of the United States naval north polar expedition, I do hereby solemnly promise and agree to conform to all the orders and instructions as herein set forth by the Secretary of the United States Navy to the commander," it read. Break that oath, Davenport's presence hinted darkly, and Meyer would swing from the yardarm.

But then Hall once again backed down. After pinning Meyer like a butterfly in a collection box, Hall gave the man what he wanted. He relieved Meyer of his duties as secretary and appointed a young man named Joseph Mauch. Bessel won after all. From that day onward, Captain Hall would relinquish the scientific studies he had worked so hard to teach himself. To Bessel and his scientific corps would fall the pleasures of collecting the specimens, bones, rocks, and Native artifacts that Hall so loved.

Something else troubling happened. There was a saboteur aboard. Before the *Polaris* sailed again, the ship's machinery was tampered with. The special boilers designed to burn seal oil and whale blubber vanished. Someone had thrown them overboard, it seemed. Now the vessel could run the engines or heat the crew's quarters only by burning coal. And where they were headed, there were no coal stores except what they carried in their hold. All Hall's ingenuity to provide that backup plan went for naught.

Even the Reverend Newman weighed in to pour oil upon the troubled waters. The day before the *Polaris* sailed, he came aboard to read one of the prayers he'd written for blessing the enterprise. It borrowed heavily from the Psalms, especially the part about those who go down to the sea in ships and do their business upon the great waters seeing the works of the Lord and his wonders in the deep. Whoever wrote that psalm had been upon the sea.

But the wise Newman had added something else—a plea for harmony. In deep, resonant tones, the minister's rolling voice sang out the lines:

Give us noble thoughts, pure emotions, and generous sympathies for each other, while so far away from human habitations. May we have for each other that charity that suffereth long and is kind, that envieth not, that vaunteth not itself, that is not puffed up, that seeketh not her own, that is not easily provoked, that thinketh not evil, but that beareth all things, hopeth all things, endureth all things; that charity that never faileth.

That about covered it. If the men aboard the *Polaris* followed that exhortation, they would be all right. But it would take a strong sailor to live up to those words—once the dark and cold of the Arctic worked on them.

In his diary notation for August 10, George Tyson wrote:

Captain Davenport and Rev. Dr. Newman, who came up in the *Congress*, have had their hands full trying to straighten things out between Captain Hall and the disaffected. Some of the party seem bound to go contrary anyway, and if Hall wants a thing done, that is just what they won't do.

Out in the bay a squall line swept sleet and rain across the sea like a giant's whisk broom. Wind advancing before the rain tore wisps of spindrift from the tops of the short waves and roiled the sullen water. Patches of pewter sky, overwhelmed by the lowering clouds, merged with the leaden sea. Davenport watched the *Polaris* slip into the curtain of rain and fog.

Not a ship heading for trouble, the navy captain must have realized, but a troubled ship going in harm's way.

Chapter Four

FIRST ICE

There are two parties already, if not three, aboard. All the foreigners hang together, and expressions are freely made that Hall shall not get any credit out of this expedition. Already some have made up their minds how far they will go, and when they will get home again—queer sort of explorers these!

—GEORGE TYSON, DIARY, AUGUST 10, 1871

August 18, 1871, the *Polaris* reached Upernavik. The vessel dropped anchor in a shroud of mist and fog. For those new to the far North, the gray skies and barren, windblown coast of Greenland offered a sour taste of what lay ahead. Strewn with bits and pieces of driftwood and salvaged scraps, the village resembled a dump rather than the last notable link with civilization. After Upernavik only the harbored settlement of Tasiussaq lay between them and the unknown. Whereas the sunlit rocks and shadowed tidal pools of St. John's underscored Newfoundland's rugged beauty, the coast of Greenland presented a far gloomier picture. Barren, desolate, and dank, the colorless harbor existed uneasily between the threatening sea and the brooding peaks that scowled down upon it. These *nunataks*, or mountain peaks, pierce the omnipresent mantle of ice that dominates the region. Scoured of snow by the winds, the jagged projections of hard Precambrian rock rise above the ice like somber crystals, making them the inverse of the picturesque, snow-covered peaks of the Alps or Rocky Mountains.

As the largest island of the world, Greenland suffers from two dubious distinctions. To the eye, it is neither green nor land. First, two-thirds of its land mass lies within the Arctic Circle, so most of

Passing Fitz Clarence Rock, August 26, 1871 (Culver Pictures)

Greenland is white. Erik the Red lied to his fellow Icelanders on his return from Greenland in A.D. 985 to encourage them to settle there. Later travelers would marvel at the irony of the place's name.

Besides not being green, there is precious little land either. A massive ice cap, second in size only to Antarctica, covers more than 85 percent of the land. Like a colossal melting block of ice, varying in places from one to two miles thick, the ice cap flows ever outward from the center toward the sea. Snowfall of up to eighty centimeters blankets the cap, compressing the underlying ice into dense layers. Heat is generated during this process, and the ice begins to slide outward. Friction from the moving sheets generates more heat. Melt from this heat lubricates the interface, but the sheer weight and bulk of the sliding ice scour the underlying rock and grind it into fine silt, called glacial flour. This powdery dust turns the melting water into white, milky streams. One of Greenland's fastest-moving glaciers, the Jakobshavn Glacier, slides along at one hundred feet per day. All this ice heads for the ocean.

Eking a tenuous existence between these wandering walls are scraps of exposed high ground. Spared by the glaciers, the land is scourged by the wind. No trees of note grow there, only stunted and dwarfed birch, scrub alder, and willow. Mainly the barren rock is carpeted with cotton grass, sedge, and lichens. The drier parts are termed tundra, while the wetter hollows are called taiga.

About this bleak landscape, Arctic foxes, hares, musk ox, and lemmings struggle to survive.

Well after dark, Mr. Chester's well-traveled whaleboat thumped against the side of the *Polaris*. The first mate, sent to search for the second Inuit sled driver, had returned. A lantern held aloft by the deck watch revealed an astonishing sight. Beaming upward in the reflected light were five round faces and a dozen sled dogs. Awkwardly, the first mate explained to Captain Hall that Hans Christian, while willing to join the expedition, refused to part with his family and all his worldly possessions. Hans saw no difficulty in this. With an Inuit's straightforward logic, he decided to take everything with him. Settling his wife and three small children in the boat, Hans then crammed the craft to its gunnels with his furs, guns, lamps, grass baskets, harpoons, sled, kayak, and his entire dog team. In addition to this was more unwelcome cargo: within the Inuit's hair and among their furs crawled hundreds of lice.

After the new additions were hauled aboard, a touching reunion took place. Hans shook hands all around with Hall and the officers. When he came to William Morton, he paused. Both Morton and Hans had accompanied Elisha Kent Kane's expedition seventeen years before.

Those seventeen years at sea had been hard ones for William Morton. It was Morton and Hans who had mushed overland while the rest of the expedition wintered in their icebound ship, the *Advance*. Near Cape Constitution open water halted their foray. Morton returned and reported his findings to Kane. The delusion of the Open Polar Sea was popular at that time, and Morton's findings seemed to confirm that such an open waterway existed. However, the expedition led by Hall's nemesis, Isaac Hayes, seven years later found only ice. Morton was labeled a liar and his beloved Kane faulted for taking the word of an enlisted man. Morton's loss of credibility weighed heavily on him, aging him severely.

Morton's seamed face had so changed that Hans failed to recognize his old friend. Then Morton showed his hands to the Inuit. An accidental explosion of black powder during the Kane exploration burned and scarred the seaman's hands. Hans took the hands and ran his fingers over the raised scars. Instantly Hans identified the injury and with it his past companion. The two men embraced warmly and shook hands while tears moistened the old explorer's eyes.

Two days passed while Hall struggled to buy more sled dogs. Without adequate animals to haul the sleds, overland advance would be impossible. No other animal could live and work in the harsh conditions as well as the tough, thick-coated dogs bred by the Inuit. Years later Robert Scott would use ponies instead of dogs to haul his sledges in his quest for the South Pole. That would cost the lives of the entire Scott expedition.

The commander used the time to strengthen his position. After the Sunday services given by Mr. Bryan, Hall resolved to bell the cat. He rose and addressed the gathering, intending to reaffirm his command over all aspects of the expedition, especially Bessel's group. Instead of unifying his men, as was his intention, the speech did little good. The split had occurred. His words fell upon different ears with differing impact. What German and American heard was very divergent.

To Joseph Mauch, the young German assigned to be Hall's stenographer, the lecture dissolved into a diatribe directed against the ranking Teuton, Emil Bessel. "Capt. Hall made some remarks insulting Dr. Bessel most severely," Mauch wrote in his journal.

To the American Noah Hayes, his captain's speech reflected his steadfast resolve and noble principles. Hayes remembered Captain Hall asserting "his determination to maintain order and obedience to all lawful commands." Prophetically Hayes recalled Hall's vowing "if necessary to die in the performance of his duty as commander rather than yield a letter."

Hall had cast his gauntlet down and backed his oath with his life.

Another day's steam found the ship anchored at Tasiussaq, a collection of huts more than anything else. Hall purchased more dogs, bringing the total up to sixty. He had hoped to convince a man named Jansen to join the group, but Jansen refused.

All around them signs of autumn showed. Yellow laced the curling willow and alder leaves, and the white caribou moss rose in stark contrast against the red-and-orange–tinged lichen. The air carried a sharper bite. Each evening the land breeze wafted the pungent tang of high bush cranberries among the tarred rigging lines. Hall grew more anxious with each sign. His window through the sea ice was closing. Any day now the mountains of floating ice would slide down from the north to crash and collide while they sealed Smith Sound until the next summer.

Two days of solid fog blocked their departure. Cold, white, and impenetrable, the fog descended on the harbor without notice. Hall chafed at the bit, finally deciding to trust the ship to the local knowledge of a pilot. Hastily he amended his last report to Navy Secretary Robeson. Gov. Lowertz Elberg had promised to see the report safely aboard the next ship to the United States. On August 22 he had written optimistically, "The prospects of the expedition are fine; the weather beautiful, clear, and exceptionally warm." A landsman, he failed to realize the warm air was a mixed blessing and might bring fog. Now he penned a more somber note: "The *Polaris* bids adieu to civilization. God be with us."

Through the fog and into the open sea of Baffin Bay, *Polaris* headed north for the neck of the bottle called Smith Sound. With Von Otto's report that the ice pack had receded still fresh in his mind, Hall made way through the open water, following the most direct path to his goal. Like a silent hunter lying in wait to spring the trap, Smith Sound remained open, luring the ship ever northward. Fading astern, the faint oil lamps of Tasiussaq shimmered over the rolling waves until they became no more than a memory. With those lights faded all contact with their modern world. Behind lay hospitals, electric lights, telegraph, civilized comforts, and safety. Ahead waited the cold and darkness and danger.

Inside Smith Sound the first icebergs appeared.

Saint Brendan, the seafaring Irish monk, first mentioned encountering "floating crystal castles" during his far-flung voyages in a cowhide coracle. Saint Brendan often exaggerated and was given to flights of fancy as he rocked along in his fragile craft. Unfortunately for mariners to this day, what he saw was real, and nothing he wrote about icebergs conveyed their majesty or the utter terror they invoke in a sailor's heart as they slide silently through the water with the help of current and wind. The nip in the air that precedes an iceberg can chill a mariner to his marrow. Before radar and the Global Positioning System (GPS), only a keen eye and a quick hand on the helm prevented a collision with these floating monsters. In thick fog the faint echo of the foghorn might be the only thing to give adequate warning.

But Greenland is infamous for producing very large tabular icebergs. Flat and expansive, these ice islands, often miles across, drift along barely showing above the surface. No sounds echo from these. A vessel driven aground on one has no chance. If the ship is not instantly holed and sunk, its rocking rips the hull apart on this floating island.

And where the *Polaris* sailed was iceberg country, indeed. Unlike the eastern coast of Greenland, where icebergs are few and move north with the current, western Greenland wins the prize for calving icebergs. Shearing off the moving face of the glaciers, massive blocks of ice escape the fjords to sail south along the western face of Greenland with the Labrador Current. Appropriately enough, given their potential for destruction, all up and down the coast thundering booms and cracks herald their birth, resonating for miles from the fjords.

Rolling over so that the bulk of ice lies below the waterline, these watery battering rams head for the shipping lanes. More than 7,500 icebergs train down Davis Strait. Fewer than 1 in 20 sails past Newfoundland, but the vagaries of wind and surface temperature can dramatically prolong their lives. In both 1907 and 1926, icebergs traveled as far south as Bermuda.

From the deck of the *Polaris*, the crew watched pale battalions loom on the horizon. More and more ice appeared as the water developed a dark and sinister cast. Jagged icebergs mingled with spinning plates of fractured floe ice. Steaming along in the dark, the *Polaris* narrowly missed a low tabular iceberg. The lookouts were doubled and instructed to keep a sharp eye for areas of dead water. As the lowering clouds and fog hid the moon, only the absence of whitecaps exposed the giant saucers of ice skimming along at sea level.

Dawn brought a surprise. Directly ahead lay an ice floe littered with rolling, grunting, reddish-brown lumps. The foul stench of rotted fish and dung blew ahead of the floe, announcing the arrival of a pod of walrus. Warily the animals regarded the ship as they drifted closer. Inuit hunted the animals for their meat, tusks, and skins to make their *oomiaks*. Besides the few humans who paddled their fragile boats, only killer whales and polar bear threaten these large mammals, but the vigilant males who guarded the group failed to recognize these men as a danger. Still cautious, the walrus watched the dark hulk of the *Polaris* sail closer.

These were Arctic specimens, so Dr. Bessel induced George Tyson to shoot one for scientific study. But the walrus has a thick, spongy skull like the elephant that encases a tiny brain. Now Tyson learned what the Inuit already knew. Walrus are difficult to kill unless shot through the eye. If not killed instantly, they slide off and sink. The Inuit used harpoons with braided skin lines. Even then, more than one hunter died beneath the slashing tusks of a wounded walrus or drowned when the animal shattered his *oomiak*. Both Tyson's shots missed a vital spot, and the animals vanished into the safety of the black water, leaving behind only an empty, brown-streaked floe.

Threading through the ever-increasing floes of ice, the *Polaris* beat northward, aiming for the eye of the needle. Passing through Smith Sound, the vessel entered the ice-cluttered narrows that separates Greenland from Ellesmere Island. Tapering in places to a mere sixteen miles across, the three-hundred-mile gauntlet widens north of Smith Sound into Kane Basin, a massive bite taken out of the western side of Greenland by the Humboldt Glacier. Beyond Kane Basin the passage constricts again into Kennedy Channel. Beyond that passage lies the Lincoln Sea, sweeping north of Ellesmere Island and the northernmost tip of Greenland. No land exists north of here. Here is truly the end of the earth.

Ancient mariners might leave the unknown edges of their charts white and fearfully mark "Here be dragons." But this is land's end. And dragons do live here in the form of frightening gales, building-size bergs that bulldoze down the straits, and numbing cold. A man lost overboard is dead within fifteen minutes from hypothermia. Within minutes the 38°F seawater so cools the small muscles of the hands that a man overboard cannot grasp a lifeline. Anyone lucky enough to reach shore or climb aboard floating ice freezes just as quickly without a fire or shelter.

The elusive goal of the North Pole that Charles Francis Hall sought actually sits above a depression at the top of the globe. Like a hard-boiled egg with one end smashed in, the North Polar region is one vast frozen sea overlying an irregular dent in the earth. Subterranean ridges roughly divide this scooped-out depression into three basins: the Nansen Basin, the Makarov Basin, and the Canada Basin. The highest ridge, the Lomonosov Ridge, runs from the top of Greenland across to eastern Siberia.

For those used to the security of terra firma, this region offers little solace. The ice is restless. Twisted by the rotation of the earth and pushed by the winds and currents, the polar ice field drifts endlessly. Above Ellesmere Island the ice spins ponderously clockwise like a massive frozen pinwheel called the Beaufort Gyral Stream. Closer to the Pole itself, the ice moves along the Greenwich meridian from east to west at three to four miles a day. A party pressing against this drift can struggle forward all day only to find it has progressed backward.

This constant movement fractures the ice and crumples it upon itself. Miles of pressure ridges traverse the ice plain like miniature Rocky Mountains, creating barriers impossible to cross. Sharp-edged *sastrugi* like twenty-foot piles of broken glass litter the journey, cutting dogs' feet, lacerating boots, and shattering sled runners. Deep crevasses and open lees of water mingle among the blocks of ice.

Of course, most of this was unknown to Captain Hall and his companions at the time. His journey north was much like what a trip to Mars would be today. Every mile he moved past where civilized man had gone was a mile into the unknown. Even his instruments were primitive by modern standards. In the 1870s the finest tools with which to measure one's position were the sextant, the magnetic compass, and the hand-wound chronometer.

As far north as the *Polaris* sailed, the pull of the magnetic pole on the compass needle rendered it almost useless, deflecting the needle more than 47° to the west of true north. Measuring longitude accurately required an accurate timepiece. While you could measure your latitude fairly correctly on the surface of the earth with a sextant by taking a noon sun shot, measuring the sun when it was directly overhead, to calculate your longitude required the accurate time. Every four seconds off the correct time equaled an error of one nautical mile.

Once again the British government, in 1728, rising to a challenge, offered a reward to whoever built the most accurate chronometer, one that met its strict requirements. After all, how was the British Lion to rule the seas if it couldn't tell where it was? As usual, the prize money amounted to twenty thousand pounds. An amateur mechanic and carpenter named John Harrison surprised the Royal Society by building such a timepiece. The Board of Longitude equivocated, so Harrison improved his designs, making them more accurate and, more important, small enough to be carried aboard ship. In 1762 Harrison's number 4 marine chronometer erased all doubts. During a test cruise from England to Jamaica, Harrison's clock showed an error of only five seconds. The problem of longitude was solved. Even so, the government paid Harrison only five thousand pounds at first, holding back on the remainder until 1773.

But for these hardy Arctic adventurers, special problems existed. Cold temperatures played havoc with the lubricating oil and finely tuned springs of the chronometers, affecting their accuracy. Using the sextant was even harder. The cold, bare metal of the sextant instantly froze any exposed fingers, necessitating cumbersome gloves. The slightest wisp of breath will fog the instrument. The Arctic sun by late summer runs low on the horizon and vanishes entirely in October. Without a horizon of open water, a plate of liquid mercury must be used to reflect the sighting. The navigator must lie on his stomach on the ice, sight into the shimmering dish, and try to match the sun or star with its reflected circle in the dish. Using a mercury horizon in the twilight to sight dim stars is almost impossible. This compounds errors in the sighting. Any result is then divided by two to get a reading. And any accidental error doubles.

The whole exercise is akin to trying to align the reflection of two swinging lightbulbs in a saucer of water while balancing on your elbows. Only your life may depend on your accuracy.

Years later Robert Peary, with better chronographs and sextants, would still struggle with this difficult means of measurement. Even today his readings that prove he reached the North Pole trouble some historians.

To solve these problems, Hall planned to use Polaris, the North Star, as his guiding light. When asked by members of the academy how he intended to tell when he reached the North Pole, he blithely answered that he would look overhead at Polaris. When the star no longer moved southward as he trekked north but stayed constantly overhead in the firmaments, he would be directly beneath the Pole Star and standing on the exact North Pole. The scientists accepted his logic, for everyone knew the Polar Star hung in the sky directly over the Pole and never wavered. Had Hall actually reached the North Pole, he would have been puzzled by his findings. To the observer standing beneath it, Polaris oscillates back and forth in a small ellipse while the earth wobbles on its axis.

Whatever misfortune Captain Hall suffered with his officers and crew, good fortune favored his advance up the narrow straits. The floating bergs parted, and no pack ice blocked their way. On the evening of August 27, the *Polaris* steamed past the highest point that Hall's nemesis Dr. Hayes had reached. In 1860 gales and ice had forced Hayes's schooner the *United States* to winter over at a place Hayes named Port Foulke near Hartstene Bay. Dr. Kane's exploration aboard the *Advance* in 1853 nearly met disaster when a sudden storm forced ice around the ship, causing it to take refuge in that harbor. Both Hayes and Kane pressed northward by sled while their ships wintered over. Eventually Kane was forced to abandon the *Advance* and retreat south. Within three more hours the *Polaris* continued past Rensselaer Harbor.

A jubilant Hall paced the decks as the sightings confirmed they had reached 78°51' N, where Kane had grounded his ship and made his winter camp. Dawn found them passing through the narrowing of Kennedy Channel. Beyond this the channel widened again.

William Morton and Hans pointed and laughed as the ship beat through the water. Here was the place they had reached seventeen years before and reported on only to be ridiculed when Hayes later found it frozen. Kane's Open Polar Sea, they called it, and their enthusiasm brought them only reproach. Now the *Polaris* cruised where Hayes had declared sea travel was impossible. They were vindicated.

Ahead in the swirling mists, the Open Polar Sea narrowed. It was not a sea after all but another of the basins that populate the passage like a string of misshapen pearls. Expansively, Hall renamed the place after himself, calling it Hall Basin. He could hardly wait to see the look on Hayes's face when the man learned the *Polaris* had sailed where Hayes said no ship could.

Exiting the northern end of the basin, the ship brushed aside slabs of floating ice and entered another channel. Now it sailed where no ship had gone before. With mounting exuberance, Charles Hall began naming everything in sight. The channel became Robeson Channel, after the secretary of the navy; an indentation along its eastern side became Polaris Bay. Ahead another, larger bay was named Newman's Bay, after the good reverend. Headlands rising from the southern edge of Newman's Bay became Sumner Headlands, after the senator from Massachusetts. For all his excitement, Hall covered all bases, political patrons along with ecclesiastic supporters. A sealed brass cylinder noting their northern progress was thrown overboard on August 27.

While Hall, Morton, and Hans congratulated themselves and laughed like schoolboys, the master of sail failed to share their glee. Each nautical mile the ship sailed north weighed like a pound of lead on Sidney Buddington's mind. Not in his wildest nightmares had he expected to sail this far. When they reached Port Foulke, Kane's winter quarters, he strongly urged Hall to put in. There was a snug harbor where the ship could winter over in relative comfort, and he could raid the pantry and sample his drink while Hall could sled north to his heart's content. If that madman and his allies wished to freeze to death on the ice, so be it. That was not Buddington's cup of tea. He was sailing master, and his responsibility began and ended with the safety of the ship. Port Foulke was a very nice, safe spot. They should put in there and prepare for winter. That was what all prudent whaling captains did when faced with ice.

Yet Hall was no prudent whaling captain—in fact, no sea

captain at all. He brushed aside Buddington's pleas and persisted in sailing on. No doubt that recklessness rankled Buddington. No one but a landsman would endanger the vessel and all aboard, especially in these unknown waters. If he wrecked the ship, they would all be lost. The ship was their only means of returning to safety.

But Hall continued his perilous course, and George Tyson encouraged him. Tyson climbed the mast, waved his arms from the crow's nest, and shouted down to Hall and the helmsman that he could see more open water ahead.

Tyson's assistant navigator commission did little to clarify his function. Tyson's acting like another captain must have been a thorn in Buddington's side more than a help. The whaler could only imagine that Hall had brought Tyson along because he didn't trust Buddington. In truth, Tyson had been Hall's first choice to skipper the ship. Probably every man aboard, including Buddington, knew that by now. Buddington would later describe Tyson as a malcontent, always criticizing his handling of the ship while toadying up to Hall.

But the crew knew who had the sea experience, and so did Hubbard Chester, the first mate. Like Buddington, they were mariners with little taste for sinking their home just to climb a few more degrees of latitude north. Every Jack Tar of them knew shipmates who had frozen to death or simply vanished with their ships in these waters, and they were not anxious to join the long list of missing sailors posted on the walls of the Whaleman's Chapel in New Bedford. The ghastly white faces and clawlike frozen fingers of seamen who had died on the ice surely haunted their nightly dreams.

Buddington recruited them to his side whenever he could. Not openly, of course, but with subtle gestures and snide remarks, and always behind Hall's back. Direct insubordination could lead to losing one's master's papers, something Buddington feared. He had to admire the craftiness of the German, Emil Bessel. The chief scientist bested Hall at every turn. Disdainful, aloof, almost imperial in his actions, Bessel unnerved Hall with a combination of ridicule and contempt.

Tyson's shout caused the helmsman to spin the wheel and head the ship back across the channel to where Tyson pointed. Ahead

Buddington saw only forests of floating bergs, shifting and grinding against one another in the failing light.

Even if George Tyson realized that his exuberance nettled Captain Buddington, he couldn't have cared less. Hall's passion to reach the North Pole had infected him. While Buddington fretted, Tyson enjoyed the danger of zigzagging up the channel. Every nautical mile they made brought them closer to their goal and spared them sledding an equal mile over the rugged *sastrugi*. When Mr. Chester informed him just before midnight that an impassable barrier of ice lay ahead, Tyson went aloft and proved him wrong. Spending his entire watch in the rigging, Tyson piloted the *Polaris* through a narrow lee and along that channel until open water reappeared.

By now they had sailed farther north than any white man had ever gone. Here the differences between Buddington and Tyson grew obvious. Like Hall, George Tyson enjoyed the unmarked chart, the undiscovered land. And especially like their commander, Tyson had adapted to dogsled travel with the Inuit. For him the fields of unbroken ice and barren, snow-covered land held no special terror. Other than Hall, no one else aboard felt that way. To the rest, the ship meant safety. To Hall, Tyson, and the Inuit, the ship was only a means to move them higher before they took to their sleds.

Carried along on the ship's rolls in a position that ill suited his rank as captain in his own right, Tyson felt like a fish out of water. Buddington, Chester, and even old Morton fit neatly into the ship's chain of command. But he did not. What exactly did an assistant navigator do if the navigator was sound?

However, as master of the sledges, he had a role, albeit a role off the ship. Like Hall and quite unlike Chester, Buddington, or Bessel, Tyson felt comfortable driving a dogsled over the crackling ice. His heart did not leap into his throat when his sled skated across water overflowing on the ice or hurdled across opened cracks in the floes. He could handle a team almost as well as Hall, a tall accomplishment for a white man. Hans Christian, Ebierbing, and even Tookoolito had run sled dogs from the day they could walk, and Hans handled the teams like the master he was. But Hall and Tyson could steer and control the dogs and eagerly anticipated venturing away from the *Polaris* on sledding explorations. In that they were quite different from the rest of the crew.

To most mariners, their ship is their home, their substitute wife, their mother, and at most times their strong-willed mistress. Demanding, unforgiving, but always supportive, each vessel has its own personality. Ships are always referred to as "she" or "her" and described as "tender" or "forgiving," terms applied to women. In a faceless, heartless ocean, a sailor's vessel provides food, warmth, shelter, and his only means of survival.

For these reasons most seamen are reluctant to step off their vessel except in port. Even in dire emergencies with the ship afire or sinking, many refuse to abandon the only security they know— even if staying aboard means certain death.

Extrapolate that mind-set to the *Polaris*: a well-found ship, strong and modified with the latest modern equipment to survive in the Arctic. What sailor in his right mind would exchange that security for the shifting ice fields and wind-whipped whiteout conditions surrounding them? There a man might vanish in a second into a crevasse, and shelter meant a cold, dark igloo heated by a single, sputtering seal-oil lamp.

So in the end three divergent groups rode aboard the *Polaris* as the ship beat northward. Buddington, Chester, and the English-speaking seamen saw their future in the safety of the vessel. The scientific corps with Emil Bessel, Frederick Meyer, and the German crew believed they could study the Arctic from the ship or nearby land. No need for them to risk life and limb in lengthy forays away from the *Polaris*. Only Charles Francis Hall with George Tyson, a few exuberant sailors like Noah Hayes, and the Inuit desired to leave the ship once the ice locked around it. Tyson ridiculed the others' fears. "I see some rueful countenances," he noted in his diary. "I believe some of them think we are going to sail off the edge of the world, or into 'Symme's Hole,' " he wrote, referring to a mythical whirlpoollike aberration in the ocean that sailors feared could suck down an entire ship, leaving no trace.

Hall had crossed his Rubicon. He could not turn back. He would rather die than forgo his quest to reach the North Pole, he had told his crew. His unbending ambition and goal threatened the safety of two of the three groups. Unwittingly, by pressuring them, Hall put his own life in jeopardy. In the back of his mind, the leader of this flawed party must have realized this. Grave foreboding crept into his thoughts.

One evening Tyson found Hall working at his writing desk. Already an author of one book on his first Arctic travels, Hall had shown Tyson the notes and drafts of his attempt to find the lost Franklin expedition. Hall brought them aboard when the ship left New York. What better place to finish a manuscript than during the idle hours aboard the ship, both men realized.

"Are you writing up your Franklin search book?" Tyson asked.

Hall stopped writing. For a minute he regarded the papers before him. "No," he said flatly. "No," he sighed, "I left those papers in Disco."

In Disko! The reply shocked Tyson. In New York all Hall could talk about besides reaching the North Pole was his unfinished manuscript. With drawings, detailed notes, maps, and etchings of the varied artifacts recovered from Franklin's trail of death and disaster, Hall's work held valued insights and poignant relics. The public eagerly awaited his book. Now it might be two to three years before he could work on it again.

And leaving it in Disko in the hands of the Danish governor made no sense. An uneasy knot turned in Tyson's stomach.

"Why?" he blurted out.

A mask of gloom spread over Hall's face. Even in the pale light of the guttering oil lamp, Tyson watched the shadow of darkness settle across his leader's features and the ruddy color drain away. The depression and anguish reflected in the man's face made Tyson truly uncomfortable. He would later record his feelings that night in his diary.

Without raising his head, Hall whispered, "I left them there for safety. . . ."

Feeling as if he had accidentally stepped on his companion's soul, Tyson backed out of the cabin. Hall never raised his head, never made eye contact. Instead, he returned to writing his journal.

Back on deck Tyson shivered, but not from the cold. What was Captain Hall thinking? What safer place could there be for the man's manuscript than by his side? Was there something bad that Hall sensed? Did he believe disaster lay ahead for the ship? Did he fear someone aboard might maliciously destroy his precious notes . . . or even do him harm?

"I saw the subject was not pleasant, and I made no further remark," Tyson wrote that night of their discussion, "but I could not help thinking it over."

Chapter Five

NIPPED

The ice had got us, we were frozen in for the winter, 'glued up' . . .

—ELISHA KENT KANE, 1850

On August 29, 1871, the *Polaris*'s run of luck ended. Geometric slabs of ice forty feet thick drifted down Robeson Channel to fill the gaps between the heavier bergs. Birthed amid overhanging ledges and wrenched from the shallows by tides and winds, these blocks cascaded into the narrowing channel. Floating slush and brash ice the ship could brush aside, and its reinforced beak could ram past inches of newly formed sea ice. This liberated land ice was another matter. Weighing tons apiece, these miniature icebergs could easily ram through the hull planking. To make matters worse, a thick fog settled over this shifting minefield just as the sun slipped below the peaks to the west.

Engineer Emil Schuman looked up from his gauges at the first clang of the ship's communicator. The lever spun to ALL STOP with a final ring. He wiped the sweat from his eyes with the back of his hand and signaled to John Booth and Walter Campbell, the firemen, who were blackened from head to foot with coal dust. Their eyes shining like agate stones from their dusted faces, they wearily set their shovels aside and settled atop the piles of coal.

Spinning the bypass valves, Schuman diverted the steam from the pistons that drove the ship's screw. Warily, he watched the needles on the pressure dials rise. This was always a tense moment. Any weakness in the boiler's plating could lead to disaster. Even the tiniest pinhole might bathe them in superheated steam. Vapors that hot would boil the skin right off a person in the blink of an eye.

Boiler explosions occurred frequently. Only six years before, the paddle wheeler *Sultana* had exploded on the Mississippi with the loss of seventeen hundred lives. Schuman must have considered the irony of cooking to death while the temperature outside the hull remained below freezing.

The screech of ice grinding along the length of the hull filled the close chambers. With the engine quiet, every contact with the solid water reverberated through the engine room. More ice raked the sides, one block after another. If the seams split, freezing water would pour inside. Then the boilers would explode. Death by fire and ice—neither one a pleasant way to die, as Robert Frost would later note.

On deck seamen cast grappling hooks to an adjacent floe and made the ship fast while they waited for an opening. The wind freshened, then backed. A gale was brewing.

By 7:30 P.M. a lead opened near the eastern shore. Like a shadow amid the shimmering ice fields, the channel challenged them. At Hall's urging Buddington reluctantly steered the ship up the gauntlet until the stem grounded against the ice. Ahead jumbled blocks and shards packed the channel amid mountainous icebergs. The way ahead was impassable.

They had gone as far as possible by ship. The ice made this decision for them; neither Hall's exuberance nor Buddington's reluctance played a part. The wind rose again, swirling down the passage and pressing heavy ice against both sides of the *Polaris*. Within minutes thick ice hemmed in the sides of the vessel.

Hall checked his calculations against Tyson's and got 82°29' N. They had sailed farther north than anyone before them. Still, he wanted more, if possible. Launching a whaleboat, the two men rowed to the Greenland side. From the deck of the *Polaris*, a notch in the land looked inviting. If the ship could winter there, Hall thought, so much the better.

What looked like a harbor turned out to be a shallow bight, nothing more than a subtle curve in the coastline, without protection from wind or icebergs sweeping along the shallow bay. Hall waded ashore and raised an American flag. With little thought that this wind-scoured spit might belong to Greenland, the explorer claimed this northern land for the United States. When the harbor proved unsuitable, he ironically named it Repulse Harbor.

Dejectedly the two men struggled with the boat back through the howling wind to find the *Polaris* tightly caught in the icy jaws. A full-fledged storm fell upon them now. Driven by the gale-force winds, the shore ice ground and compressed the hull like a vise. Planking groaned and seams opened until streams of water sprayed into the bilges.

The ship appeared endangered as the ice layered about its sides. Just to be sure his achievement did not die if the ship sank, Hall noted their latitude and cast the report overboard in a second brass cylinder, in accordance with his written instructions. To the sailors who beat back ice piling over the deck, that cylinder had as much chance of being found as they had of remaining afloat—next to none. They were correct; none of the brass containers cast adrift was ever seen again.

The wind veered to the east. Shifting counterclockwise as it did was a sure sign of an approaching storm. Now the floe that had provided safety threatened the ship, becoming the anvil to the rampaging ice's hammering blows. Smaller, swifter pieces of ice crashed into the ponderous ice island and rammed the side of the ship against its mooring. The bow and stern hawsers snapped, and the ship swung around like a drunken sailor. A sudden rush of twenty-foot-thick blocks drove the vessel high onto the ice shelf until it lay heeled over on its side. Crests from the froth-filled waves broke over the railings and ran along the scuppers. The *Polaris* creaked and groaned as ton after ton of ice squeezed its sides.

It looked as if the ship might be crushed. Hall ordered provisions placed on a wide floe wedged against the ship. Blankets, tents, medicines, and tins of salted pemmican piled on the ice. Rifles, cartridges, and two suits of dry clothing for each man joined the supplies. If the ship rolled or sank suddenly, these provisions would prove lifesaving.

Around the *Polaris* hummocks, pressure ridges, and open leads rose and fell, twisting and buckling under the wind and water like land rippled by an incessant earthquake. Snow fell, slanting horizontally through the fog to sting the men's faces like nettles. As the landscape shifted and buckled, Hall ordered the emergency stores divided and half moved to another hummock as an extra precaution. While the world about them bucked under their feet, the frightened and exhausted sailors struggled through the clouds of swirling snow to move their precious goods.

Schuman kept the boilers fired to run the steam pumps, but the leaks remained minimal. The shipyard repairs were proving sound. By morning the storm abated, and the supplies were returned to the deck but kept ready if the situation worsened.

On September 1 the temperature plummeted well below freezing. Ice covered the topsides and formed over the open leads. Hall ordered the propeller unshipped. Raised through the special slot in the hull, the shaft and bronze screw reposed out of harm's way.

The storm alternated its attack among ice, wind, and snow. While the ice rested, heavy snow showers filled the air. First gales, then charging ice vied with periods of eerie calm and fog until the men's nerves frayed like the overtaut hawsers. The pressing need to move supplies onto the ice, then back aboard, disrupted the normal ship's routine of four-hour watches, adding to their disorientation.

Men prayed in earnest. Hall held his usual Sunday service and exhorted the crew to pray even harder for the ship's safety. The captain's zealousness and religious fervor led him to assume even the role of chaplain. Herman Sieman wrote in German in his diary: "Ship and crew appear to be ready prey to the ice. But there is a God who aids and saves from death; to Him I trust between these icebergs and ice-fields, although I do not deserve all the good he grants me." The Lutheran Sieman found good need to pray for everything. Before the *Polaris* departed New York, he penned a prayer in his journal: "Then, even if the icebergs cover our mortal part, or the fierce polar bear tears it, we shall have Thee, Savior, and the best guide of our heart's ship."

Lacking Sieman's faith, Captain Buddington was battered all the harder by the storm. He fretted about the harbor at Port Foulke they had passed up.

The day after the propeller had been raised, a fresh northeastern wind opened a tantalizing new channel along the eastern coast. Immediately Hall called a conference. George Tyson recorded it word for word in his diary. In his small cabin Hall expressed his desire to press northward once the storm ended. His zeal infected Mr. Chester this time. Both the first mate and Tyson supported the notion. But the ice rasping along their wooden walls was too much for Buddington.

"We'll never get back again," he protested. "We have no business to go!" Before Hall could reply, Buddington ended the meeting. "I'll be damned if I'll move this ship from here!" he swore. With that oath ringing in the others' ears, he stomped off.

Chester and Tyson looked at Buddington's receding bulk before turning back to Captain Hall. They had to follow Buddington's orders, but Hall held overall command of the expedition. He could overrule Buddington, and the officers must obey.

But the rent in the fabric of command started earlier at Disko made that unlikely. Hall hurried after Buddington like a chastened schoolboy. The two talked animatedly out of earshot. For awkward minutes Chester and Tyson waited. But the council had ended. There was to be no further attempt to sail the ship farther north. Nothing more was left but to find the best spot to winter the vessel.

That evening Hall unburdened his fears to Tyson, admitting, "I'm worried."

Tyson shook his head. "Well, I've got nothing to gain, but it would be a great credit to you if we made another two or three degrees north."

Hall nodded slowly and backed away. For the first time Tyson sensed that his commander feared offending someone in the party. Who could that be? Tyson wondered. Buddington or Dr. Bessel? What hold over the captain did they have that he feared more than the ice itself? Bessel seemed a dark shadow as he moved about the ship, his presence like the breath of cold air off an iceberg. He was rarely overtly defiant but was never supportive of the captain, and that sufficed to produce a chilling effect.

Buddington, on the other hand, clearly feared what lay ahead and showed it. While he might sneak around the pantry to steal sugar, he wore his emotions plainly on his sleeve. The ice and the storms frightened him to death. The steward and cook saw his fear, and the word quickly spread, adding to the men's unease. A worried ship's captain inevitably leads to a worried crew.

Tyson half expected the whaling captain to voice concern that they would sail off the edge of a flat world like the sailors of old. To Tyson, Buddington's actions recalled Sir Edward Belcher's words:

> If they entered the Polar Sea on the range of these islands, with comparatively open waters for one hundred miles, they might drift to and fro for years, or until they experienced one of those northern nips which would form a mound above them in a few seconds! The more I see of the actions of the ice—the partially open water and the deceitful leads into pools—the more satisfied I am that *the man who once ventures off the land is in all probability sacrificed!*

Obviously Buddington feared the same things.

Men with those feelings ought to stay at home, Tyson snorted.

Locked in the ice and without propulsion, the *Polaris* now drifted backward with the ice floe. The relentless blows of the northeastern gale forced the ship to relinquish each precious mile for which it had struggled so hard. Over the next seven days, the vessel found itself carried down inside Polaris Bay, almost fifty miles south of its highest sail.

As if to mock their timidity, the ice opened again the next day. This time the open lead ran along the eastern side of the bay. Quickly the propeller was lowered. The bay rang with the sounds of hammers chipping ice from the frozen shaft as the men worked feverishly to free it. By evening the *Polaris* steamed into a small bite. After midnight Hall and five others rowed out to take soundings. The spot proved sufficiently deep to support the draft of the *Polaris,* and the whaleboat landed. Ever the explorer, Hall murmured a brief prayer and planted another American flag on this land he had discovered. The *Polaris* steamed closer and dropped anchor. For better or worse, this barren cove flanked by steep cliffs would be home for the winter.

Perhaps satisfied that its secrets were still guarded, the Arctic weather relaxed its hold on the expedition. The clouds parted, and the sun shone brightly. The fresh snow melted to expose the stunted willow and lichen battling for a grip on the shale and gravel beach. Lemmings and voles scurried about stocking their burrows while musk oxen grazed warily along the far plateau. In spite of the sun, the cold bite remained in the air, so the denizens of this site continued their preparations for winter. This far north summer could end any day. During this relentless freeze-thaw cycle, the scientists began their routine of measuring the hourly temperatures with specially coated "black-bulb" thermometers designed to reduce radiated warmth from the ground along with the usual "naked-bulb" mercury thermometers.

Four days passed while the ship maneuvered for better shelter inside the bay. Each reanchoring brought the vessel closer to land. But the holding ground was poor. The rough gravel and shale proved not sticky enough for the anchor. Another gale and the anchor would drag.

However, within sixty yards of the shore, a large iceberg lay grounded in about thirteen fathoms of water. Rising roughly 60 feet above the waterline, the iceberg offered a shelter 450 feet long and 300 feet wide. Many times the weight of the *Polaris*, it could provide the needed protection, especially against sea ice sweeping along the shallow curve of the harbor. In a land where ice is the predominant feature, a berg thus grounded appeared ideal as a mooring platform. Slipping inside the shadow of this frozen wharf, the ship dropped anchor. Here Buddington declared the ship would stay. Other storms would rock the ship until the men finally secured the vessel to the iceberg with ice anchors and screws driven into the ice and connected to hawsers and cables.

After the next Sunday services, Captain Hall named their new home Thank God Harbor and their frozen guardian Providence Berg. Besides sheltering the beleaguered ship, the iceberg proved providential in another way. During the terror of the storm, moving the emergency supplies had engaged all hands, and the firemen neglected their touchy machines. The small boilers nearly ran dry and hovered on the verge of exploding. Luckily the problem was noticed before another disaster occurred. The firemen hastily fed freshwater ice from their mooring into the tanks, thus cooling as well as replenishing the boilers.

Any thoughts of leaving their secure harbor vanished by September 11. Winter arrived. A cold snap descended upon the harbor. By morning ice inches thick encased the hull of the *Polaris*. In the cold, metal turned into a common enemy that burned the unwary at the slightest touch like a hot poker, freezing the skin hard and producing blood-filled blisters when the frozen part thawed.

As if the ship were entering a cocoon, her shape changed, and she began to merge into her surroundings. Canvas tenting housed the deck, blocking the wind that howled through the rigging with each new gale. Hans and Ebierbing showed the men how to cut blocks from the wind-packed snow to bank against the sides of the ship. Slowly, inexorably, the ship's dark wooden sides vanished behind the mounting blocks of snow. With a constant temperature of 32°F, the snow offered excellent insulating properties against the cold.

Internally the *Polaris* contracted on itself like a cat curling up for warmth. The Inuit families moved below decks to warmer quarters, for their staterooms on the upper deck had little insulation. The location of the galley on the forward deck proved even more troublesome. William Jackson, the black cook, and John Herron, the steward, risked their lives daily to bring food aft to the dining salon. Chained along the narrow deck were sixty hungry sled dogs. These dogs were bred for their stamina and ability to pull a sled— not for their manners. Anyone passing close by with food risked loss of limb or worse. While the ship battled northward, the diminutive Herron beat his own treacherous course through snapping jaws and lunging brutes. Several times the animals robbed him of food and tore his clothing.

Once *Polaris* anchored for good, the dogs were brought ashore. But another problem arose: the deepening cold. Jackson struggled hourly to keep the stoves going as the mercury dropped, and no amount of sprinting across the icy deck by Herron could keep the grub from growing cold before it reached the crew.

To solve this problem, Captain Hall gave up his own stateroom. His generous move increased the size of the galley, moving it closer to the mess hall, and further aided the passage of warm air into the crew's quarters. His action thrust him into the lion's den. He moved into a cramped cabin with Bryan, Meyer, Bessel, Schuman, and the mess crew. Now Bessel and his Teutonic brethren surrounded the commander. Hall slept beside the three hostile Germans. Only the cook, William Jackson, and Herron, the steward, remained friendly besides young Bryan. Fresh from the seminary, the ship's chaplain and astronomer overflowed with Christian charity toward everyone and everything. Wandering about like Percival after the Holy Grail, the undiscriminating Bryan remained well liked by all factions. The galley crew, not being officers, largely kept out of sight.

While the men prepared the ship, an unnerving pattern recurred in the surrounding ice. Existing leads and open pools froze solidly enough to support men and loaded sleds during wintry snaps. Clear, cold nights, lit by sinuous northern lights and eye-burning stars, accompanied these drops in the thermometer. Then, with little warning, fierce gales and blinding snowstorms raked through the bay. The ice buckled and cracked as the underlying waves roiled their frozen covers. Treacherous crevasses, fissures, and pressure ridges reappeared, while massive blocks of ice broke and cascaded about like tumbling dominoes. More cold air followed, and blown snow soon concealed these openings. Then the ice would thicken once more to await the next storm.

As a consequence, the bay surrounding Providence Berg and the *Polaris* took on the characteristics of a lunatic's garden. Like everything in the North, Buddington's secure anchorage was proving dangerous in itself.

Under Hall's direction supplies were moved ashore, again as a precaution. A small, prefabricated shed manufactured in New York was dragged the three hundred yards over the dangerous ice onto land. Bolted together and anchored to the ground, the wooden hut became Emil Bessel's scientific observatory.

Extending back from the bay, a flat, windswept plain climbed gradually until it collided with mountains bordering the north, south, and east. Eroded by wind and water, the sides of these surrounding peaks were steep while the tops remained flattened. Deep ravines and fissures scarred the face of the slopes where melting runoff and glacial streams had cut into the rock. Water creeping into the cracks of dislodged boulders split these stones into flinty shards as the water froze and expanded. The debris from this incessant war between the earth and the elements littered the beach, carried there by wind, water, and gravity.

Powdery glacial flour, silt, pebbles, and coarse shale filled the basin. Furrows cut by glacial streams raced from the headlands to the restless sea. Clumps of lichen and moss battled for every toehold with spidery roots of stunted willow. A tree in its own right in more hospitable climes, the willow here was reduced to twisted scrub. Minute blue and red flowers, killed by the first frost, littered the beach like fallen soldiers. On viewing this depressing sight, Herman Sieman wrote in his diary: "But, why should we fear the darkness around us, if light remains only in our hearts? Yes, my Lord, if I have only Thee, I do not care for heaven or earth."

The heaven and earth surrounding Sieman were hardly inviting. Unfortunately for him and all the others, the heaven and earth he viewed cared even less for them. All too soon they would demonstrate that fact.

The ice thickened and snow fell until only the windswept bluffs retained their dull gray color. Unleashed to do what they did best, Hans and Ebierbing and their dog teams spread out across the basin to hunt. Returning with a seal and four geese, the hunters demonstrated their skill and another fact about the Arctic: animals grow large where the climate is cold. Being bigger reduces their surface area in proportion to their volume, notably cutting their heat loss. One day the two Eskimo returned with an Arctic hare weighing eighty-one pounds.

Encouraged by the seeming ease with which the Natives moved about, Frederick Meyer decided to survey the mountains to the south. He enlisted the help of Mr. Bryan and Joseph Mauch. Captain Hall warned Meyer that the mountains were close to twenty miles away and not an easy trek. The experienced explorer knew that distances can be deceiving in the clear Arctic air. Meyer disregarded the warning. The hike would take only a few hours, he reasoned. The survey party set off at eight the next morning.

Nine hours later the party had only just reached the foothills. Exhausted, with night fast approaching, they turned back. Now they discovered what many a climber knows: going down a mountain is often harder than going up.

By the time they had descended to the inlet, a storm struck. The wind rose, howling through the darkness like a lost soul. Blowing snow blinded them, stinging their eyes until they watered constantly. Their lashes froze together, and white patches of frostbite speckled their cheeks. Ice covering the bay shifted and split with resounding cracks like rifle shots as swells and waves rolled into the harbor. Fissures opened and closed, and blowing snow disguised these dangers.

Struggling through snowdrifts and crawling over ice hummocks, the three men lost sight of the ship. Stumbling about in drunken arcs, they used the glowering mountains behind them for reference. Hour after hour they pressed desperately onward, but each time they turned back to gauge their progress, the dark mountains seemed just as close.

Exploiting every weakness, the Arctic had turned a simple excursion into a life-threatening rout. Like men before them, they had underestimated the power of the Arctic. Any such error exposes the maker to severe punishment.

Crossing the quivering ice, all three men fell into open cracks. Meyer was the first, sinking up to his knees before he pulled himself to safety. Next Bryan leaped across a crevasse only to break through where he landed. Mauch fell through twice.

The icy water that soaked them to the skin chilled the men to the bone and robbed their clothing of its vital insulating properties. They were already dehydrated from their efforts, and now their body temperatures began the deadly slide into hypothermia.

With each dropping degree in core temperature, the body fights desperately to keep the heart warm. Over eons the human organism has learned to make hard choices to survive. Without a beating heart, life ceases. What are a few fingers or toes compared to the pumping heart? Chill the heart below 90°F and it fibrillates. Death quickly follows. So when faced with its temperature dropping, the body begins to circulate its warming blood in an ever-tightening circle close to the heart, shunting the warmth away from areas of lesser importance to survival and those sites most likely to lose that vital heat.

The skin, fingers, limbs—all have their circulation drastically curtailed. The cerebral cortex, a comparatively new addition to the brain, is also on the hit list. That region—which is responsible for thought, judgment, and reason and separates man from animal—

ranks below the brain stem, which processes vital functions. With hypothermia blood shunts away from the cortex, impairing clear thought.

Panic set in. Tantalizingly, the clouds of snow parted just enough to offer them a glimpse of their ship. Befuddled and robbed of clear thought, the men broke into a terrified run. Stumbling, falling, slipping, they stampeded toward the *Polaris*.

The fortunate Meyer and Bryan wore Inuit mukluks, light and designed for the ice. Tough *oogrik* hide lined the soles of these boots. On some the natives sew a strip of sealskin along the bottom with the hairs facing backward. With each step the hairs grip the ice and resist sliding backward yet easily slip on the forward motion—the precursor of modern waxless cross-country skis. A skilled hunter can skim across the ice using his mukluks like skates.

Unfortunately the two men had neglected to tighten the drawstrings at the tops of their knee-high boots. When they fell through the ice, seawater rushed inside. Being waterproof works both ways. While the mukluks kept the water inside from freezing and prevented frostbite, the weight of several pounds of water sloshing around with each step added to the men's exhaustion.

Joseph Mauch wore heavy leather boots, which had become soaked through. Ice encrusted the tops and soles, adding pounds to the already cumbersome boots and making the smooth leather bottoms slick as polished glass.

In the race to safety, Mauch fell farther and farther behind. The other two sped on without thought for their companion's safety. It was every man for himself. Soon Mauch vanished behind them.

Meyer and Bryan reached the *Polaris* at one-thirty in the morning. Layered in ice, the young theologian collapsed and was carried unconscious to his bunk. Heated water bottles and cloths were applied to his chest and under his arms while Hall paced about anxiously.

Modern methods of treating hypothermia use warmed intravenous fluids, heated gases from a respirator, and even warmed fluids via peritoneal dialysis. When the core temperature drops too low, external heat is essential to rewarm the body.

During the rewarming process, dangerous shifts of potassium out of the cells occur, which can lead to fatal cardiac arrhythmia.

One well-documented case involved nearly a dozen Swedish sea-men rescued from the North Sea. When brought on board, all the men were talking and able to walk without assistance. They were sent below to rest. The rescuers found every single man dead an hour later.

Hall and Dr. Bessel knew nothing of potassium shifts and resorted to the usual methods. The Inuit use body heat to warm a victim, stripping naked and climbing in bed with the patient. While highly effective, this method proved too shocking for the white man.

When the party returned without Mauch, Captain Hall immediately dispatched the Inuit men to find him. They returned dragging the half-dead Mauch. When they found him, he was staggering in circles, incoherent and severely hypothermic. An hour later and they would have found him dead.

Fortunately neither of the two men developed cardiac problems. Mauch recovered under a mountain of blankets, and Bryan eventually opened his eyes. Seeing Captain Hall, the young man stammered, "Captain, traveling in this country is very discouraging. . . ."

After that, no party ventured far from the ship without Hans or Ebierbing as a guide.

Daylight shortened with each passing day, and the mercury slid lower as the sun departed the region. Bessel's observatory nearly blew over until cables and beams braced it against the howling gusts of wind that would sweep down from the mountains or lash inland across the bay.

Sextant readings placed the winter camp at 81°38' N, roughly forty-seven miles south of their highest sailing. Though they were still higher than any white man had placed his foot, exploring the shoreline revealed the presence of prior travelers. Circles of stones marked where Inuit hunters following the herds of musk oxen and reindeer had anchored their summer tents. Digging among the shale, the men discovered part of a broken sled, spear points carved from walrus teeth, and bone awls. Eagerly, Bessel added these to the expedition's collection. How Hall viewed this is uncertain. On all his past expeditions, he was the one who had collected artifacts. Being excluded from collecting probably strengthened his desire to press on to the Pole. While Bessel gathered artifacts, Hall renewed his zeal for geography and named the distant shores of Ellesmere Island Grinnell Land and Grant Land. The prominence marking the north tip of the bay became Cape Lupton to honor a man who had helped finance Hall's earlier expeditions.

No one gave a second thought to the fact that they were claiming and naming land where the indigenous people had traveled and lived for hundreds of years.

On the eighteenth of September, Bessel and Chester left for a weeklong hunt. Wisely, they took both Hans and Ebierbing along. Encountering a herd of musk oxen, Hans released several of his dogs. The animals attacked the musk oxen, and the valiant Arctic beasts instinctively formed a protective circle, heads outward with their young calves inside. Shooting a musk ox took little skill, although several lead bullets from the men's Sharps rifles were needed to bring down the unfortunate bull.

The party returned with three hundred pounds of fresh meat, a trophy head, and hide. While Hall had taken special pains to ensure that the expedition's tinned meat was the best available, Arctic explorers knew that only fresh meat protected against scurvy. In his living with the Inuit, Hall had adopted their custom of eating his meat raw. In fact, whenever he felt under the weather, a bloody slab of meat returned his vigor.

This addition to the crew's table provided welcome relief from the salted beef and tinned ham. Since fuel for cooking was precious, most of the meals consisted of warmed meat, bread, and soups removed from tinned cans and flavored with dried apples and other dried fruits. Box-size loaves of baked bread, stored in bags, alternated with tins of stone-hard, unleavened crackers called sailor's biscuit. On another voyage Tyson had sampled musk ox meat from the Labrador coast and found it "scarcely edible" because of the strong odor of musk. This young bull, however, tasted "very much like other beef."

The fresh meat, warm surroundings, and relative security fostered good feelings among the party. Buddington, freed of the constant fear of shipwreck, resorted to his old habits of devious raids on the pantry and closet drinking. The new observatory and the plethora of samples kept Dr. Bessel and Frederick Meyer busy collecting specimens and taking measurements. Hall and Tyson consulted over forays along the coast, while the Inuit hunted over the ice pack. Hunched patiently over the holes in the ice, which the seals used for breathing, the Inuit hunters returned almost daily with fresh meat, whereas the sailors, who chased after the animals in whaleboats, had no success at all.

During this period one of the standard methods of returning specimens to the museums for scientific study was to preserve the horns and hide and the skeleton. Salt or drying handled the hide, but removing flesh from the bony parts required great care. Scarab-type beetles proved helpful, but no such insects served aboard the *Polaris*. Boiling might loosen the flesh but could easily dissolve the skull sutures and spoil the result.

So an unlikely ally was put to good use in separating the uneaten parts of the trophy from its skeleton. The bay where *Polaris* lay at anchor teemed with hundreds of shrimp despite the frigid water. These voracious eaters would strip flesh from the bones of any animal lowered into the water. An appropriate hole in the ice already existed. Since the freezing of the bay, the crew maintained an opening in the ice as a source of water should the ship catch fire. Grateful for the free meal, the shrimp readily cleaned the bones not used in the cooking. On more than one occasion, Dr. Bessel would enlist these crustaceans in preparing musk ox skeletons for the collection.

All in all, the newness of their situation, the awesome surroundings, the preparation for winter, and the gathering of scientific material kept everyone busy. With all hands far from idle, there was little work for the devil.

Captain Hall continued his daily religious services, with special attention to Sunday's observances. The earthy seamen used profanity like a second set of clothing, much to the distress of Herman Sieman and Noah Hayes, and Captain Hall constantly urged them to improve their speech. But his efforts to keep them whole and fit generally pleased the men.

For weeks the sailors had grumbled over a common complaint: food. The preferential treatment given to the officers by the galley irked them. Jackson, the cook, knowing which side his bread was buttered on, naturally spent more time and imagination preparing the meals for the aft mess, where the officers dined. Some of this is to be expected. Sailing vessels never were democracies.

However, as time passed, the difference between what the men ate and what the officers ate grew more and more striking. In fact, Buddington abetted the inequity by encouraging Jackson in his lavish preparation of the officers' table. He may even have ordered him to do so.

Before the ship sailed from Washington, it was Buddington who had ordered the sailors to direct all questions concerning the mess to him and not to Captain Hall. So here was the perpetrator of the injustices acting as the magistrate; naturally nothing was resolved, and the problem grew. Captain Buddington never complained, but the men did. In desperation, they spoke to Hall.

When the men brought the inequity to his attention, Captain Hall acted promptly. The change had occurred without his knowledge, he assured them. It was contrary to his wishes, and he did not approve of it. Everyone would eat the same food, he vowed. They should all live together as brothers, and Jackson would prepare identical meals for forward and aft messes.

After his gratifying sermon to that effect one Sunday, the crew wrote a letter of appreciation to Captain Hall. Herman Sieman penned the note:

The men forward desire publicly to tender their thanks to Capt. C. F. Hall for his late kindness, not, however, that we were suffering want, but for the fact that it manifests a disposition to treat [us] as reasonable men, possessing intelligence to appreciate respect and yield it only when merited; and he need never fear that it will be our greatest pleasure to so live that he can implicitly rely on our services in any duty or emergency.

Deeply touched, Hall responded in kind:

Sirs,

The reception of your letter of thanks to me of this date I acknowledge with a heart that deeply feels and fully appreciates the kind feeling that has prompted you to this act. I need not assure you that your commander has, and ever will have, a lively interest in your welfare. You have left your homes, friends, and country; indeed you have bid a long farewell for a time to the whole civilized world, for the purpose of aiding me in discovering the mysterious, hidden parts of the earth. I therefore must and shall care for you as a prudent father cares for his faithful children.

YOUR COMMANDER, C. F. HALL,
UNITED STATES NORTH POLAR EXPEDITION
IN WINTER QUARTERS, THANK GOD HARBOR
LAT. 81°38' N., LONG. 61°44' W. SEPT. 24, 1871

As is often the case, what went unstated revealed as much as what was written. Interestingly, Hall's letter dealt with the "men" and did not include the officers. Neither Captain Buddington nor Dr. Bessel considered himself among the "faithful children" to Hall's father figure.

Chapter Six

DEATH

Joseph Mauch, captain's clerk, came into the cabin in the morning and told us that there had been some poisoning around there.
—HENRY HOBBY, TESTIMONY AT INQUEST

The morning of September 27 the barometer plummeted, and one hour before noon a fearsome storm struck. Swirling walls of sleet and snow engulfed the *Polaris* and erased all view of land or sea. Wind jangled the rigging and tore at the canvas tenting. Attempts to clear the lines of ice failed, since the sleet cut the men's eyes so badly, they were forced to retreat below decks to safety. The gale lasted three days. During that time the surrounding ice broke and crowded the anchored vessel. While Providence Berg shielded the ship from direct assault as the ice rolled into the bay, nothing could protect the ship from the rolling blocks sweeping in from the sides. Once again the icy jaws clamped down on the vessel.

For three days the frightened men huddled below and listened to the slabs of ice crashing and grinding along the hull. Hourly, Schuman and Alvin Odell, the assistant engineer, scoured the bilge looking for leaks as the planking groaned and complained while tons of ice pressed upon all sides. The ice and snow banked against the sides for insulation vanished. What little the wind failed to wipe away fell into the frothing sea as cracks and fissures opened around the hull. Roiled by wind and waves, the *Polaris* rocked from side to side, lifting at times when bergs wedged under the stem and stern.

On Sunday, October 1, the maelstrom subsided as suddenly as it had arrived. A cobalt-blue sky, devoid of clouds and sharp as crystal, filled the heavens. Slanting rays from the low-hanging sun striped long purple and violet shadows across the blinding white landscape. For all the surrounding beauty, everyone aboard realized how dangerous this harbor could become and how precarious the safety of the *Polaris* was.

More provisions, including some precious coal, were moved ashore. Several feet of drifted snow had buried those supplies previously placed on the beach. A day passed while these were moved beneath the shadows of bluffs farther inland.

The fractured ice field re-formed, mending the cracks brought by the storm. Captain Hall's thoughts turned to probing along the coastline by land. On October 10 Hall led an exploratory party of two sleds, each pulled by a team of seven dogs. He and his faithful Ebierbing had one sled while Chester sat in the sled basket of the second, driven by Hans. Before he left, Hall took Tyson aside. He pointed to Captain Buddington, who wandered just beyond earshot, and whispered to Tyson, "I cannot trust that man. I want you to go with me, but I don't know how to leave him on the ship."

Tyson shrugged. "I would like to go," he admitted, biting back his desire. Inwardly he hoped his disappointment did not show. Duty came first, he realized. "But, of course, I'll remain and take care of the ship," he added.

Hall nodded. "I'd like to reach a higher latitude than Parry did before I come back from this trip," he said. He then explained to Tyson that this foray would seek out the best route for the main thrust in the spring. He hoped to find the land route that would be better than traveling over the ice floes and pressure ridges of the ever-changing straits.

Under diamond-bright stars the two teams raced off into the velvet night on a northeasterly track. Clouds rolled in later that night, and another snowstorm layered a foot of fresh snow over the sled tracks.

The next morning Hans Christian returned with his empty sled. He carried a note from Captain Hall. In his excitement the meticulous planner had forgotten several vital things. The party camped five miles from the ship, waiting for Hans to return with the items. The letter, addressed to Sidney Buddington, read like a shopping list:

Sir,

Just as soon as possible attend to the following, and send Hans back immediately:

Feed up the dogs (14) on the seal-meat there, giving each 2 pounds.

In the mean time order the following articles to be in readiness:

> My bearskin mittens
> 3 or 4 pairs of seal skin mittens (Greenland make)
> 8 fathoms lance warp
> 20 fathoms white line for dog lines
> 1 pair seal skin pants, for myself
> 12 candles, for drying our clothing
> Chester's seal skin coat
> 1 candlestick, 1 three-cornered file, 4 onions
> 1 snowshoe
> 1 cup, holding just one gill
> 1 fireball and the cylinder in which it hangs
> Have the carpenter make, quick as possible, an oak whip handle, and send the material for 2 or 3 more.
> A small box that will hold the 1 pound of coffee which I have
> A small additional quantity of sinew
> Try and raise, if possible, 2 pairs of seal skin boots that will answer for both Chester and myself

Hall then ordered Bryan to calibrate his watch with the ship's chronometer and send it with Hans. He wrote more detailed instructions for Tookoolito to sew a bag for the timepiece, which Hans was to wear around his neck on the return trip.

As an afterthought, he wrote, "Tell Dr. Bessel to be very mindful that the chronometers are all wound up at just the appointed time every day."

Whether he meant to or not, Hall's letter surely rankled both Buddington and the good doctor. The long list of demands—some vital, others trivial—made the sailing master appear to be his servant. Who was Buddington to be packing C. F. Hall's things like a mother sending her boy to summer camp? The men must have muttered below decks. And what was Hall thinking while he sorted his own gear that he should forget so many things? In his efforts to micromanage everyone else's work, was he being overwhelmed? The sailors must have shaken their heads over a commander who would focus on the winding of a watch yet forget his essential mittens and pants.

Overlooking the forest for the trees, the saying goes. Hall's actions must have shaken those of the crew who supported him and strengthened the innuendos cast by Buddington that their commander was dangerously in over his head. The ice's incessant chewing on the ship's hull served as a constant reminder to all aboard that disaster hovered around the corner, waiting for just such an omission or a mistake to destroy them.

Distressingly the reminders to Buddington and Bessel reflect the siege mentality developing aboard the ship. Hall sensed sabotage of his efforts to press northward. Without the dogs and an accurate chronometer, he could not reach the North Pole. The letter's tone smacked of imperialism and treated Buddington like a dolt. Surely he would know enough to feed the dogs before sending them back. But the note also raised questions about Hall's own competence. All those odds and ends for him, yet nothing needed for Hans or Ebierbing. Apparently the Inuit knew how to pack their kits.

Far worse, that offhanded remark to Bessel stung the haughty Prussian. As with the instructions for Buddington, Hall's reminder to wind the chronometers assumed that the doctor would otherwise forget. For a man who had a string of degrees from Heidelberg, Stuttgart, and Jena and served as the head of the scientific corps, it was a deep insult.

Here was another example of Hall's attempting to micromanage his expedition. Even before he left on this first overland trip, he presented Buddington with a long, detailed list of instructions on how to manage the ship in his absence. It ranged from instructing Buddington (the experienced sea captain) as to what to do in an emergency to how to feed the newborn litter of puppies with canned pemmican. Too much coal was being burned to heat the ship, he complained. Only enough to keep the temperature at 50°F was to be used. All lights were to be out by nine P.M. except for a single candle forward for the night watch, and nothing was to be burned without the permission of Noah Hayes, who was to record every scrap.

Tellingly he appointed William Morton as quartermaster and ordered that only Morton could open supplies. For a final slap in the face, he commanded Buddington to keep a journal of any and all violations of this fiat, as if Buddington would be stupid enough to report his own pilfering. Nothing survives of the response that Buddington or Bessel made to either of Hall's letters. No mention is found in any of the recovered journals or diaries. One can easily assume, however, that their bitterness toward Hall only increased.

The requested supplies raced back with Hans, and the men worked at banking more snow and ice against the sides of the ship. On October 17 the sun sank behind the mountains of Greenland, not to be seen again until February. From then on each shrinking hour of daylight would be marked only by the rosy glow that shimmered along the southern horizon. Blackness and gloom began to permeate everything, slowly sapping the expedition's strength.

Captain Hall's party mushed northward along the foot of the mountains until they struck a frozen river. Since the river drained northward, they traveled along its relatively smooth surface, following the twisting riverbed until it emptied into the head of a bay. There Hall read a special prayer written for the occasion by John Newman and named the bay after Newman. He must have reflected bitterly over the lines in Reverend Newman's prayer that said: "And here in this far-off northern clime Thou givest snow like wool and scattereth the hoarfrost like ashes. Who can stand before Thy cold?" For a cleric who had not sailed north of Disko, Newman's words proved remarkably accurate. Already the trip was bogging down. Although Hall had planned to travel a hundred miles, the sleds had made less than fifty.

Sledding over the frozen water, they reached the mouth in two days and turned north again. Scaling a mountain, Hall and Chester viewed the surrounding land. Below lay the ice-choked Robeson Channel. Across the straits Ellesmere Island ran north by west in a curving arc while the earth beneath their feet rounded to the east.

Hall correctly surmised he was standing on an island and looking at the northern ends of both Ellesmere Island and Greenland. Here was the end of land. Ahead lay the Lincoln Sea and the North Pole. No solid earth remained above water between the tips of these two islands and the top of the world.

Hall's viewpoint of the top of the world was dutifully named Cape Brevoort, after his generous benefactor J. Carson Brevoort of Brooklyn. Hall sat among the rocks on a windswept portion of the mountain to draft a dispatch to Secretary of the Navy Robeson.

Below him stretched a missed opportunity, one that might never come again. Sanguinely he wrote:

> On arriving here we found the mouth of Newman's Bay open water, having numerous seals in it, bobbing up their heads. This open water making close both to Sumner Headland and Cape Brevoort, and the ice of Robeson Strait on the move, thus debarring all possible chance of extending our journey on the ice up the strait.

The collusion between his troublesome Captain Buddington and the ever-shifting sea ice had cost him dearly. With his own eyes he watched the fading light fingering across the open water. *The route farther north by sea still lay open!* Had Buddington the stomach, they could have laid to, set the ship in irons, or anchored while the storms passed, then steamed on! At the very least they might have pushed their way into this fine bay to winter over. Deeper than Polaris Bay and guarded by the sheer headlands, Newman Bay offered far better shelter than the shallow scallop of Thank God Harbor. By whatever quirk of nature, Newman Bay remained open, even now, where thick ice gripped the *Polaris* fifty miles farther south.

Most disheartening was the fact that the open water now blocked any farther progress by dogsled. From the speed of the icy cubes sweeping south in Robeson Channel, Hall realized that the current of more than two knots would keep the straits open for days to come. It would do no good to wait for ice to seal the sea. Weeks might pass before the ice grew thick enough for safe sledding.

He was blocked by land and by sea. Clouds the color of hammered pewter, reflecting the dark mood, closed in as the men descended. Like Moses, Hall had been to the mountain and had seen the promised land. Like Moses, he would never set foot on it.

Huddled inside an igloo hastily built by Hans and Ebierbing before the storm broke, Hall finished his dispatch. He neglected to mention two close calls that had nearly spelled disaster for the probing mission. One night in particular almost proved deadly as they sat inside a snow house. Expertly crafted by Ebierbing and Hans to retain the warmth of a single seal-oil lamp yet block the howling Arctic wind, the house matched the Inuit's usual specifications of being airtight. With everyone inside, the Natives dutifully sealed the door with a block shaped for that purpose. Tired, preoccupied, or perhaps careless, no one had bothered to cut a vent hole in the top.

While Hall calculated his dead reckoning and star sights, the kerosene lamp flickered and went out. Assuming it had run low on fuel, Hall continued by the light of the one candle while Chester and the Inuit dozed. Then the candle sputtered and died. Exasperated, Hall struck a match to relight the taper. Match after match extinguished as soon as it was struck. Puzzled by this, Hall suddenly became dizzy. The candle and lamp had consumed all the oxygen in the sealed igloo, he realized. They were out of air.

"Kick down the door!" he ordered Ebierbing, who was closest to the entrance. The Inuit obeyed, and fresh air rushed into the room to revive them. It had been a close thing. Had they been sleeping, they would have suffocated.

Danger and death lurked at each turn. Back at the ship, Chester picked up a pot of coffee boiling on the portable metal stove, called a conjurer because it resembled something a magician might use to brew a potion. Finding the pot handles too hot to hold, the first mate dropped the pot and splashed boiling coffee over his face. Blisters immediately formed. Luckily Chester's eyes were spared, and his burns responded to Cosmoline, the rust-inhibiting grease, wiped from the rifles and metal tools and applied to his burned skin.

If anyone on the trip needed a reminder of the harsh nature surrounding him, he had only to look about. Grim evidence abounded.

During the sled passage one of the dogs had given birth to a full litter of pups. As the animals slept in harness, tied to the sled, the tracings kept the mother from moving her babies to safety. In the night the other dogs killed and ate all the puppies.

"Up to the time I and my party left the ship all have been well, and continue with high hopes of accomplishing our great mission," Hall wrote the next morning. In his heart he knew he could not account for the actions of Captain Buddington or Emil Bessel while he was absent from the ship.

Hall must have feared that Buddington would sail the ship south at the first opportunity. The skipper had wanted to winter over at Kane's winter camp, farther south. Perhaps the fact that Kane had survived the winter at that location provided Buddington with assurances, whereas their advanced position did not. Bessel, however, appeared happy collecting and measuring where the ship now lay anchored. With his feet on land and overseeing the construction of his observatory, the Prussian scientist seemed fully occupied. But his apparent contentment worried Hall. The man detested him, he and Tyson realized all too well. Bessel hated taking orders from someone he rated far beneath him. Since the episode at Disko, Bessel looked as if he were biding his time, waiting for the right moment to strike.

Up to the time Hall had left, everything was fine. But what mischief awaited his return he could only guess.

Nothing of Hall's concerns survived, but George Tyson's diary and testimony as well as that of the men paint a picture of growing acrimony between the chief scientist, the skipper, and Captain Hall.

Trying to end on a positive note, Hall added:

> I have omitted to note that our sleeping-bags, our vestments, everything that we wear, are all saturated with the moisture, and frozen stiff. But these kinds of difficulties we do not mind much. So long as we can forward the service we are engaged in, so long will we laugh at such obstacles as these mentioned.

Reluctantly they turned back in the morning. Before departing the men scraped away the snow until they found enough rock to build a cairn of stones. Placing the dispatch inside a copper cylinder as prescribed by his orders, Hall sealed the opening and trudged away. His dispatch was written on a form instructing the finder in six different languages to forward the message to the secretary of the navy. Chester further marked the site with an empty two-pound meat tin and a condensed-milk can filled with sand. The rough draft of the letter Hall cached remained inside his portable writing desk and so survived for us to read. His scribbled notes tightly fill all four corners of the printed official paper.

The pack ice and icebergs jostling within Robeson Channel mocked any idea of crossing by sled. The rugged slate-gray mountains lining the tip of Greenland blocked farther travel overland. He would have to wait until spring, Hall realized. Already this short trek was proving more arduous than expected.

George Tyson dropped the snow block he held and looked up. The sled dogs tethered on the ice and near the observatory barked and strained against their leashes. Beside him Morton and Sieman continued their work of hauling the cut squares to bank against the sides of the ship. Whenever the weather permitted, insulating the *Polaris* continued. This was the fourth day, and the snow bank measured ten feet thick in parts. Still, much more needed to be done.

Tyson scanned the horizon. The thick twilight restricted his vision to a few hundred yards. Something had disturbed the animals. No musk ox would be foolish enough to blunder into camp. Polar bears were another matter. He squinted harder. The white bears blended so well with their surroundings as to be almost invisible. Only their black eyes and black nose stood out. But he saw nothing.

The dogs renewed their yelping. Now they all stood, howling and facing to the east. In the cold, dense air, sound carried for miles across the jumbled ice field. Faint barks returned from the base of the foothills. Tiny dark dots crested the rise of a snow ridge and sped toward the ship. Captain Hall and Chester had returned.

Instinctively Tyson fished his pocket watch from the folds of his sealskin coat. It read one o'clock. Two weeks to the day, the advance party was back. He waited as the sleds drew nearer.

Expertly Ebierbing brought the team to a halt alongside the observatory building. Hall rolled out of the sled basket and sprang to his feet. Walter Campbell, one of the firemen, greeted him. To Campbell, the commander looked unwell.

Hall shook his head. "No, I'm pretty tired, but quite well in health."

Emil Bessel emerged from the hut. The two shook hands, and Bessel walked beside Hall, talking about several of the experiments. Frederick Meyer and Noah Hayes stopped stacking provisions to welcome their commander. Hayes thought Hall looked "very much exhausted." Once again Hall insisted he felt fine.

A crowd gathered as Hall walked toward the *Polaris*. Buddington and Morton approached. "Do you think the Pole can be reached along the shore you just explored?" Buddington asked.

"It can," Hall answered firmly. He then clasped Tyson's outstretched hand and smiled warmly. Patches of hoarfrost silvered Hall's beard and eyebrows, contrasting with the ruddy complexion of his flushed face.

"How was the trip?" Tyson asked.

Hall grinned widely. "Wonderful time. Only went fifty miles instead of the hundred miles I planned. But, all went well. Didn't lose a single dog."

Tyson nodded.

Hall wiped his running nose with the back of his mitten. "Going again," he said. "And I want you to go along."

Hall shook hands with everyone in the work party. Before climbing the gangplank, he addressed the men. "Men, I thank you for your good behavior during my absence," he said.

Ebierbing and Mr. Chester, both covered with snow and frost, climbed the platform with Hall. Campbell and Morton followed. At the tumble home Bryan and the steward, Herron, waited as the reception party. Hall exchanged a few words with the chaplain before crossing the tented deck and making his way below to his shared quarters. Joseph Mauch greeted the captain at the doorway. In his hands he held a bound ledger recording the events that had taken place during Hall's exploratory trip. Before he left, Hall had ordered Mauch as secretary to keep an accurate log of all happenings. Proudly Mauch thrust the book at Hall.

Hall eyed the ledger. He nodded his approval but waved off the book. "I'll read it as soon as possible," he said. Perusing the log was not on his mind. He was thirsty.

"Have you any coffee ready?" Hall asked Herron.

"Always enough," the steward beamed. "Under way down stairs in the galley. Would the Captain care for anything else?"

"No. Just the coffee."

Herron rushed off to find the cook, Jackson. But the pot was empty. Dinner would not be served to the working parties for another two hours. The thirsty crew stacking provisions by the hut and banking the ship had drunk the morning's coffee to keep warm. Campbell, acting as assistant cook, watched as Jackson brewed a fresh pot. Later, under cross-examination, Jackson would claim that the captain's cup was filled from the same pot everyone else had sampled. Whether he lied or had a lapse of memory, the truth remains that the cook brewed a fresh cup for Captain Hall. Both Campbell and Mauch remembered watching him make one.

In the cabin William Morton pulled off Hall's mukluks and washed his feet. The commander sat on his bunk. Going from minus-zero temperatures to the relative warmth of the ship caused him to sweat, further drenching his already damp shirt. Throughout their trip moisture had plagued Chester and Hall. Without modern synthetic fibers to wick perspiration away from their bodies, the two men had steamed inside their clothing as they ran beside the dogsleds. Furthermore, the wet wool lost all of its insulating property.

By evening their undergarments had literally dripped. Each morning they had awakened to sleeping bags frozen into stiff cocoons from the water vapor. Hans and Ebierbing avoided this problem by sensibly wearing nothing beneath their furs and sleeping under the hollow-haired caribou robes.

As an afterthought Morton went out to retrieve a change of dry clothing for his commander. Bryan and Bessel stood inside the cabin. When the mate returned, Hall sat drinking his cup of coffee. Herron had returned with the brew. Captain Hall drank his coffee sweetened with sugar—"white lump sugar," as the steward described it. How many hands beside Jackson's and Herron's passed the cup to Hall is unknown, but Dr. Bessel and Mr. Bryan were present.

As Hall gulped down the coffee, he grimaced. Those present saw him do so. The taste was awful, unlike any coffee he had drunk before, far too sweet and metallic in character. He mentioned it to Morton and again, later, to Tookoolito. He set the cup aside and rose to pull his shirt over his head. Suddenly his stomach burned, a visceral fire deep inside as if he had swallowed molten iron.

"Something is the matter with me," Hall stammered. "I . . . I feel sick." Abruptly he doubled over as the pain struck even harder. He vomited suddenly. But the pain continued, and he collapsed onto his bunk.

The vomiting continued unabated.

Helplessly Morton and the steward watched as wave after wave of pain and nausea swept over the captain. Bryan wrung his hands, while Bessel studied the attack with medical detachment. Within minutes Hall appeared to improve. Emptying his stomach seemed to relieve the symptoms.

Fearing that something in the coffee had affected him, Hall asked Dr. Bessel for an emetic. If his vomiting had left anything harmful behind, further regurgitation could only help. With problems in food handling, preparation, and preservation rampant in the nineteenth century, food poisoning was common. On an Arctic vessel with little water used for hand-washing, the problem was compounded. Emetics were a common way of dealing with contaminated foods.

Surprisingly Bessel shook his head. "No. You are not strong enough," he said. "One would weaken you too much." Bryan blinked at this unexpected recommendation. Purging was standard practice, and the captain's vomiting had seemed to help him. However, he deferred to Bessel's medical experience. Since he had not examined Hall, the Heidelberg-trained physician had no basis for such a pronouncement regarding Hall's relative strength or weakness, unless he was trying to keep the contents of the coffee cup inside Hall.

Captain Buddington arrived. Hall looked up from his bunk,

pale and shaken. "I felt a little sick coming in from the cold to this warm cabin," Hall explained, "and I've been vomiting slightly."

Buddington frowned. The man looked sicker than what he described.

"I still plan on going north again after a few days," Hall insisted. "This may be a bilious attack." Then he enlisted Buddington's support for a purgative. "Don't you think I need an emetic, Captain Buddington?"

"Yes." Buddington, like all the rest, believed in purging the body of noxious elements.

Both men turned toward Bessel, but the physician remained adamant. Folding his arms across his chest, he shook his head again. "It will not do for you to take an emetic," he stated flatly.

George Tyson stopped supervision of the snow-banking as soon as he learned of Hall's attack and visited the cabin. Hall asked him also if a purgative might not help, and, like Buddington, Tyson thought it would. But Bessel still refused.

Denied what he believed his best chance to cure the burning in his stomach, Hall finally turned his face to the wall, rolled onto his left side, and drew his knees up. Buddington, Bryan, and Bessel filed silently out. Herron and Morton took stations outside the door to the cabin in case their captain needed them.

Strangely, just after that first onslaught of vomiting, Bessel told Buddington that Hall's illness was fatal. This was an extraordinary thing for him to say. He had not examined Hall. While the vomiting was sudden and severe, nothing else pointed to a fatal outcome. Either Bessel was an incredibly bad physician, or else he knew something about the attack that no one else did.

Word of Hall's sudden illness quickly spread. A palpable feeling of uneasiness flowed outward from that darkened cabin and seeped throughout the ship, spread into every corner, onto the ice to the men banking the sides of the ship, and across the frozen bay to the sailors working around the observatory. Men whispered to one another: the skipper was down. Within minutes everyone knew. In this isolated anchorage, ill news traveled fast.

As soon as he heard of Hall's collapse, Herman Sieman uttered a silent prayer for his commander's speedy recovery. From the most religious to the most blasphemous member of the crew, each sailor probably echoed similar sentiments.

On any ship the captain's words and deeds can save or sink the vessel. Few other places on earth bestow such awesome power on a single individual, but the merciless, unforgiving nature of the sea demands that a ship have one ultimate authority whose word is law. While some of the crew might not recognize Hall as that ultimate authority, everyone realized they depended upon him. Captain Hall knew more about surviving in this bitter wilderness than anyone else aboard. His years in the Arctic had proved that. His expertise strengthened the odds they would all return home alive.

Everyone on board knew that three factions divided the *Polaris* expedition, and even the dullest Jack among them realized that Captain C. F. Hall was the only thing that held them all together.

By morning, October 25, Hall felt better. Although the cramping pain had continued throughout the night, it subsided somewhat by daylight. He ate some chicken and arrowroot. An anxious Tookoolito and Ebierbing reached his side.

"Did you drink the coffee, Joe?" Hall asked his friend. "I don't know. I took a cup of coffee, and then I got very sick and vomited."

He looked at Tookoolito. "I think the coffee made me sick. It tasted too sweet." Drawing the two Inuit closer, he whispered, "I think there was something bad in the coffee. It burned inside my stomach. I never tasted anything like it before. Not like the coffee you make for me, Hannah."

The two Natives backed away as Dr. Bessel entered the cabin. For the remainder of the day, Hall rested in bed while Bessel hovered about applying cold compresses to the captain's head and mustard plasters to his legs and chest. No record is made of Hall's eating anything that day, but he steadily improved, according to Morton and Bryan.

Nevertheless, Bessel wrote in his diary that Hall suffered from paralysis of the left side of his body, including his tongue—something no one else saw on that day. With minute detail Bessel recorded his findings and treatments. Later he would use his notes to defend his care of Captain Hall.

Furthermore, Dr. Bessel recorded an irregular pulse and now

decided to purge his recovering patient. How massive diarrhea might correct an irregular pulse is a mystery. If Bessel had been worried about weakening Hall before, he must have gotten over his concerns. He administered castor oil mixed with four drops of croton oil. Presumably copious glasses of water followed to wash down the objectionable concoction. To solidify his diagnosis even more, Bessel announced that Captain Hall had suffered from a fit of apoplexy and was not expected to live. Other than Bessel's questionable findings of paralysis, little documentation exists that the captain had had a cerebrovascular accident, or stroke.

Granted, medicine has progressed considerably in the last 130 years. And granted, cathartics and purgatives were commonly prescribed at that time. But Bessel's treatment is inconsistent and without good foundation—even for that time. If Hall's irregular pulse was the result of electrolyte imbalance from his vomiting, knowing what we do now, inducing further loss of sodium and potassium through diarrhea only worsened the problem.

By evening the stomach pain returned. Hall resumed vomiting all night. With the arrival of morning, once again, he improved. Although still weak, Hall inquired about the ship and speculated on his next trip by sled. The paralysis that Bessel described had vanished, although the doctor noted that Hall had difficulty swallowing. What trouble the captain had nevertheless failed to prevent him from taking some sustenance. His appetite had returned somewhat, as the stomach pains were also gone. He ate some preserved fruit, peaches or pineapple.

During this time Dr. Bessel checked his patient's temperature. Taking both oral and axillary readings, the doctor recorded wildly diverse measurements, ranging from lows of 83°F to highs of 111°F. What sort of thermometer had Bessel used? Certainly it could not have been one of the carefully calibrated "black-bulb" or "naked-bulb" mercury thermometers that the National Academy of Sciences admired for their superb accuracy. The numbers Bessel recorded are unbelievable. His readings are incompatible with survival. The heart fibrillates when the core temperature drops below 90°F, and the brain cooks when temperature rises past 107°F. More worrisome is the fact that Bessel used these findings to initiate further treatment. Because of the elevated temperature, the physician prescribed quinine injections.

In the 1870s quinine was used for a variety of ills, fever being just one. By dilating the small blood vessels in the skin, quinine will lower an elevated temperature. Other than its primary use in combating malaria, the drug also produced pain relief by depressing areas of the central nervous system. It can also produce digestive upsets, visual disturbances, and a skin rash. Bessel gave Hall an injection, which he described as "a hypodermic injection of one and a half grains of quinine, to see the effect."

The doctor's choice of quinine is open to question. Certainly Hall did not suffer from malaria, the drug's primary usage, nor did he complain of pain, another indication for quinine during that time. With the captain's temperature all over the map, quinine probably should not have been used, and it could be expected to further upset an already disturbed stomach.

According to Bessel's notes, the effect was beneficial, and the captain's appetite and mental acuity improved over the next day. Not wanting to let well enough alone, Bessel injected Hall again, even though the man's temperature was no longer elevated. During this time Morton and Chester stayed at the sick man's bedside and clearly remembered the injections. Both men recalled Bessel's mixing a white powder into the solution before injecting it.

The fact that the treatment improved the captain's appetite and mental condition—just the opposite of what might have been expected—raises the question of whether the white powder was quinine or something else.

Trouble began the next day. Hall leaped from his bed suddenly and shouted that Chester, Tyson, and Buddington planned to shoot him and that Bessel and the cook were poisoning him. For the next four days, Hall ranted and raved about his cabin.

When Jackson, the cook, entered the cabin to fetch his pipe, Hall mistook the pipe for a pistol and cried out that Jackson meant to shoot him. The frightened man fled when Hall ordered Buddington to strip the cook's bunk and search it for weapons. Hall also refused a change of stockings from Chester, fearing they might be laced with poison.

Focusing primarily on Bessel as the ringleader of a plot to kill him, Hall finally refused to let the doctor treat him. Pointing directly at Bessel, Hall told Jackson, "That man is trying to poison me!"

Bessel abandoned his previously haughty demeanor and now suddenly adopted the patience of Job, affecting an air of extreme kindness toward his ranting leader. That appears to have been out of character for the brusque man. When Captain Buddington offered to drink a glass of medicine first to prove to Hall that it was safe, Bessel strangely would not allow it. Why was that? A sip of any medicine would have allayed Hall's fears and would not have hurt Buddington. Were the contents of the glass harmful instead of helpful? If it did contain poison, Bessel certainly would not wish to kill Buddington, a man whom he could readily control and who was needed to ensure their safe return.

To the men around him, Hall appeared to accuse everyone, especially Bessel and Buddington, but he never laid any blame on his Inuit friends.

Hoping to cure himself by tried-and-true methods, Hall asked for raw seal meat. Bessel refused to allow it, and Hall accused the doctor of starving him. To avoid the poison he feared, Hall refused all food unless it was proved safe. Like the Roman emperors with their food testers, the explorer ate only after Chester, Morton, or Herron had first sampled his meals. Tookoolito assumed the task of preparing his soups and teas. Hall even suspected that the water used to wash him might have been harmful.

During this time Noah Hayes and Herman Sieman asked to visit the captain. Sieman wished to pray over a fellow Christian and Hayes to comfort his idol. Buddington and Bessel refused their requests. Why is unclear. The disturbed Hall might have garnered comfort from friendly faces. Was this a kind of psychological warfare being practiced on Hall? Or was it meant to prevent Hall from poisoning the crew with innuendo and accusation? No matter the reason, the skipper and doctor managed to isolate Hall from the crew during this time, allowing only the Inuit and officers access to the sick man.

In the close confines of the ship, engulfed in darkness and hundreds of miles from help, the captain's raving unnerved the crew.

One day Joseph Mauch took Henry Hobby aside and whispered darkly that "there was poisoning around there." Mauch had studied some pharmacology in Germany and recognized the odor of a certain poison within the captain's cabin. Unfortunately Mauch could not recall the English word for the poison he smelled.

Concurrent with the captain's illness, a strange affliction struck a litter of newborn sled dogs. One by one the previously healthy pups developed prolapsed intestines. With their protruding entrails dragging behind, the unfortunate creatures fell victim to the other dogs, which attacked and pulled on the exposed organs. To end their suffering, the animals were killed. Death and dying permeated the atmosphere of the entrapped ship and further unnerved the sailors. To the superstitious seamen, what befell the puppies was just another sign that their ship was unlucky. No one stopped to consider that someone might have been testing poisonous mixes on the unfortunate creatures.

Meanwhile, Captain Hall teetered between the brink of madness and guilt for his outbursts. To Emil Schuman he apologized repeatedly—up to ten times, according to the engineer. "Mr. Schuman," he lamented, "if I ever did wrong to you, I beg your pardon. I'm extremely sorry." With Schuman's limited English, most of Hall's invectives went unnoticed; Hall's profuse apologies did not.

Hall's hallucinations peaked one night. Awaking suddenly, he jumped up and seized Buddington by his collar. The startled whaler shouted to Tyson and Chester for help. But Hall barred their way. With his left hand (the one that was supposedly paralyzed), the captain held the door closed, grasping the doorknob so tightly that the men outside could not turn it. Showing remarkably good strength for a "paralyzed" and weakened person, Hall kept the two men at bay while he questioned Buddington.

"There are blue vapors surrounding the cabin lantern," he insisted to his captive audience while the other officers hammered at the door. "Do you not see it?"

"Sir!" Buddington stammered.

Hall's wild eyes rolled toward his captive. His already waxen face tightened, and his mouth gaped in horror. "What's this? Blue flames shooting from your mouth, sir!"

Hall's grip on the handle relaxed, and Tyson forced the door ajar. Chester and he rushed inside and pried Hall's fingers from Buddington's throat. Gently they forced Hall back into his bunk. The stricken man wiped futilely at Chester's coat, brushing away the cloud of blue vapor that drifted around the first mate and clung to his coat. After anxious moments the men quieted Hall and covered him with his blankets. Tyson sat beside him.

Weakly Hall raised on his elbow and ran his fingers around Tyson's mouth. "What's that coming out of your mouth?" Hall whispered. "It's something blue . . ."

Bryan hurried to the cabin. Seeing him, Hall pointed to the bunk Bessel used. "Doctor Bessel had an infernal machine in his berth that emits blue vapor. Don't you see it? It is there. Can't you see the vapor coiling around in the air? I know the machine is in there because I can see blue vapor hanging along the edge of the berth. Don't you see it, Mr. Bryan?"

The distraught chaplain looked about. Only smoke from the kerosene lamp circled inside the small cabin.

Hall inclined his head toward the other bunks. A look of madness crept into his eyes. "Bessel has put his machine somewhere inside here. He is pumping his blue vapor into my berth." Fear filled Hall's stricken face. "It is killing me," he said slowly. Then a conspiratorial look replaced the terror. "That little German dancing master doesn't think I know that he is at the center of this, but I do."

During this time the "thin-skinned" and "sensitive" Bessel demonstrated remarkable equanimity. Before, he took offense at the smallest slight; now he seemed inured to the poison charges. The chief scientist wandered around the ship casting dire prognoses about Hall's chances of survival. Before Hall dismissed his services, Bessel had remained close by his patient, often sleeping in a chair by the captain's bed. On one occasion the doctor tied a string to Hall and then to his own arm to awaken him if his patient needed care. The men assumed that this was to spare the others sleeping in the cabin from loss of their rest, but the string arrangement conveniently enabled Bessel to treat the befuddled Hall without arousing possible witnesses.

In lucid moments the explorer fed himself from tins of food stored under his bunk, which he opened himself.

After treating all other foods as poisoned, drinking only water or tea directly from Tookoolito's hand, and not letting Bessel near him, C. F. Hall began to improve. From November 1 through November 3, he steadily regained his strength. His mind cleared, and he resumed his plans for another trip northward. If Bessel was poisoning the captain, this improvement when out of the good doctor's hands is damning evidence.

On November 4 Hall kept his secretary, Joseph Mauch, busy revising the ship's logs and bringing his journal up to date. Throughout the day he chatted with anyone who passed about his plans for reaching the North Pole. His appetite was strong, and all signs of the mysterious stomach pains had vanished.

At this time Dr. Bessel prevailed upon Mr. Bryan to intercede with the captain on the doctor's behalf. Bryan, acting mostly in his role of ship's chaplain and conciliator, implored Hall to let Bessel resume treatments. It was Dr. Bessel's highly skilled talents, learned in Heidelberg, that had brought about Hall's miraculous cure, Bryan argued.

No one could doubt that Hall had improved remarkably. But was this due to Bessel's injections and solutions or to Hall's paranoid actions? Bryan's arguments must have been convincing, for the captain relented and allowed the doctor he had accused of poisoning him to resume his care. Years later Bryan would express doubts about whether he had done the right thing.

By that evening Bessel once more injected his medicines into the captain's thigh. In his journal Bessel wrote that Hall had difficulty speaking, appeared slow, and had numbness of his tongue that day, and that is why he restarted his treatments.

The next two days Hall walked about on deck and continued amending the ship's journals with Mauch. As a seaman passed his porthole with a freshly killed seal, Hall laughed and pointed to the man. He seemed well on the road to complete recovery.

He ate a full meal before turning in. He told Buddington he would have breakfast with him in the morning and added, "Mr. Chester and Mr. Morton need not sit up with me at night. I'm as well as I ever was."

Near midnight Hall developed labored breathing. Alarmed at this sudden change, Chester awoke Bessel and relayed his findings.

Strangely, the doctor who had tied himself to his patient now appeared unimpressed with Chester's report. In the words of the startled first mate: "I asked the doctor about it. He said it was all right and started out quick as he could to the observatory."

What was so important for Bessel to do in the observatory in the middle of the night? Whatever scientific observation he needed could not have been that crucial, for Bessel would have slept through the night if Chester had not aroused him. Was he just trying to get in a few observations while awake? Was the good doctor trying to establish an alibi, one that put him in the science hut when Hall died? Most important, why would he ignore Chester's report when respiratory depression is frequently a terminal sign?

When Chester returned to his charge, he found Hall muttering incoherently around a dangerously swollen tongue. The captain's condition so unnerved Chester that he ran on deck to dispatch the first man he saw to retrieve the errant Bessel from his observatory. The first mate then rushed to find Captain Buddington. "Captain Hall is dying," he blurted to the ship's master.

Both men reached Hall to find him sitting upright, legs dangling, and his head wobbling from one side to the other. The man's glassy-eyed stare and cadaveric appearance were "frightful to look at," according to Buddington.

"How do you spell . . . murder?" Hall rasped. He kept spelling the word over and over, using different and incorrect spellings. Buddington and Chester could only look at each other in confusion. As Bessel returned and entered the cabin, Hall straightened up. "Doctor, I know everything that's going on," he whispered. "You can't fool me."

Calling for water, Hall choked on the drink, then vomited before collapsing back onto his cot. Bessel immediately diagnosed a second attack of apoplexy.

Hall remained unconscious. They rolled him onto his stomach to keep him from swallowing his tongue. Then he lay, facedown in his blankets, drooling and breathing heavily. Chester and Morton continued their bedside vigil. Hall's breathing grew heavier.

For the first time Chester noticed blisters and sores developing around Captain Hall's nose and mouth. Soon blisters encircled his entire mouth. Blisters such as these would not be the skin rashes possible from quinine; however, certain types of poison do produce circumoral blistering.

All that night and throughout the next day, the stricken explorer lay on his stomach, his face almost buried in his blankets. No words issued from his mouth until evening. Then he raised his head as Dr. Bessel straightened his blankets.

Recognizing the doctor, Hall murmured, "Doctor, you have been very kind to me, and I'm obliged to you." He then sank back into his coma. Around midnight the faithful Morton took his turn on the dreadful watch.

Chester looked up at his relief. "He's asleep, and I don't think he's any better," the first mate responded to Morton's unspoken query. He shook his head sadly. "He's very bad."

Morton slipped into the chair. He watched the sweaty tangle of dark hair and unkempt beard half buried in the pillow. Heavy gurgling sounds came from the body. The shoulders rose and fell as the captain fought for each labored breath. The air inside the cabin tasted stale and reeked with the odors of unwashed bodies. The gurgling grew more pronounced.

Fearful that the captain might be choking, Morton called out to him. There was no reply. Gently, gingerly as a rough-handed worker might raise a newborn infant, Morton lifted Hall's head. The eyes remained closed, and saliva dripped from the man's half-opened mouth. Moisture matted the mustache and beard surrounding the pallid lips. Morton wiped the crusts and drool away with a cloth and rolled the unconscious man more onto his back. He propped Hall's head against his pillow to give him a better airway. On a table beside the bed rested a glass containing liquid. It might have been medicine left by Bessel or tea, for all Morton knew, but he hoped some fluid might relieve the awful sounds that accompanied the captain's labored breathing. With infinite care the old traveler ladled a spoonful between Hall's lips. His efforts produced little effect. The fluid dribbled between the opened lips onto the pillow. Morton returned to his seat to resume his watch.

At 2:25 in the morning of November 8, 1871, Hall's breathing stopped. Morton rose and examined him. Leaning over, he placed his roughened cheek close to detect any movement of air. There was none. Morton stepped back and gazed upon his friend.

Charles Francis Hall was dead. In death his face resumed the sallow complexion it had held in life. Neither blotches nor flushing nor contortions distorted the peaceful face. Sadly the mate roused Dr. Bessel. The doctor confirmed the diagnosis and placed the official time of death at 3:35 A.M. Morton awoke Buddington and Chester. Within minutes everyone sleeping in the cabin was up.

Word spread to the forecastle. One by one the seamen filed into the crowded room to pay their respects to their fallen leader. Quietly they gazed upon the still face before shuffling out. What feelings Bessel and Buddington had they kept to themselves at this time. Later their true sentiments would emerge.

For all their rebellious actions, every one of the common seamen professed a genuine grief. Whatever Hall's shortcomings, the men's best interests occupied his central thoughts, next only to his desire to reach the North Pole. Unfortunately some among them believed that his zeal to conquer the Pole threatened their lives.

The death of any member of a ship strikes hard at the core of the vessel. By the very nature of its small size, the *Polaris* fostered familiarity among officers as well as crew. Everyone aboard had shared experiences with Hall and felt his touch. Furthermore, his death amid the dark shoulders of the threatening icebergs and icy fingers of the remorseless Arctic served all the more to remind them that death and disaster shadowed every foray into the far North.

The blow of Hall's death came even harder since the men had dropped their guard. His wonderful recovery from a malady that Bessel said was fatal had inspired them. Only the previous day, Hall had looked strong and fit. He had walked on deck and resumed his plans. Now he was dead, less than three months into the expedition.

Morton and Chester dressed Hall in a fresh navy uniform. Dark blue wool with double rows of brass buttons, it looked like official U.S. Navy issue, but like Charles Francis Hall, it was ambiguous, for no gold braid adorned the sleeves. Like Hall, the commander's uniform was incomplete, lacking a full commission.

Down below, Nathan Coffin, the ship's carpenter, who had struggled so hard to recover from his illness in New York in time to sail with his shipmates, began his grim task. Using his plane and saw, he built a pine coffin from spare wood.

Morton, Tyson, Chester, and Noah Hayes began digging a grave. Picking a level spot near the observatory and depot of ship's stores, they commenced to dig. The rock-hard frozen ground resisted all efforts. A few shovelfuls of scree and coarse gravel lay beneath the snow. That much was easy. After that there remained nothing but frozen ground, cemented in ice since the first Ice Age.

An entire day passed while the men battled with pick, crowbar, and ax to chisel a hole deep enough to hold the coffin. While the men labored, Hall received one final viewing before Coffin nailed the lid shut. Progress on the grave proved agonizingly slow. Worried that the dead man might begin to decompose in the warm cabin, Captain Buddington ordered the coffin moved to the poop deck.

By the end of the second day, a depression barely more than two feet deep existed. That would have to do. Further efforts gained little. Noah Hayes, in frustration, rammed the crowbar he was using into the ground near the head of the grave.

The burial service took place in the dark. The Arctic sun no longer shone even at eleven o'clock in the morning. The ship's bell rang the departing of the captain, this time forever, and the coffin was loaded onto a waiting sled. Somberly, the line of men hauled the sled and coffin along while Tyson led the procession with his lantern. Shuffling behind the body of their friend walked the Inuit, with Hans's children led by their mother. Chaplain Bryan read a simple service. The men piled the loosened gravel and stones over the half-buried coffin, and the procession wended its way back to the darkened ship. The soft weeping of Tookoolito faded into the distance with the shuffling sound of her mukluks, leaving only the cold, lonely Arctic night.

The American flag that Charles Francis Hall had hoped to plant at the top of the world now hung at half-mast over his grave.

Chapter Seven

DISORDER

There was good discipline while Captain Hall lived, but we put discipline along with him in his grave.
—GUSTAVUS W. LINDQUIST, TESTIMONY AT INQUEST

Captain Hall's sudden death jerked the linchpin from the *Polaris* expedition. For all his shortcomings, his presence had held the factions together. Even before the lichen crept across Captain Hall's fresh grave, trouble began.

His old enemies could hardly conceal their delight at Hall's passing. Typically the tactless Buddington spoke first, mere hours after the captain's death and while he lay aboard still warm in his coffin.

"Well, Henry," he chortled to Seaman Henry Hobby, "there's a stone off my heart."

The grieving Hobby asked, "How so?"

"Why, Captain Hall is dead."

Startled, Hobby could only stare in disbelief. Their leader, a Christian gentleman, was dead, and the sailor could not imagine the skipper's rejoicing over the death. "How do you mean by that?" he finally asked.

Buddington rambled on. "We're all right now. We shan't be starved."

Hobby fled down the gangway. Over his shoulder he hurled a rebuttal, knowing he teetered on the brink of insubordination. Still, his conscience made him voice the trust he had had in Captain Hall. "I never thought we would," he said.

Unwittingly Buddington had let slip to Hobby the overpowering fear that haunted him: dying a long, protracted death on the ice by starvation. Like Columbus's sailors who feared that he might drive them off the edge of the world, Buddington must have feared that Hall's ambition would drive them beyond the limits of their provisions. Even with the tons of provisions stored on the ship, his fears were not totally unreasonable. The sudden crushing and sinking of the ship by a rogue iceberg could leave them destitute. The dark rumors of cannibalism still haunted the tales of the lost Franklin expedition. Buddington and the entire crew were well acquainted with them—those and tales of doomed ships with ghostly white crewmen frozen to the rigging washing ashore off Newfoundland.

Next Frederick Meyer let slip his inner feelings. Since Disko, when he had challenged Hall's orders with Bessel's backing, Meyer had held a grudge. His attempt at insubordination might have worked had it not been for the intervention of that stiff-backed old commander, Captain Davenport of the United States tender *Congress*. Facing Davenport's threat to take him back in irons, Meyer retreated and signed that humiliating statement, but he never forgot nor forgave the slight. Having to bend to the wishes of a self-made nobody from Cincinnati must have deeply galled Meyer, who had been trained as a Prussian military officer.

Strutting about the decks, Meyer griped to anyone within earshot that Hall had never followed the proper chain of command. "He consulted with the sailors and not the officers," Meyer complained, "giving the sailors command." That was not the Prussian way of doing things.

With the egalitarian Hall gone, things would return to their proper order, Meyer insisted. The officers would resume their positions of power, and the men would do as they were ordered without having any say. The whole ship would be better off with the chain of command once more forged into continuous links.

Strange, incongruous words for a man who had bucked his own superior officer when Hall lived. Probably the German sailors understood Meyer's position, but the meteorologist's sudden arrogance went against the grain of the Americans like Noah Hayes and Hobby. But now with the American expedition leader gone, the German element of the assembly, especially the officers and scientists, flexed their muscles.

Dr. Emil Bessel grew almost giddy with relief. Since they first laid eyes on each other, he and Hall had shared an antagonistic connection. Aristocrat and commoner, academician and self-taught man, the two had nothing in common, not even a mutual respect for the other's accomplishments. Hall's paternalism galled Bessel, while the doctor's condescension needled the explorer.

Within days of planting Hall beneath the frozen earth, Bessel skipped about his observatory lighthearted and laughing. More than once he remarked laughingly to Hayes that Hall's death was the best thing that could have happened to the expedition.

Of all the men who didn't mourn Hall's passing, Buddington is the one whose relief is most understandable. More and more the grinding, wallowing walls of moving ice frightened him. Somewhere along the way, he had lost his nerve to sail among the icebergs. Maybe he never had it. Maybe he never had the experience everyone assumed he did.

For on all his numerous voyages to hunt the whale, Buddington operated his ships in the time-honored way. He would sail as far north as necessary to take the marine mammals—but no farther than absolutely needed. He would then seek a secure harbor, anchor, and loose his whaleboats to wreak havoc among the migrating humpbacks and California gray whales. If caught by the weather and onset of ice, he would sail closer to land and winter the ship over.

Blasting through rotten ice, dodging icebergs, and constantly endangering his ship while navigating through shifting leads were not in his repertoire.

More important, Buddington had never sailed these waters alone. Fleets of whaling ships prowled these waters during the hunting season. Most often they sailed together and anchored together. If one vessel burned or sank, others were close by to rescue the crew.

Sidney O. Buddington was no William Scoresby. He never exhibited any desire to see beyond the far horizon. Scientific discovery never enthralled him as it did that ancient mariner. He had no imagination for those things, but he did imagine all too vividly what might happen to his ship.

Regrettably the goal of the *Polaris* expedition demanded that Buddington now beat northward into the ice on his own, without backup, something he was not prepared to do. Were the ship to founder, only the cold, empty expanses of the Greenland coast awaited those lucky enough to reach shore. To a man used to the sea, this inhospitable land was as fearful as the ice floes. So Buddington resisted moving his ship northward like a man who fears his life is threatened, for that is what he fervently believed. Nothing awaited him on shore, he was convinced, but a slow, painful death by starvation.

In contrast, Charles Francis Hall loved the moving islands of ice and wind-scoured peaks as much as life itself. He could live on and travel across the wastelands like the Inuit. His incessant pressure on the frightened Buddington served as a constant thorn in the man's side. Not just that, but Hall's enthusiasm only underlined Buddington's lack of courage.

Buddington's release from C. F. Hall's mandate to push farther north meant that he could anchor in the safety of Thank God Harbor and drink himself into a stupor. After all, his work of protecting the ship was done, and Bessel appeared content to investigate from their snug winter camp. No wonder Buddington felt a stone had been lifted from his heart. With ample stores and a secure moorage, his passage back home was assured, and there was no danger of starvation. Perhaps that is what he meant when he commented to Henry Hobby about not starving to death.

But the Fates had far different plans for the new commander of the *Polaris* expedition.

And why was Bessel so delighted? In his constant clashes with Hall, the doctor had got what he wanted. Essentially the scientific corps acted as an autonomous unit within the *Polaris* group. His haughty attitude and the shadowy threat of intervention from Hall's superiors in Washington had kept the explorer at bay.

Still, by his very disposition to micromanage, Charles Hall had constantly interfered with the scientists. His practical knowledge of the far North greatly exceeded theirs, and he used every opportunity to inject his suggestions into their work. Bessel's one trip to Spitzbergen accounted for the sum total of the scientific corps's prior experience. Neither Meyer nor Bryan had ever visited the Arctic. Even George Tyson, an ardent supporter of Hall, sensed that the captain had prevented them from doing their work. If Hall had been a thorn in Buddington's side, he had been a stone in Bessel's shoe.

Yet was there more to Bessel's elation than the removal of a meddlesome opponent? The impression lingers that Bessel actively strove to keep Hall from reaching the North Pole. By his constant support of Buddington, he thwarted Hall's intention to sail farther north. Perhaps Bessel harbored ambitions beyond mere scientific discovery. Later he would offer Henry Hobby two hundred dollars to help him be the first to reach the North Pole. Perhaps Bessel's motive was more sinister. Perhaps the former Prussian officer followed orders to scuttle the trip or took it upon himself to do so. Just as the men aboard the *Polaris* faced a formidable foe in the natural elements that threatened their survival, they also faced a fight with their own human nature and its darker elements.

If Emil Bessel thought he was the one chosen to reach the top of the world, the Arctic soon demonstrated its reluctance to award that prize.

Within days of Hall's demise, the mechanism to devolve the *Polaris* command took effect. The Navy Department, so lax in so many other ways, had spelled out what to do if Hall died:

You will give special written directions to the sailing master and ice master of the expedition, Mr. S. O. Buddington, and the chief of the Scientific Department, Dr. E. Bessel, that in case of your death or disability—a contingency we sincerely trust may not arise—they shall consult as to the propriety and manner of carrying into further effect the foregoing instructions, which I here urge must, if possible, be done. In any event, however, Mr. Buddington shall in the case of your death or disability, continue as the sailing and ice master, and control and direct the movements of the vessel; and Dr. Bessel shall, in such case, continue as chief of the Scientific Department, directing all sledge journeys and scientific operations. In the possible contingency of their non-agreement as to the course to be pursued, then Mr. Buddington shall assume sole charge and command, and return with the expedition to the United States with all possible dispatch.

Navy Secretary Robeson's orders were quite specific. Control of the vessel fell to Buddington, and Bessel assumed complete control of all scientific studies and journeys overland. If they disagreed, the whaling captain was to sail home immediately. Dutifully the two men issued a written notice to that effect. There it was: both men got just what they wanted. Officially the *Polaris* expedition now had two heads. It would be only a matter of time before this two-headed chimera quarreled with itself.

Meanwhile strange happenings continued to occur.

One cold midnight, cries from the forward compartment drew the men to Nathan Coffin's bunk. Since he had fashioned Captain Hall's coffin, the carpenter showed increasing signs of instability. Described as "sensitive," Coffin had taken the captain's death hard. That night they found the carpenter cowering beneath his blankets in the corner of his berth. Wide-eyed and shaking with terror, Coffin babbled that voices were calling to him from the adjacent storage locker. The sailors unlocked the room and searched it to pacify Coffin, but to no avail. He continued to hear the voices. A rapid bedside consultation diagnosed the man's problem to be related to the isolated and exposed nature of his bunk, which was far forward of the main sleeping quarters, cold and damp. A change of sleeping arrangements was prescribed. Showing an astonishing lack of sensitivity, Captain Buddington moved the unbalanced Coffin into the dead Captain Hall's old bed. As might be expected, Coffin recalled Hall's ravings about murder and naturally assumed he was next on the list. Within days the carpenter began to fear that unknown persons aboard ship would kill him.

Then Noah Hayes fell down the gangway and twisted his knee so badly that he could not perform his duties for an entire week. Three days later an old frostbite injury on William Morton's heel reopened. During one trip with Dr. Kane, Morton had frozen his heel. The wound remained closed in temperate climates. Now the parchmentlike scar split apart, forcing the man to remain in bed until it healed. As a precaution against scurvy, lime juice joined the daily rations.

For some time now, Arctic explorers had understood that the lack of fresh vegetables and sunlight fostered scurvy. Plants and most animals can synthesize vitamin C from glucose, but humans cannot. The lack of vitamins C and D prevents the production of collagen—the main component in fibrous and elastic tissues. Teeth loosen and fall out, and healed scars break down. Bleeding into the skin and muscle follows as the walls of the blood vessels weaken. Since the Inuit ate fresh meat that contained vitamin C and never suffered from scurvy, except during periods of starvation, the Western explorers adopted their practice. Lime juice helped as well. James Lind, a Scottish surgeon serving in the Royal Navy, first discovered this association in 1753. Forced to drink a mix of lime juice and sauerkraut, the British tar soon acquired the moniker of "Limey."

With each passing hour, the days and nights merged more tightly into one black, faceless event. The thermometer sank incessantly, and the wind grew dangerously sharp. The sinuous winding of greenish-purple and rose-colored auroras appeared with increasing frequency in the skies overhead, confirming the Inuit's feelings that evil forces were at work.

The galley stove broke down. A constant wind raking across the deck and rattling the ice-rimed rigging now forced downdrafts through the chimney. Clouds of smoke, sparks, and burning cinders drove Jackson and his helpers out of the galley. The small stoves in the forecastle and below decks replaced the galley. Each mess therefore cooked their own meals. This solution further conspired to divide the crew. Buddington unwittingly aggravated the problem when he canceled the daily services that Hall had held. No longer would the various watches and teams on the *Polaris* come together in one place.

A series of gales raked across the bay beginning on November 18. Winds increased to almost fifty knots. The wind instruments tore apart under the impact. Herman Sieman, a stout figure, left the ship to measure the tidal change through the fire hole, an opening kept from freezing over in case seawater should be needed to fight a fire on board the ship. A gust blew his feet from under him. Crashing onto his back, Sieman shot across the ice in freezing water that had overflowed from fresh cracks in the ice. Each new blast pushed him farther from the ship. Using his ice ax, he barely made it back to the safety of the ship.

The fury of the storm trapped Emil Bessel in his flimsy observatory. Each hammering of the wind threatened to rip the prefabricated shack apart. By nine o'clock the next morning, Bessel had not returned. Since the observatory had a small coal stove, his tardiness caused little alarm.

As time passed, concern mounted until Meyer volunteered to reach the house. Each attempt he made, the storm foiled. Struggling through a milky white world where he could not even see his hand, he never found the building. The force of the storm drove him back with mounting savagery. One of his eyelids froze solid during his struggle. Finally Hans and Ebierbing joined the attempt. The swirling snow taxed even their expertise. Creeping along on hands and knees, the three finally reached the observatory.

Inside they found Emil Bessel on the verge of freezing to death. He had burned his last lump of coal more than eight hours before and then huddled inside the rattling building while his ear froze. As they battled back to the ship with the petrified doctor, Ebierbing's right cheek turned white from frostbite. Only Hans escaped unharmed. With the temperature reaching minus 20°F and the wind howling at fifty knots, exposed skin froze within fifteen seconds.

All day the men huddled inside while the ship creaked and groaned with the buckling ice. Far out to sea, the thinner sea ice shattered as the ocean's fetch allowed waves and swells to grow under the increasing pressure of the wind. The rolling sea jacked the thicker bay ice until leads and fissures crisscrossed the harbor. By afternoon the *Polaris* rocked inside her frozen cradle as the walls around her splintered and shattered to the accompanying rifle-shot cracks of breaking ice.

At two-thirty in the morning, a convulsive jerk rippled throughout the ship. All hands rushed topside to find the vessel surrounded by a frothy well of black water. Its icy cradle had shattered to pieces. Freed of its constraints, the ship rocked wildly with each wave. The open water quickly swallowed the ice wall that the men had spent days banking against the ship's sides. In an instant all their work vanished.

Blinded by the swirling clouds of snow, the men waited like sightless creatures as block after block of bay ice rammed against the sides of the ship. Soundings with a lead line confirmed an even worse fear: The *Polaris* had dragged her anchor and was drifting. The soundings read deeper water under the keel with each throw. With the bay ice broken, the entire pack was drifting out to sea—carrying the *Polaris* along with it.

Even more frightening was the presence of Providence Berg. Once a shelter from the wind and seas, the massive iceberg now threatened the ship. All the turmoil of waves and wind had not dislodged the iceberg. Firmly grounded in the bottom of the bay, the frozen mountain still straddled Thank God Harbor.

Now the current and wind carried the ship directly toward the stationary iceberg. Drawn like a floating leaf, within minutes the *Polaris* would be smashed against the iceberg. Once the hull began sliding along the underwater portion of Providence Berg, the contact would be fatal. The underwater spur of the iceberg, frozen water polished to a slick surface, would act like a deadly ramp, flipping the ship onto its side while wind and waves cascaded over the opposite railings. The *Polaris* would roll over until water rushed over the leeward rail, overwhelmed her pumps, and she sank.

Frantically the sailors broke open chain lockers and bent on heavy chain to bow and stern anchors. Ice coating the lockers had to be chipped off to free the chains. If anchors could be set in the powdery bottom, the hopeless drift of the ship toward the iceberg could be slowed or stopped. Fore and aft anchors splashed into the water—with no relief. The anchors continued to drag across the poor holding ground.

The men braced themselves for the grinding crash. But none came. Almost docilely *Polaris* sidled under the protective shoulder of Providence Berg. The following ice floes parted and flowed past the ship on their way out to sea. Soberly the sailors realized their respite might not last more than an hour unless the ship was secured. Since the anchors refused to bite into the soft bottom, mooring the ship to the grounded iceberg remained the only option.

William Lindermann stripped off his fur clothing and squeezed through the forward porthole on the starboard side. Just beneath him, the ship's prow jutted across part of Providence Berg. From there he grasped a projecting spur of the iceberg and dragged himself onto the ice. Ebierbing followed close behind him. Using knife and hatchet, the Inuit cut footsteps so they could ascend to the flat saddle of the iceberg.

Under the light of a burning kerosene-soaked hawser set in a pan, the two men drove an ice anchor into the berg and secured the bowline. Three more men scampered across and placed two more anchors. Secured fore and aft, the *Polaris* nestled beneath the protective shoulder of the frozen giant while the men aboard listened to the thumping and crashing of waves and floating ice hammering against the outer side.

By late afternoon the storm blew itself out. When the air cleared sufficiently for the men to look about, they took stock. The change was remarkable. The bay—once frozen solidly with two-foot-thick sections of ice—now lay open. Black water lapped against the ship's hull and stretched as far as the eyes could see.

The sudden breakup of the surrounding ice had cost the party dearly. Two sleds vanished into the dark sea, and two dogs were missing along with numerous parcels. The wind and snow wreaked havoc with the instruments left on the bank. The declinometer lay on its side, half buried in snowdrifts. Several small igloos were blown down, and Dr. Bessel's prefabricated observatory was totally buried by snow. Burrowing a six-foot-long tunnel to the door proved the only way to enter the laboratory.

Satisfied that it had demonstrated its power, the Arctic abruptly ceased its savagery and started to preen. The sky cleared to expose a dazzling display of northern lights. Electric clouds, as the seamen called them, floated above their heads. Coiling and snaking, the bands of pale blue and violet danced from one horizon to the next. Folding and writhing like a living thing, the lighted curtains arced across the clear air, appearing to hover just outside of fingers' reach, although they actually waved more than two hundred miles overhead. Using the latest instruments available, the scientists measured the mysterious sight. Their magnetic instruments showed no effect, probably because they were not sensitive enough, and the black paddles of the electroscope remained still. To the men on the *Polaris* expedition, the aurora borealis remained an unexplained phenomenon.

It would take another hundred years for men of science like Sun Akasofu of the University of Alaska to unravel most of the mysteries of the northern lights. Still not completely understood, the dazzling display results from charged electrons and protons reaching the earth in the solar wind emanating from the sun. The magnetic fields surrounding the earth pour out from the north and south magnetic poles like unseen fountains and draw the charged particles toward the top and bottom of the earth. During intense periods of solar activity, gust after gust of solar particles blow out from the sun to concentrate at the poles and bombard the earth's upper atmosphere. Slamming into the atmosphere, these charged particles collide with oxygen and nitrogen atoms, split off their electrons, and knock those electrons into excited states. As the electrons drop back into their normal state, they emit characteristic light waves of violet, green-blue, and red. At the exact moment a display of northern lights flares over the North Pole, an identical display—the aurora australis, or southern lights—dances over the South Pole. In some ways the magnetized air over the poles acts like one enormous fluorescent bulb lighting up the heavens.

Magnetic fields do accompany the aurora borealis. Intense light displays will send power surges along high-tension electric lines running between Anchorage and Fairbanks, Alaska, and magnetic fields do flow down the Alaska oil pipeline. So why the scientists of the *Polaris* failed to detect magnetic changes is uncertain. However, the pipeline and power wires act as giant conductors, concentrating the aurora's magnetism.

That the *Polaris* escaped major damage from the storm amazed all hands. The ship narrowly missed being dragged out to sea with the ice pack. Without a full head of steam, the ship would have drifted without power until crushed amid the jostling ice. If divine intervention had played any part in the ship's salvation, the idea was lost on Captain Buddington. The following Sunday, over the objections of Mr. Bryan, the captain announced that attending Sunday services was no longer required.

Two days later an eerie sight greeted all the men. A strangely shaped full moon rose and shone brightly across the covered decks. Refraction of moonlight on ice crystals suspended in the air, aided by the density of the cold air, produced an optical illusion called a *paraselene*. Three identical images of the full moon hovered in the dark sky, surrounding the real one, one on each side and one above. A fourth image, the lowest one, was hidden by the mountains. The four visible images connected by the rays of light from the real moon, aided by the mind's eye, formed a cross. The Inuit took this to be another omen of bad things to come.

They didn't have long to wait. Providence Berg, once the protector, turned on the ship it sheltered. Another storm struck—this time from the south. Heavy snow fell, adding to that blown by the wind, and soon the visibility dropped to a few feet. Wind and waves attacked both ship and iceberg from their unprotected side.

Under constant pressure from the ice floe, Providence Berg split in two. The advancing ice floe wedged the halves apart until more than eight feet separated them. The half that sheltered *Polaris* swung on its grounded foot while the smaller island of ice rammed into the ship's side. Every man held his breath as the *Polaris* creaked and groaned against the point of this frozen lance.

Buddington rushed back and forth along the covered deck, peering over the side with each protest from the straining oak planks. Was the side cut through? he wondered. Were the ribs staved in? Miraculously the wood withstood the pressure. Seams opened, but the ship's flanks remained intact.

However, another, more dangerous, event occurred. What the ice could not break, it sought to overturn. A shelf of ice protruded from Providence Berg below the waterline, close beside the ship's nose. Slowly the force of the storm drove the *Polaris* onto the underwater projection, lifting her keel until the bow rose into the air, exposing the copper sheathing and barnacle-encrusted iron plate of the prow. Shaking and quivering like a whipped dog, the ship advanced with each blow from the thundering waves.

In time the *Polaris* keeled to one side, coming to lie nearly on its

Fastening to Providence Berg, November 21, 1871 (Culver Pictures)

beam end. Men slid down the icy deck to crash into the aft cabins. The deck canted so steeply that walking proved difficult without using the lifelines. When the *Polaris* finally came to rest, the stem jutted two and one-half feet above the sea. Here the ship remained, careened to one side like a trader run on a reef. When the tide ran out, the ship's stern dropped and the bow rose four feet in the air. On the flood tide the stern rose again, lowering the stem to two and one-half feet once more. All the while this teeter-tottering worked its damage on the keel. The pitch and yaw of the ship so frightened the Inuit that they moved from the ship to the observatory. There they took up residence, scattering their skins and oil lamps among the crates of brass instruments.

Thanksgiving arrived with no special services to celebrate their deliverance from another near disaster. As George Tyson wrote acerbically in his diary, "Thanksgiving was remembered at the table, but in no other way." Opened cans of lobster, turkey, oyster soup, pecans, walnuts, plum duff, cherry pie, and wine punch made up for the lack of spirituality. While the men feasted, no one considered the extra fuel they were using. Ominously, 6,334 pounds of coal were burned during November, 1,596 pounds more than the previous month.

December brought deepening cold. The men amused themselves by playing cards and racing sleds on the refrozen bay. Captain Buddington wrote in his journal: "All possible preparations are being made to succeed with our sledge parties next spring." His notes must have been for public consumption. Already the skipper was doing his best to paint the brightest picture possible for the men in Washington. No other journals mention such preparations. Tookoolito's sewing of new skin anoraks and pants appears to be the only measure taken.

Chester wrote glowing praise of the men, describing them like cheerful Boy Scouts, always industrious and especially neat: "They are all *good* men. They keep clean and take good care of themselves. Everything about their quarters looks clean and neat. There is not much danger of such men being troubled with scurvy."

His rose-colored glasses are impressive. First, soap cannot prevent scurvy. Second, stability aboard the *Polaris* had all but vanished. Increasingly Captain Buddington was drunk, and the men, taking their cue from the captain, pilfered the ship's alcohol stores. Gallons of ethanol intended to preserve scientific specimens simply vanished. Duplicate keys to the storage lockers sprang up throughout the ship. Boisterous, drunken parties reigned nightly.

Order and discipline suffered. Day and night became the same. One long, ongoing period of darkness engulfed the crew. Day and night activities bled slowly into each other. Now when the need was greatest to establish regular routines to prevent the malaise that follows the loss of these normal cycles, there were none. Buddington had no stomach for order, preferring to drink in his cabin. Tyson, Hayes, and Hobby regularly visited Hall's grave and lamented his absence. "Captain Hall did not always act with the clearest judgement," George Tyson wrote, "but *it was heaven to this*."

Tyson saw things quite differently from Chester. "There is so little regularity observed," he lamented. "There is no stated time for putting out lights; the men are allowed to do as they please; and, consequently, they often make nights hideous by their carousing, playing cards to all hours." He took to walking on the ice in the darkness "longing for a moment's quiet." But the heartless isolation and oppressive darkness weighed heavily on him. "The gloom and silence of every thing around settles down on one like a pall," he wrote.

Nathan Coffin turned worse. When he was sane, he worked diligently repairing sleds in the aft-galley space, which had become the carpentry workshop. During those times he appeared normal. At other times a black mood fell over him. His deranged mind remained convinced that someone on board intended to murder him.

Their method for doing him in was bizarre by any standards. Coffin imagined that after boring a hole in the bulkhead where he slept, they would insert a nozzle through the opening and spray him with carbolic acid, thus freezing him to death. Such a death would be ascribed to the Arctic cold rather than to a murderer, he reasoned, and would go unpunished. The open questions about Captain Hall's recent demise gave credence to his theory. Hall's ravings about poison still remained fresh in everyone's mind. Many still wondered if their commander had been murdered.

Many nights Coffin lay awake, cowering in fear from that anticipated sound of a wood bore. He changed sleeping places nightly, hiding in lockers and behind bulkheads. Other times he would pretend to sleep in one place only to move to another site while the others slept. Gaunt and hollow-eyed from lack of sleep, the carpenter stalked about below decks like a wraith. His madness served as a constant reminder to the crew of Captain Hall's sudden, suspicious death.

In the face of the ship's crumbling discipline, Captain Buddington did a curious and unexplained thing: he issued revolvers and rifles to the crew. What purpose this served is unknown. No external threat from Natives or animals existed. Hunting parties had need of firearms, and armed guards could be posted against the occasional marauding polar bear, but arming the crew during peacetime is unusual. Tyson would later surmise in his diary that Buddington armed the crew to curry their favor, intimating that Buddington might have feared that Tyson would snatch command away from him. But Tyson was no great favorite of the men either.

On December 6 the Arctic almost snatched Emil Bessel. Showing the same general contempt for the North Country that he had showered upon Captain Hall nearly cost him his life. Without carefully checking the weather one night, he departed the ship for his observatory. Normally the walk over the ice took half an hour, with the hut always within sight. The distance was a mere 1,307 feet, roughly a quarter of a mile. The onset of a sudden storm caught the doctor in the open. Pressing onward instead of turning back in the whiteout conditions, he missed the shack. Disoriented in the blowing snow, he could neither find the house nor locate the *Polaris*.

Forced to shelter behind an outcropping of ice, Bessel spent the night trying to keep warm. Undoubtedly his Inuit clothing and boots kept him from freezing in temperatures close to 30° below zero. During that time he no doubt realized that a guide rope from ship to shore would have prevented his problem. Four hours later the snow diminished enough for him to find the observatory. Alarmed when he heard he had almost lost his chief scientist and ally, Buddington ordered a hastily constructed line of rubber-coated wire strung between the two points.

The remainder of December passed with little note. "Nothing occurring that is pleasant or profitable to record," Tyson wrote. The oppressive darkness continued to exert increasing pressure on all, and the North showed its total disregard for these interlopers. Alternating periods of misery and elation washed over the crew like irregular waves. The northern lights flashed brighter and clearer with each passing day, taunting the men, while frost and ice infested the sleeping quarters.

When the *Polaris* broke free and drifted against Providence Berg, the ship had lost the insulating layers of snow so carefully banked along its sides. With the ship rocking up and down on its keel with each rise and fall of the tide, no amount of work could keep a new layer of snow in place. Without proper insulation, frost and cold crept quickly through the wooden walls. The dark interiors of the berths soon sported crystal layers of hoarfrost and ice. Water vapor from the stoves and human breath condensed everywhere. Showers of snow and icy crystal flakes fluttered down with every movement when the stoves were unlit. Lighting the heaters made matters only worse. The heat melted the rime and filled the quarters with a dripping, soggy haze of fog and dew that penetrated wool clothing and chilled everyone. When the stoves died out, the frost reformed, and the cycle repeated itself.

Christmas arrived to elaborate preparations but once again without any religious services being held. As at Thanksgiving, the table groaned under the weight of food and drink.

The divisiveness that set the crew at odds with one another raised its head briefly over the celebration. Since Christmas Eve was on a Sunday, some of the crew objected to celebrating on the Sabbath, preferring to have the party on Christmas night. The Germans absolutely refused to go along with that idea, wanting their party. Being the majority, they flexed their muscle. Rear Adm. C. H. Davis, in his *Narrative of the North Polar Expedition*, wrote of this incident that "the others cheerfully yielded." That they did seems unlikely. One does not usually give up religious preferences "cheerfully." Davis's work under the direction of Navy Secretary Robeson paints a rosy picture of every aspect of the expedition.

A drawing distributed Christmas packages to the crew, and everyone opened theirs at exactly ten o'clock. The presents turned out to be toys and trinkets bought by Captain Hall as gifts for any Eskimo children they might encounter. In a macabre twist, the dead explorer's specter rose over the occasion. Few noticed, and most were too drunk to care.

All the while the onshore wind continually stacked additional pack ice against the outside of their protective iceberg. The growing weight levered the shelter farther onto its side, and that, in turn, raised *Polaris* ever higher out of the water. Cracks developed in the stem and along the keel. One worrisome leak opened near the bow, where ice had staved in the planking. Located near the six-foot watermark, the shattered beam teetered tantalizingly just out of reach as the bow dipped in and out of the water.

And just as the wind and water wore away at the ship, the cold, isolation, and Arctic night worked to divide the crew. Buddington and Bessel soon quarreled over control of the dogsleds. Robeson's orders directed Bessel to conduct the sled trips, but the Prussian's lack of Arctic experience left him open to question. His frostbitten ear and recent fiasco while attempting to reach his hut highlighted his inexperience. To Buddington the haughty foreigner acted too proud to admit his ignorance. To Bessel the ship's captain, on the other hand, was no more than a drunken lout. While neither man openly confronted the other, animosity radiated out from each like light from the oil lanterns.

While Bessel and Buddington jockeyed for overall command, neither could muster a constant group of supporters to his cause. George Tyson, brooding about his lost chances for promotion under Hall, loathed them both and refused to back one or the other. Frederick Meyer took the side of his fellow Prussian in arguments with Buddington but in private argued with Bessel. First Mate Hubbard Chester disliked George Tyson. Tyson returned the compliment. Buddington cared little for his chief engineer, Schuman, and all four American officers viewed Meyer and Bessel with suspicion. Only Mr. Bryan appeared above the petty differences, which steadily grew out of proportion.

Naturally the attitude of the officers spilled over to the enlisted men. Men who had prospered under Captain Hall felt they were punished for their loyalty to their dead leader. Joseph Mauch, elevated to the role of secretary to Captain Hall, found himself returned to the forecastle. Having more education than the other sailors, he lavished sarcasm on his fellow shipmates. He developed a special dislike for Emil Bessel, accusing the doctor of being a "damned imposter," of being too lazy to do his job properly, and of making up false data to cover that fact. Later, Captain Buddington reappointed Mauch to act as his scribe.

Noah Hayes struggled under the harsh control of Walter Campbell, the fireman. Hayes had hoped Captain Hall would promote him out of the black gang, but the commander's death left the cheerful neophyte trapped in the boiler rooms with the bad-tempered Campbell and the martinet Schuman. In time Hayes's spleen would vent itself in his diary, filling page after page with invectives.

And so it went, round and round, slight piled upon slight, anger added to anger. This splintering of loyalties and introspected resentment frequently infects groups subjected to the long Arctic winter.

When the sun disappears from October 17 to February 28 and a crew lacks strong direction, the results are predictable. Loss of orientation, isolation, and constant discomfort unhinge even the best of intentions. Strong leadership, well-defined goals, and motivation are the antidotes. None of that remained in the *Polaris* expedition.

Add to this the physiology of light deprivation. Unknown to anyone at that time, the effects are striking on susceptible individuals. Without a certain quantity of daylight hitting the human retina, the brain stops producing melatonin. This hormone, besides stimulating pigment production, aids in sleep regulation and mood elevation. Lowered levels lead to loss of energy, listlessness, and depression in some people. Overeating and heavy drinking occur in others. Modern medicine has coined a term for the problem, *seasonal affective disorder,* spawning a whole line of treatments. Some people are highly sensitive to changes in sunlight, whereas others are not. Staring at light boxes emitting the same spectrum of light as daylight helps the problem. One enterprising Alaskan cured his own disorder by staring into his car's headlights for twenty minutes a day during the winter, although this treatment is not recommended. Perhaps Captain Buddington was afflicted by this disorder instead of alcoholism.

The Arctic winter is an equal-opportunity destroyer. All that affected the *Polaris* crew had touched those who went before them and those who would follow. Some reacted better to the stress; others reacted worse. Henry Hudson's crew mutinied. Royal Navy discipline held Sir John Franklin's expedition together until the bitter end, as it did with Robert Scott's small band in the Antarctic. Even Charles Francis Hall, who adapted well to the Arctic, had grown moody and troublesome on his previous explorations. How well or how poorly the men of the *Polaris* rate in dealing with the stress of the Arctic winter is open to discussion.

December ended with a whimper. Tantalizingly the sea opened a distance from the stranded ship, but three to four miles of ice still lay between them. To compound matters, a new fear arose. The status of the steering was uncertain. Encased in ice, the rudder stock and its chains could neither be examined for damage nor repaired.

Many feared that the rudder had snapped off when the *Polaris* heeled over.

Buddington filled his personal journal with excuses, emphasizing the constant danger to the ship and lamenting that Hall had not followed his advice about a more secure anchorage. With remarkably selective recall, he forgot his desire to sail south to Port Foulke and remembered wanting to anchor in Newman Bay. There would be no drifting ice pack, no daily rocking on the ice spur, no danger from anything had he been listened to, he postulated.

Two days before and two days after the New Year, attempts to free the ship ended in dismal failure. The men chiseled holes in the surrounding ice and placed four bottles of black powder. Their first effort failed to split off the spur of ice that lifted the keel. Their last attempt nearly broke the ship's ribs. The four feet of solid ice entrapping the vessel remained unaffected.

Captain Buddington now fastened on a new excuse for failure. During December the ship had burned close to one ton of coal more than in November. Characteristically Buddington blamed Hall's previous estimate of the available coal in the coal bunkers. Only eighty tons actually remained, Buddington claimed, not the one hundred tons that Hall had estimated. "If the consumption of this fuel is continued at the same rate, a stoppage of which, without endangering our health is not possible, we will hardly have enough for two winters, to say nothing of using steam on our return," Buddington carefully noted, adding, "The idea of piloting the vessel through Smith Sound with the aid of sails is an absurdity."

Again he carefully painted himself into a corner, limiting his options. Despite Hall's careful efforts to outfit the expedition for at least two years, the new commander deemed there were barely enough provisions to get them to the next sailing season. And what could he do differently? His hands were tied by circumstances beyond his control. Surely the men in Washington would understand that he must see to the welfare of his men before that of the mission.

Drunk almost daily since Hall's death, S. O. Buddington no doubt increasingly worried about covering his failings. In his mind he had no intention of spending another dreary winter in the Arctic if he could help it. His journal writings resound with reasons he could not complete the mission. Rather than constituting a journal, his entries shifted to a preparation for his defense.

Faced with a similar decision, Captain Hall would have cut back the coal usage, perhaps looked for alternative fuels to burn. But C. F. Hall was dead, and the special boiler designed to burn whale oil or seal blubber was gone as well, mysteriously thrown over the side back at Disko.

While Bessel and Buddington languished in their separate commands, the other men moved about aimlessly. At long last, whether through boredom or through rising courage, the officers and crew began to mount dogsled forays away from the ship without the help of Hans or Ebierbing. The sailors' lack of skill in handling dogs soon became painfully apparent. While the Inuit made it look easy, controlling the fractious animals over broken ice proved tricky for the neophytes. Few of the mariners' trips achieved more than a dozen miles. Nothing new was discovered, and each team returned with conflicting reports of the sea to the west. The shifting condition of the water and ice, which appeared open to some and closed to others, stymied any coordinated plan to move the ship. Of course, that suited Buddington's strategy of inaction.

January ended much as December had. Everything submerged beneath the gray mantle of the long Arctic night. Tasks and days blurred into one protracted period of depressing darkness. The strain of taking nightly meteorology readings finally exhausted Frederick Meyer, so Mauch gratefully assumed the task. Working in the observation hut freed him from having to act as Buddington's secretary. On a positive note, the more careful burning of coal paid off, saving 798 pounds over that burned the prior month.

By February shimmering glimpses of twilight crept back into the days, increasing with each passing hour. February 28 saw the sun peek over the rim of the Greenland mountains to the east. One hundred and thirty-five days of darkness had passed. The arrival of the sun reenergized the expedition, or at least some of its members. What is interesting is that Dr. Bessel, who had frustrated Captain Hall's attempts to reach the North Pole, now seemed bent on reaching the top of the world himself. Emil Bessel sent a note to Captain Buddington:

Sir:

As with the return of the sun the further operations of the expedition must be begun, and as, in regard to all these, a consultation between us should take place, I forward herewith to you a sketch of a plan by means of which, as I think, we may best fulfill the mission upon which we are sent.

Very respectfully,
Emil Bessel

Whereupon the chief scientist enclosed five pages of detailed instructions for mounting further probes northward. March or April would be a good time to start, Bessel imagined, and the chance of the *Polaris*'s breaking loose from its iceberg's grip by then seemed unlikely. Therefore, exploring by small boat or sled offered the best option. Here the German physician was proceeding on faith instead of experience. If the *Polaris* could not break free of the ice, how did he expect his small boat teams to progress northward?

Bessel suggested that Buddington should wait until conditions permitted to steam the ship northward to Newman Bay to rendezvous with the advance party. Since the primary purpose was to discover the North Pole, a geographical goal, Bessel reasoned that land travel best suited that purpose. Bessel then outlined a plan approaching the Normandy invasion in complexity. He has boat teams and sled groups crisscrossing north and south before meeting with the *Polaris*. Boats and shore supply depots would be left if the parties missed one another—a highly likely event given the vagaries of the Arctic weather and the difficult terrain. If the *Polaris* broke free before the teams returned, it was to sail north to Newman Bay and await the others. If the ice pack drifted south with the ship still entrapped, Buddington should cache "documents of the further route they intend to take" near the observatory. Presumably the men on the boats or dog teams would read the notes and race down the coast after the drifting *Polaris* to reunite with her.

Bessel continued to detail his attack. However, his ignorance of Arctic exploration revealed itself. He wrote:

It cannot be denied that it is a great advantage to use dogs for draught, but as we are compelled to travel over a poor country and make large distances the dogs will prove hindrances rather than help. We must, then, as the English expeditions have done, almost exclusively use man for draught.

Nothing could be more disastrous. In his inexperience Bessel intended to commit the same error that had doomed Sir John Franklin and would later lead to the deaths of Scott and his men in the Antarctic: he would substitute manpower for dogs.

If a man could do a better job pulling a sled, why did the Inuit use dogs? A thousand years of experience backed their decision to use canines. Generations of Natives had spent their lives refining sled design and breeding dogs to yield the most efficient combination for hauling goods over the ice, and the Eskimo's survival in the Arctic attested to the success of their methods. High spirits notwithstanding, a man cannot pull a two-hundred-pound sled for long in the Arctic. The expenditure of energy is just too great.

Furthermore, Bessel intended his sled journey to be a one-way affair. Expecting the ice pack to break up before the men could pull their sleds back, the Prussian planned to camp along the shoreline and wait for the *Polaris* to find them. "They will keep up a continued watch and signalize by flags and smoke, while the vessel fires a gun several times a day," he proudly wrote. Somehow, the scientist believed the blinding snow squalls and smothering fog that harassed them would go away. It is not hard to imagine the ship and land parties' never connecting.

The complexity of Bessel's planning would have scattered the expedition's men and limited resources widely along the coastline of Greenland, overextending their lines of supply and communication, a further prescription for disaster. An axiom of Arctic travel is to keep needed supplies as close at hand as possible. The lifesaving cache is always the one too far away, the one that is never reached, as Scott would later reaffirm. He and his men died less than eleven miles from all the food and supplies they would have needed.

Not content merely to trample over centuries of Inuit wisdom, Bessel went on to tell Captain Buddington how to sail his ship. "Now, a few remarks upon the operation of the vessel," he wrote. "It would undoubtedly be best to use as little as possible of our coal, and to proceed north by sail." Ironically Bessel had replaced Captain Hall in attempting to micromanage Buddington.

Buddington must have choked when he read those lines. First, the landlubber Hall had deigned to instruct him on handling his vessel, and now the "little German dancing master" was weighing in as well.

"If it is *possible* for the vessel to advance along the coast of Grinnell Land *it would be profitable to do so*," Bessel wrote condescendingly. One can almost see Buddington taking another drink as he read these directions. Take a running survey along the coastline, Bessel ordered, *"as there certainly will be some one on board who can conduct a work of this kind."*

Bessel continued to rub salt in the wounds his words undoubtedly reopened. He proceeded to remind Buddington the sailor that the magnetic pole would affect his compass. "The determination of the local attraction of the compass before the vessel starts should not be neglected *as heretofore*, because without this an able survey cannot be made." In all the fanfare and hurry to leave Washington and the Brooklyn Navy Yard, the ship's compass aboard the *Polaris* had never been swung to determine its deflection and deviation—a grievous oversight, and one that Captain George Tyson used to belittle Captain Buddington.

"It should be considered as a matter of the highest importance to take deep-sea soundings, or soundings in general, whenever practicable," the doctor concluded, as if Buddington might forget to test the depth of the unknown waters into which he would be sailing. Any prudent master always used soundings to measure the depth of the water. It was the surest way to keep from running aground.

Lost in his own self-importance, the physician neglected to close his "sketch" with "Respectfully yours," the usual courteous ending, signing the letter merely "Emil Bessel."

The obvious insults aside, Buddington readily consented to Bessel's plan. It gave him just what he wanted. He could stay aboard the *Polaris* with the hateful chief scientist out of his hair, dragging his two-hundred-pound sled over the knife-edged *sastrugi*.

If the ice the captain feared carried him south, so be it. All he had to do was leave supplies and a message of his general intent. He probably wished to leave Bessel to freeze, but he could not write that down. If the ice receded, that was all the better. He could steam up to Newman Bay, pick up the exhausted survivors of Bessel's death march, and claim his share of the glory for saving their lives. Then a speedy retreat back to Washington.

"Your suggestions as to an early trip to Cape Constitution and the inland meet with my entire approval," Buddington wrote back. Using the opportunity afforded by Bessel's "sketch," the captain jumped at the part that spared him from driving his ship against the ice floes. "The expedition to the north, will, in all probability, proceed by the aid of boats," he agreed. Ever aware that his actions would be carefully scrutinized on their return, he added stoutly, "It is my decided intention, in such a case, to take command of the boat party." Then he slyly scribbled an ending that kept him off the hook: "To come to any conclusion as yet to the details of this boat journey and the proceedings of the ship appears to be useless, inasmuch as circumstances will generally govern our actions."

Once again Buddington had fashioned a passive role for himself. Whatever the conditions permitted, he would acquiesce to those events instead of pressing onward without regard to his safety, as Charles Francis Hall might have done—a far, far different mind-set from that of the late commander.

Still, the sled forays could leave within a matter of weeks, far earlier than any whaleboat expedition, and that would get Bessel out of his hair. It would be at least June before water travel was likely. The sooner Bessel left, the happier Buddington would be. A three-month gap would separate land and water exploration, giving the ship captain a much-needed respite from the chief scientist.

Relations between Bessel and Buddington remained strained. Not only did each man openly despise the other, but Bessel used every opportunity to humiliate the captain. One such opportunity presented itself over the scientific corps's specimen alcohol.

Having consumed all the rum and wine he had secreted in nooks and corners of the storerooms, Captain Buddington increasingly turned to raiding the alcohol used by Dr. Bessel for his scientific specimens. In fact, he remained drunk almost daily.

Others stole a drink or two, using their unauthorized duplicate keys, but the captain proved the most frequent and serious offender, and he had an official key with unlimited access to the stores. Luckily for all concerned, the scientific corps preserved its finds in pure grain alcohol, following the accepted methods of preservation. Had it used wood alcohol or methanol, Buddington and his fellow drinkers would quickly have gone blind.

The rapidly diminishing supply of his preservative alarmed Bessel. Besides, he relished the chance to exercise his authority over his troublesome captain. The physician soon discovered that Buddington was stealing bottles of alcohol and hiding them in the pantry. From there it was only a leisurely stroll from the captain's cabin to the pantry for a quick drink.

The doctor set his trap. Quietly he crept below and hid himself behind the crates and barrels. He had not long to wait. Buddington slipped down the ladder and went straight to his hidden supply. The instant the captain retrieved the specimen bottle and brought it to his lips, Emil Bessel sprang out and seized him by the collar.

Caught red-handed, Buddington could only stare open-mouthed as the little Prussian berated him like a child with his hand in the cookie jar. For a man "built on rather too small a scale," Bessel with his sudden attack succeeded in cowing the larger man. Seeing this terrier shaking the heavyset mariner must have been amusing to those of the galley crew who witnessed it. However, the event did nothing to bolster what little confidence the sailors still retained in their officers.

So it was decided: sled expeditions would be mounted at the first opportunity. Coffin poured his energy into making small sleds for the men to pull and larger ones to haul the boats. March, however, came in like a lion. Gales lashed the ship on the first and second and threatened to drive the *Polaris* off her precarious perch. Temperatures plummeted to minus 50° while the wind tore through the canvas and riggings at fifty knots. The recently installed window in the observatory blew out, and stones the size of hens' eggs blew across the ice.

More ice lifted the vessel, so that the six-foot marking on the hull remained clearly out of the water. However, Buddington issued no orders to repair the visible hole in the side. The timbers groaned constantly, protesting the weight they had never been designed to hold. The tilt of the deck grew more extreme. In the officers' mess in the lower cabin, sitting down to eat proved impossible. Men took their meals standing, propped against the bulkheads for support. Cleats fastened along the deck and atop the cabin's roof aided the men in moving from bow to stern.

Sleeping became a constant nightmare, as the cracking and groaning of the timbers kept the men awake by the sheer intensity of their sounds. Besides, the incessant noise reminded those below that their ship was breaking apart. Finally the ship started its stem, springing the planks from the bowsprit and opening leaks to the icy seawater. Cracks in the beam ends and rib joints followed, adding an increasing stream of water to the bilge. Ever more worrisome was the tilting's effect on the ship's engine. Designed to rest squarely on its engine mounts, the machine strained against its fittings until they loosened. An alarmed Schuman discovered that the engine had shifted three inches to starboard.

Buddington ordered the coal-driven steam pumps started to deal with the leaks. While only a few minutes of pumping per hour would clear the holds, starting the engines and keeping them running and free of ice consumed much-needed coal. When the pumps stopped, the cast-iron parts quickly cooled, and ice formed over the engine and seized the valves. Chipping ice from the mechanism with hammers and chisels caused the sound to reverberate throughout the ship at hourly intervals like a time clock.

Despite the severity of the weather, signs of a returning spring grew increasingly apparent. The twilight brightened until reading without a candle became possible at midnight. Flocks of ptarmigans and Arctic hares invaded the basin. Since these animals were still wearing their white coats, with only their black eyes to give their position away, they provided challenges to the men who hunted them. Seals also returned to the bay, and Ebierbing and Hans eagerly hunted them.

Return of the daylight produced one unpleasant and unwanted effect. The prolonged darkness and dim oil lamps had damaged the vision of many of the men. The arrival of constant light caused their eyes to water and produced such spasms of the eyelids that the lids could not be kept open under the bright illumination. Emil

Bessel especially suffered from this light sensitivity and often could not read his instruments.

By the end of March, Bessel led an expedition south toward Cape Constitution. Here Dr. Bessel demonstrated that his abrasive nature would work no better with the Natives than it did with the officers and crew. The party proceeded in fits and starts, first forgetting the India rubber blankets needed to spread under their new sleeping bags and then breaking a sled runner. From the onset Ebierbing pointed out that the one sled was too heavily laden and asked for Hans to drive a second one. Bessel sharply rejected that advice.

At day's end the men working around the ship looked up to see the Inuit and Mr. Bryan returning for another sled. Bessel later accused Ebierbing of deliberately dropping the sled on the end of the runner to prove his point. Whatever the cause, Ebierbing convinced Buddington that Hans and another sled were really needed, and the two Inuit returned to the advance camp.

Bessel's group headed back to the ship after one week, with little to show for their efforts. During their return the men crossed the fresh tracks of a polar bear. This was their first sign of polar bear, and the Natives realized that the animal had left its den and was looking for food. Besides, the *Polaris* crew had exhausted all fresh meat and was living now on canned foods. Here was clearly a case of eat or be eaten. The Inuit, understanding that a best defense is always an offense, immediately loosed their dogs.

The fight that followed saw the snow spackled with gouts of blood and matted fur. Without fear the dogs rushed in and tore at the bear's flanks. The bear counterattacked the snarling, snapping hoard that annoyed him, flinging one dog high into the air with a single swipe of his paw. One large malamute named Bear attacked fearlessly, repeatedly launching himself at his adversary despite suffering several blows. The yelping, growling battle came to an abrupt end when the polar bear rose on his hind feet and Ebierbing shot him with his Sharps rifle.

The triumphant party returned to the ship with the wounded dog Bear and the dead polar bear loaded into the sled baskets. Behind they left one dog for dead where the bear's blow had flung him against an outcropping.

The fresh meat was welcome and sorely needed. Already signs of scurvy affected the crew. Teeth had loosened and old injuries returned to plague their owners. John Herron's foot swelled so badly at this time that he could not walk. First thought to be rheumatism, the problem resolved itself with fresh meat added to his diet.

For all his troubles, Emil Bessel contracted a severe case of snow blindness. The condition results from the bright Arctic sun and its reflected rays striking the unprotected eye. Hour after hour of this bombardment produces something akin to sunburn of the skin. The ultraviolet rays burn the thin layer of cells covering the cornea known as the conjunctiva. As with any burn, the cells swell, producing blistering and cloudiness of the conjunctiva. Each blink of the eyelid swipes off the damaged layer, aggravating the condition. The eyelids clamp shut involuntarily in spasm when the condition becomes severe. Anyone who has had a grain of sand beneath his or her eyelid need only multiply that feeling a thousandfold to appreciate the sensation of snow blindness. Those eyes feel as though they have been sandblasted. Involuntary tearing, cloudy vision, swollen lids, and intense pain accompany the condition.

Five days passed with the scientist confined to his darkened room with cold compresses protecting his inflamed eyelids. Exposure to any light burned like fire and flooded his eyes with tears. Another ten days were needed before the physician could perform any experiments in the observatory. When he did recover sufficiently, Bessel moved his camera outside to photograph the ship and, strangely enough, Captain Hall's grave. The exposures went well enough, as did developing the photographic plates. But when the fixative was washed off the plates, the emulsion separated from the glass and peeled off. No photographs would capture the lonely grave of Charles Francis Hall for another hundred years.

As soon as he was well, Emil Bessel resumed his demands to head another expedition, one using the whaleboats this time. A heated argument ensued. Control of the ship and its longboats still belonged to Buddington, and he had no intention of forfeiting this remaining shard of his authority. Already, premonitions that he would bear the brunt of any failure loomed large in his mind. Abrogating his command, especially to a landlubber, was the worst thing a ship's captain could do, and he'd be damned if he'd turn over his longboats to Bessel.

Still, fear clamped its iron hand on the sea captain's heart. Sailing among the icebergs and floating islands frightened him beyond all reason. What nightmares tormented him enough to souse his brain in alcohol we can only imagine. Striking an iceberg and sinking seems to have bothered him less than being trapped within the floating islands to slowly starve to death. In those frigid waters, death comes quickly from hypothermia, within minutes. But drifting, disabled, and locked in an icy embrace meant weeks of hunger and despair and the haunting specter of cannibalism. The grisly image of men cracking the long bones of their shipmates to scavenge the last scrap of marrow lurked in the minds of every whaler who sailed north.

With a cunning born of desperation, Buddington countered hotly that he would lead the boats himself. Cleverly he appointed George Tyson and H. C. Chester to command the two whaleboats. That exempted him from leaving the *Polaris*. Washington would applaud his selection of two experienced sailors to direct the boats, and Washington would understand that Buddington could not be expected to place himself under one of his selected boat captains. He would be applauded for sacrificing his share of the glory to his duty to watch over the *Polaris*. As a final touch, Buddington named the two boats. The first would be called the *U. S. Grant*, after the president, and the second would be the *George M. Robeson*, after the secretary of the navy.

Neither Tyson nor Chester really believed Buddington would leave the relative security of Thank God Harbor. To them his protesting rang hollow. Tyson even wrote in his diary, "But no one thinks he will go." Whether by design or by chance, Buddington filled the boats with his detractors.

Chester's boat got Frederick Meyer, Sieman, Anthing, Kruger, and Jamka—all troublesome Germans. The Prussian Meyer especially detested Buddington. Having a drunken captain replace the egalitarian Hall had not accomplished the military man's prediction of a return to class rule, and Sieman's tiresome piety constantly irritated the captain. What did the man expect? His shipmates were seamen, not nuns, and strong language went hand in hand with their tattoos. As for the others, they were always gathering in the forecastle and plotting in their foreign language.

To George Tyson, captain of the *Robeson*, went the prize: he got Emil Bessel. Buddington must have smirked when he penned the second boat's list. Putting his two main detractors into the same boat had to please him. Their animosity toward each other almost equaled their dislike for him. He could picture them sniping at each other as they rowed. Finally Buddington decreed that everything must be ready to launch the waterborne expedition by the first of May.

The captain's ploy succeeded in keeping his detractors distracted. April passed with everyone occupied in outfitting the boats or trying to free the ship from the four-foot-thick ice gripping her sides. With the warming weather came a new concern. As the ice thinned and the snow melted, the ship would settle back into the water. The damaged hull would have more opportunity to leak. Partially freeing the rudder and propeller brought some relief, however. Neither appeared damaged.

At this time, Buddington, always the pessimist, penned his doubts about the ship's seaworthiness in the official log:

> I think that it will be some trouble to keep the Polaris afloat when she comes down into the water again. Her sides are much open. Her main rail is broken in one place by the heavy pressure of the whole top work of the vessel listing over so much and for so long a time.

Tyson found that two planks along the six-foot mark on the starboard side of the bow were split lengthwise. Efforts to repair the damage yielded little improvement, as the bow still rocked up and down with the tide and wave action, springing the repairs open.

Yet another diversion appeared. On April 25 the two Inuit returned with their sleds loaded with fresh musk ox meat. Spring brought the annual migration of the hairy animals along the coast. The excited Natives told of seeing thick herds crossing the valley and had shot seven animals, having cached all but the three their sleds could hold.

Hunting fever swept the crew. Work on the hull stopped as hunting parties snatched their rifles and sped inland.

Hunting these creatures brought out the worst in the crew of the *Polaris*. Months of living in fear, boredom, and depression boiled over into a wild slaughter of these hapless creatures. Under the guise of obtaining fresh meat, the crew blasted away at every animal they encountered. Their killing spree exceeded whatever game they needed for fresh meat, leading to waste. Neither Buddington nor Bessel made any effort to rein in the crew's excesses.

Apparently the slaughter finally disgusted Tyson, although from the lack of sport rather than the waste. "It is not very exciting sport," he wrote, "for there is no [more] chance of missing them than the side of a house. When they have been checked by the dogs, and got themselves in a circle, there is nothing to do but walk up and shoot them." He decried an incident where Kruger and Sieman stumbled across a family of musk oxen resting near the foothills. Their first shot wounded the female, preventing her from fleeing. To their surprise, the faithful male charged Sieman. A comedic scene ensued with Kruger and Sieman running and firing while the bull chased them. At length the three animals took up their defensive stance, allowing the two men to blast away at them.

Three hundred shots were fired. The female eventually dropped down and died of her wounds, and only then did the injured male and his offspring abandon her and retreat. Having exhausted all their cartridges, Sieman and Kruger could only watch. A party of sailors finished off the rest of the family the next day and retrieved the meat of the female. The supply of fresh meat now surpassed the capacity of the ship's icebox. While Bessel oversaw the skinning of the unfortunate musk ox family so they could later be stuffed, the animals' flesh found its way into a hole cut in the side of Providence Berg.

In their blood lust the officers, scientific corps, and crew forgot all thought of proceeding north to discover new land and plant the flag at the North Pole. Perhaps this was what Captain Buddington wanted. His deadline of the first of May came and went with nothing happening. Chester and Jamka suffered snow blindness while hunting musk oxen that day. Sleds and men rushed about along the foothills and through the low plains behind the coastal bluffs, but always in search of animals to shoot. None of the trips made more than twenty miles or lasted longer than a week.

Ice still gripped the bay while leads of dark water opened and closed in Kennedy Channel at the whim of the currents. Despite the sealed surface of the bay, strong water forces swept below it and drove blocks of ice capable of crushing a longboat along any open channel. Hopes of launching the two whaleboats dimmed. Now was the time to explore by sled when the ice was still thick, but that window of opportunity was rapidly closing while the men hunted. Clearly inertia was bogging down the polar exploration, tying the men to the uncertain safety of their ship. All this might have been expected with the loss of Captain Hall. Only he—with Tyson, Morton, and the two Inuit men—were the land explorers. All the rest were sailors or laboratory scientists.

There was simply no one to lead. Now that Hall was dead, Tyson had no authority, since he had derived his strange position from the late commander's pleasure. Thirty years in the navy had conditioned Morton to follow commands, not give them, and the Inuit withdrew to their usual defensive posture of being passive when dealing with white men. To their credit, they had come along only for their friend Captain Hall, and he was dead. No one else aboard the *Polaris* had earned their friendship and respect.

Chapter Eight

CALAMITY

We were weary for want of occupation, for want of variety,
for want of the means of mental exertion, for want of
thought, and (why should I not say it?) for want of society.
—SIR JOHN ROSS, 1831

By the end of May, three feet of water filled the ship's hold, but Bessel preferred to turn his attentions to the impending expeditions and other things closer to his heart. The men had captured two flies near the observatory, the first seen since the winter, and the physician indulged his passion of studying the insects.

Buddington did order a halfhearted repair. The split along the starboard bow was caulked and tarred over and the iron plating replaced, resulting in some improvement. Work could be performed only at four-hour intervals because of the rising tide. Moreover, at the next high tide, the leak returned unabated. At that time the carpenter discovered a similar set of cracks extending eight feet aft from the port side and leaking copious amounts of seawater. For all his nightly troubles, Coffin still managed to function as the ship's carpenter. There was nothing he could do, however, to make repairs to the outside of the ship's hull. Because of the ice spur on which the *Polaris* sat, the ship had rolled and the port side remained underwater.

The weight of the water trapped within the hold placed an added strain on the ship's keel, so Buddington ordered the pumps used. Obstinate like its name, the donkey pump refused to start just then, so the men worked a smaller pump, nicknamed the "handy billy." Four hours of pumping cleared the hold.

Distressingly, water continued to accumulate aft whenever the pumping stopped. A survey of the hold failed to pinpoint any leaks in the stern. Someone suggested the rising water might be from ice melting in the coal bunkers and running aft. The crew accepted this explanation and happily returned to their new priority—making beer.

Buddington wholly supported this endeavor, at the expense of repairing his ship, stating that the brewing "would do them good." Three days of concerted effort produced a barrel filled to the brim with the sour brew. The cask occupied the center of the galley with a sign stating NORTH POLE LAGER BEER SALOON. NO TRUST. CASH.

The men quaffed their beer anxiously and watched June arrive while the water in the hold rose to five inches. The sound of water dripping into the forward hold during high tide joined the chorus of groans and creaks from the teetering hull, probably prompting the crew to drink all the more. The water contributed to the rot attacking the spare sails stored in the hold, but so far the foodstuffs and coal remained safe.

Tantalizingly, signs of summer appeared about the ship while ice still blocked the men's use of their longboats. The temperature rose daily. Pools of melted water covered the ice, melting streams cascaded from the bluffs, and rough patches of earth poked shyly through their white mantle. Moss, lichen, and ground willow stirred into life, creeping across the barren shale. All about the ship, the land was stirring. Summer is short in the Arctic. Life that depends on sunlight and warmth must rise to the occasion or be left behind.

On a visit to Captain Hall's grave, George Tyson found ground willow rooted among the piled rocks and extending interlocking fingers across the mounded dirt.

Ironically Buddington noted the changes in his journal, too, and the expedition's inaction crept into his words:

The plain is full of fine streamlets of water that give moisture to the ground. Saxifrages are blooming, and are distributed all over the plain. Insects are getting numerous. Flies and mosquitoes are met with. This single warm day has called many into life.

On the sixth of June, the Arctic cast a lure that no one aboard the ship could ignore: open sea appeared along the spur of land just north of the observatory that they called Cape Lupton. Shining water lay dancing before them. Quickly the two whaleboats were slid over the ice to the edge of the open lead at Cape Lupton the next day. The way north by whaleboat beckoned.

Mr. Chester jumped at the chance. Euphoria abounded as by eight P.M. the evening of the seventh, he sped off with his whaleboat crew and a sled loaded with extra provisions. All winter long, plans for reaching the North Pole had circulated around the mess and throughout the forecastle. Combined with the months of inaction and darkness, the mission grew in many minds until it became not only a Holy Grail of sorts but an easy grail to achieve.

Naïveté, lack of experience, and alcohol compounded to simplify this daunting task in their minds to little more than a short row up the channel instead of a six-hundred-mile, life-threatening struggle. Rear Adm. C. H. Davis, in his official report of the *Polaris* expedition, did his best to whitewash this almost unbelievable gullibility:

> During the whole winter the boat journeys had been talked about, and it had been shown over and over again how comparatively easy it was to go to the Pole. No difficulties were allowed to stand in the way, and the route was as clearly marked out as if it were a well-known channel. Undoubtedly the warm glow of the cabin stove had much to do with the coloring thrown around this boat journey. So completely had the self-deception been effected, that people now looked with confidence to the result.

Exactly what occupied these men's minds that day is hard to fathom. Since late summer of the previous year, the expedition had stumbled and faltered whenever the Arctic showed its power. Sudden storms, cold, darkness, and ice buffeted them constantly and brushed aside their attempts at progress with uncaring force. Yet here they rushed forth eagerly to subdue the far North in fragile whaleboats where their stout sailing ship could do nothing.

Chester's crew vanished into the twilight a full day ahead of Tyson. On the eighth, Tyson dispatched his men to their boat as he and Bessel gathered last-minute odds and ends. All the while the assistant navigator fretted that Chester might beat him to the prize.

While Tyson stewed over his delayed departure and his crew waited by their boat, Chester and his crew launched theirs, the *Grant*, from Cape Lupton on the morning of the eighth. Ahead of them the slate-gray water stretched around the turn of the headlands. Pulling together, the men put their backs into the oars, and the heavily laden whaleboat knifed across the open water. Spirits soared as they rowed onward. A mile passed.

Two miles into their journey, an enormous ice floe rose out of the sunlit mists directly ahead. The white island slid silently toward the opening to which the men rowed. Driven by the onshore winds, the island would block their path unless the whaleboat reached the opening first. A desperate race ensued, the men of the *Grant* straining and cursing as they rowed while the frozen wall moved inexorably closer. Chester urged his men on, and the sharp prow of the skiff shot forward. Mere yards ahead the channel remained open.

Then a gust of wind spun the floe around, and ice met ice, closing the passage with a dull crunch. The longboat crashed into the sealed opening, and its prow rode onto the hard surface with a start.

Exhausted but hardly discouraged, Chester and his crew dragged the boat onto the floe and hauled the craft across the flat surface. Supplies spilled onto the ice, filling the grooves left in the melting surface by the boat's passage. Hastily Chester sent someone to retrieve the articles. Once across the ice, they again launched the boat and paddled on. Another mile passed.

Ahead jagged islands of ice choked the passage. Jostling, colliding, and capsizing under the wind and current, these impediments posed a serious concern. Unlike the field they had just crossed, these islands crumbled and tipped and turned and provided no level place to transit. Worse still, the heat of the summer sun, raising the temperature above freezing, attacked the floating islands until huge blocks of rotten ice sheared from their surfaces to tumble into a twisted rubble of melted slush.

Two grounded icebergs loomed ahead with a flat ice floe separating them. Amid the grinding islands, this tranquil spot beckoned. With no Inuit along to recognize the impending trap, Chester ordered his men to pull for that floe just as more ice slid into place behind them. The open channel had lured them into the ice field, but the abrupt change in the sea state and the advancing tide now blocked all hope of advance or retreat.

Chester calculated that the turning tide would draw the pack ice back out to sea and ordered camp made to wait out the rising tide. The men pitched tents, preparing to stay the night, and lit fires. Soon tea boiled over the portable tin stoves. Worn out by their efforts, the men ate a hasty meal and turned in.

Frederick Anthing, the seaman who described himself as "born in Russia, on the Prussian border," took the first watch atop a saddle of ice facing west. Chester and Meyer stretched out on India rubber sheets about twenty yards from the whaleboat. The other three sailors crawled into a tent pitched beside the *Grant*.

No sooner had Chester closed his eyes than a warning shout jarred him awake.

"The ice is coming!" Anthing cried in alarm.

Chester sprang to his feet and his crew spilled out of their tent to see an advancing wall of pack ice rising above them so high that it appeared to block out the sky. The crowded wedge struck the iceberg sheltering them from the sea with a deafening roar.

The Inuit call this rapid and deadly attack of pack ice *evu*, and they fear it above all else. Sudden storms, rising tides, and current shifts will drive hundreds of tons of pack ice ashore with awesome power—and no warning. Tumbling like dominoes, twisting, and sliding over one another, enormously dense plates advance like an army. Nothing at sea level is safe from destruction. Even camps atop the windswept bluffs lining the coast fall prey to ice rafted and stacked until it towers more than one hundred feet high. Like colossal shears, the slabs scythe and crush everything standing before them.

The ground beneath Chester's feet buckled as the *evu* struck their iceberg, and the mate struggled to regain his footing. The force shattered the berg and sundered their campsite. Frozen boulders rained down from the fractured iceberg, crushing boxes and supply bags. The floe cracked into pieces. Dark open water splashed up from the sudden fissures, and the broken plates tilted and spun as more slabs showered upon them.

The three men by the boat jumped for their lives as their floor split apart. The *Grant* danced away in the second half. Before they could rescue their boat, a mountain of ice fell upon the craft, crushing it to splinters.

For endless minutes a deadly dance ensued as men sprang from one floating chip to the next. Keeping alive meant moving, but one slip or misstep would plunge a man through the cracks into the boiling sea. Opening and closing like a living net, the cracks proved as threatening as the ice attack. Anyone falling into a fissure would be crushed to death or drowned as the ice closed over him. All the while tons of ice from the shattered iceberg and the *evu* bombarded the hapless crew and sent their slippery footholds jumping and spinning.

Abruptly the attack ended. As quickly and as silently as it had begun, the *evu* passed on. Shocked and stunned by the violent event, the men could only stand and stare at their shattered world. Miraculously all survived.

Their material goods had not. The *Grant* had vanished into a pile of matchstick-size splinters drifting out to sea. Three rifles, a boxed chronometer, and Mr. Meyer's journal were all that survived. In its fury and whimsy, the ice attack had taken all else and left these random, unrelated items.

Hours ago they had rowed northward with high hopes of conquering the North Pole, and in the blink of an eye, the Arctic had dashed their hopes. Shaken, they huddled together on broken rafts of ice, stripped of all their possessions and with no alternative but to drag themselves back to their ship.

Ironically among the goods Mr. Chester lost was the Jonah American flag that the ill-fated Wilkes expedition had carried and that Grinnell later presented to Captain Hall.

A chastened Chester and his crew slogged the seven miles back, arriving aching and footsore from climbing over the shore ice piled along the bay. Instead of receiving sympathy for their misfortune, the rest of the crew treated them with the disdain they probably deserved: carelessness lay at the root of the second boat team's disaster. Only Tyson's delay had saved his men from a similar fate, yet they acted superior to the other boat crew.

Again the divisive spirit that pervaded the ship raised its ugly head. Tyson recorded the loss with ill-concealed glee: "Chester's party have all returned, having had the misfortune to lose their boat, and nearly their lives." He continued, "I called the cape near which they lost their boat Cape Disaster, and the bay they were on, beyond Cape Lupton, Folly Bay, which I believe was rather displeasing to Mr. Chester." Here Tyson sounds more like a schoolboy reveling in a classmate's failure than an adult who recognized that teamwork was essential to the success of their mission as well as their survival.

Perversely the Arctic fostered this division. Wind and water combined to once more offer an ice-free channel of open water. Smugly Tyson, Dr. Bessel, and four men launched their boat on the evening of the tenth.

Stung by the unfair criticism, Chester begged for another boat. Camping between the two grounded icebergs had been an error, he realized now. The structural strength of a summer iceberg, weakened and fissured by melting water, differed greatly from that of a winter berg. Rotten to the core and capable of breaking apart and capsizing at any time, summer icebergs offered dangerous sanctuary. Nevertheless, the floe between was the only spot suitable to land.

Chester's pleas brought mixed results. Buddington refused to release another longboat, fearing that all remaining boats might be needed at home. With the *Polaris* sinking lower into the sea as Providence Berg's spur melted, each day found new cracks in the hull and rising water in the holds. Running the steam pumps for fifteen minutes every four hours cleared the bilges of water, but that required the steam donkey to maintain six to ten pounds of steam pressure at all times. Firing the boiler constantly consumed precious coal. The dead Hall's foresight in scrimping on fuel and the special boiler sabotaged in Disko must have haunted the men's thoughts. Burning seal oil in that unique steamer would have resolved their mounting coal problem.

For all his efforts Chester finally got the Heggleman, the patented folding canvas boat. Assembling the portable craft proved challenging, so another day passed before Chester launched the canvas craft on June 12. Paddling after Tyson and Bessel, the men were described as in good spirits and singing "We're going to the Pole" as they rowed away.

Their enthusiasm soon soured and turned to glum determination as the poor design of the Heggleman revealed itself. Square-tipped on bow and stern, the puntlike craft, which might have been ideal for a summer outing on a placid lake, proved agonizingly slow and unwieldy. Its flat nose wedged solidly into any ice floe it encountered instead of pushing the ice aside as the sharp-prowed whaleboats did. Furthermore, the high sides and flat nose caught the wind like a sail. Nose on, the wind blew the boat backward, and a beam breeze left the stern man constantly fighting the tiller to keep on course. Added to all this was the boat's flimsy construction. Hickory and ash thwarts supporting stretched canvas made the boat look fragile as an eggshell compared to the massive blocks of floating ice threatening it. For sailors used to rowing a wooden-planked whaleboat, bobbing along in a cloth contraption must have proved nerve-racking.

The Heggleman's crew battled for a whole week to reach the same spot Tyson had achieved in two days. Weather and the awkward folding boat conspired against them. After a day and a half of hard rowing, the exhausted men collapsed on another floe for the night. A strong northerly wind rose while they slept and blew their floating island back down the channel. In the morning they awoke to find themselves *south* of their starting point the day before at Cape Lupton.

Things were not all rosy for Tyson's boat, the *Robeson*, however. Threading his vessel through the sea ice, Tyson passed Cape Folly and angled along Robeson Straits as far as Newman Bay. There ice thwarted him completely. A solid sheet of white sealed the waters north. Learning from Chester's mistake, Tyson beached his craft on solid ground, pitched camp, and waited for the channel to open. Unable to trap this group as it had Chester's men, the perverse nature of the far North struck at Tyson's team in another way.

Two days of staring at the endless fields of bright snow and ice reactivated Emil Bessel's snow blindness. The intensity of the reflected light bouncing off the ice inflamed the doctor's eyes, robbing him of all useful sight. To combat this glare, the Inuit fashioned goggles of wood with narrow slits cut in them to limit the amount of light reaching the eye. Hans and Ebierbing used them, as did the late Captain Hall and Tyson. Why Bessel did not is unclear. The goggles had to be made, so no extras were available. Certainly Bessel's attitude toward the Inuit guaranteed they would not offer him a pair. He might have disdained such a primitive device. However, his failure to use this protection cost him dearly, for dark glasses were yet to be developed.

Confined to the relative darkness of the tent, the doctor fretted away the long hours with his eyes swathed in rags. Discouraged to the point of despair, Bessel forced himself to finger the scraps of driftwood brought to him by the sailors and skin the various birds they caught. Equally maddening to this entomologist were the mosquitoes and black flies that buzzed about him and bit him but that he could not collect.

Eventually Chester's men reached Tyson's camp. While the two boat teams waited, more precious time dwindled away. On the sixteenth of July, a flock of geese passed overhead. To the men's alarm, the geese were flying south this time, not north as before—a sure sign that summer was drawing to a close. The next day it snowed.

Behind them the channel leading back to Thank God Harbor closed as pack ice crowded ashore. Now they could row neither north nor south. Without dogs and sleds, the *Robeson* proved too heavy to drag overland, and no one wanted to set foot inside the Heggleman boat again.

In desperation Tyson suggested that the two teams combine forces and mount an overland attack—a "pedestrian exploring party," he named it. His plan called for squads of men leapfrogging their way north on foot, leaving caches of food as they went for the journey back. Struck again by a flash of blinding optimism, Tyson described his incredible plan: "In this way, taking our guns with us to assist in procuring food, we could have walked to the pole itself if the land extended so far, without any insuperable difficulty during the Arctic summer."

To his amazement his plan failed to inspire his fellow shipmates. "But, I could get no one to join," he wrote in consternation. "Some were indisposed to the exertion of walking, and some did not know how to use the compass, and were probably afraid of getting lost; and so the project fell through."

In their collective wisdom, the sailors realized that summer was over. Instinctively they also sensed that Captain Hall's speculation was accurate—that they stood on the northern tip of Greenland and the end of all land. Had Tyson occupied a well-defined place in the command structure, he would have built up his authority as well as earned the trust of the crew, and the men might have followed his plan. Being placed in limbo by Hall's nebulous appointment, Tyson had none of those things working for him.

An equally frightening thought lurked in the back of each man's mind: Captain Buddington could not be trusted to wait for their return to the ship. More than once Buddington had voiced to Tyson and Chester that if the way south opened for the *Polaris* and if he "got a chance to get out he would not wait." That scuttlebutt spread below deck faster than the speed of light. Even the lowest seaman clearly knew the captain's mind in that matter. If they pressed farther north, chances were slim that their ship would be waiting for those lucky enough to find their way back to Thank God Harbor.

Back on the *Polaris* Captain Buddington wrestled with his own demons. Rising water in the holds had ruined a number of provisions. The worsening leaks now required the pumps to be run every other hour. Having burned every bit of scrap wood, the captain resorted to fueling the boilers with coal bags soaked in turpentine to conserve their dwindling supply of precious coal.

Next a northeast gale struck, blasting the harbor with winds exceeding forty knots. Providence Berg shifted and ground along the shallow floor under the force of the storm, and all hands feared that their mooring platform would break free and drift out to sea with the rest of the pack ice. The captain ordered the observatory cleared of its instruments and every fragment of wood salvaged for fuel. As the advance boat parties feared, Buddington was preparing to retreat.

Complying with Bessel's impractical "sketch," he left written instructions for the two boats. Here another flaw in the doctor's plan made Buddington's message useless. Unknown to Buddington, ice prevented any movement of the scouting boats. With the crew already preparing to abandon their craft, they would be unable to follow him south.

The gale passed, clearing all ice out of the harbor and turning the way southwest into one broad expanse of water. But Providence Berg remained firmly grounded and the twelve-foot-thick spread of ice linking the *Polaris* to the iceberg unbroken.

Frantically Buddington tried another powder charge to no avail. Ashes of coal dust spread around the ship cloaked the ice like funeral bunting and aided in melting the top few inches. Resorting to ice saws, the engineers erected derricks and commenced sawing the vessel free. Close to the hull, the ice grew to fifteen feet in thickness, exceeding the ability of the saws, so the men resorted to pulleys.

Four double blocks of tackle rigged around the last remnants of entrapping ice broke loose this last impediment. A cheer rose from the men working the capstan as the *Polaris* slipped off the tongue of ice that had imprisoned her for so long and slid into the water. The ship was floating at last.

Being adrift only aggravated the ship's leaking. The steam donkey pumped all day while the crew frantically stopped whatever leaks they could.

Anxious to sail, Buddington found that retrieving his anchors proved another problem. Without them the vessel could not be stopped. Both starboard and port anchors had been deployed to save the ship. Providence Berg lay on top of the starboard anchor, so it could not be raised. Reluctantly its cable was cut. The port anchor lay so deeply embedded in the ocean floor that it could not be broken free.

While they struggled with the anchors, more and more pack ice drifted into the mouth of the bay. Buddington watched his chance for freedom slowly slipping away with each arriving block of ice. In desperation the captain ordered his last anchor marked with a buoy and unshackled.

Steaming out of the bay, Buddington quickly encountered a solid wall of pack ice blocking the passage. Throughout the night he steamed back and forth, searching in vain for an open lead. By morning the captain admitted defeat and returned to Thank God Harbor to hook onto his waiting port anchor.

To make matters worse, the ship rode even lower in the water than before. A hasty inspection revealed that the drain holes in the bulkheads were plugged by debris shaken loose while the ship sailed. Tons of seawater filled the forepeak, the chain lockers, and the main hold. Boring additional drain holes in the bulkheads allowed the water to gush forth. The water drained into the bilge, where the overworked steam donkey pumped it overboard, correcting that problem, but salt water had ruined even more provisions.

The rising tide provided mixed blessings for the beleaguered officer. The port anchor broke free, and the clear water surrounding the ship revealed the full extent of the damage done to the hull by the long winter's rocking. The heavy oak stem section of the keel was ripped loose and twisted to port, while a half-inch gap separated the two planks near the six-foot marking on the same side. Buddington retreated to his bunk that night to listen to the clank of the steam pumps and ponder what kept his ship from sinking outright.

Two gunshots the next morning announced the return of Kruger and Sieman with a note from Mr. Chester asking for supplies of bread. Buddington eagerly moved to absorb the two sailors back into his ship's company. Barely able to handle his newly liberated vessel with so shorthanded a crew, he denied the request and ordered the men to stay. He would sail north and pick up the rest of their party, he boldly announced, and then he would sail even farther north.

Two halfhearted attempts yielded nothing of the sort. While burning precious coal, Buddington steamed about but never cleared the harbor. Ice blocked his way, and the badly split stem discouraged any thought he might have entertained of crashing his way through the ice fields. After failing in his last attempt to break out, Buddington wrote in his journal that the low sun had blinded his eyes and kept him from seeing far enough ahead to navigate safely. Faced with this bumbling, Kruger and Sieman urged Buddington to release them and walked back with his orders for Chester to return at once.

North of Cape Lupton, Chester and Tyson greeted the command with contempt. "I won't go!" Chester shouted when ordered to turn back. Every man clustered around the beached boats sensed that this was their last chance to press farther north. To their embarrassment none of them had ventured farther north than Captain Hall and Ebierbing had gone almost nine months before. Repeatedly well-provisioned teams of healthy men had failed to pass the mark reached by those two in a dogsled.

Tyson overheard the sailors muttering, "if the captain got a good chance, he would sail south without waiting for anyone." Kruger and Sieman's report confirmed the crew's assessment of their drunken commander. In disgust one man spat out that he "didn't care" if Buddington left or not, that they had a better chance of escaping south in their whaleboat before winter arrived.

Ebierbing's arrival two days later settled the debate. Solemnly the Inuit stepped off his sled and handed a written order to Chester. Return at once, it commanded. Chester could not disobey a written order. Both he and Tyson knew that the crafty Buddington would have copies of that specific order safely preserved for any later hearing. Buddington's blunt command had incisively ended any further exploration by them.

With heavy hearts they turned back. Buddington would sail south as quickly as he could, they all realized. Regardless of what he boasted, he would never take the *Polaris* farther northward. No more forays north to plant the Stars and Stripes on undiscovered territory would come from their expedition, either by land or by sea.

Their mission had failed. The North Pole would remain unclaimed. The United States would add its name to that of England, France, Russia, Denmark, and every other nation that had mounted an expedition to the North Pole . . . and failed.

Nothing remained but to get back alive.

They abandoned the unwieldy collapsible boat to the Arctic, leaving the winds to tear the canvas and the lemmings and voles to gnaw the wooden struts. The remaining useful whaleboat presented another problem. The sturdy oak planking that served so well against the floating ice made the craft too heavy to drag across the broken ice fields. Loading it on a sledge would work, but Ebierbing's sled was not the heavy type built especially by the half-mad Coffin to carry sledges. Besides, the sled was gone. The half-blind Bessel snatched at his chance and rode back to the ship in the Inuit's sled basket.

They dragged the whaleboat high onto the bluffs, where the tide and the *evu* would not wreck it, and covered it with canvas. It took all hands and forty-eight hours to haul the skiff up a ravine to the safest place they could find. Caching an extra tent and boxes of provisions too heavy to carry, Meyer buried another copper cylinder nearby with their meager achievements and the record of Captain Hall's death.

Hiking the twenty miles back to the ship took two days. Worn out on arrival, Chester found Captain Buddington at his wit's end. All throughout the Fourth of July, a northeastern gale had battered the ship and driven blocks of ice against the hull. The men had spent their holiday fending off the icy battering rams with long poles.

That night the ship's company watched helplessly as an iceberg half the size of the *Polaris* cruised down on their moored vessel. Streaming directly toward the midships like a well-aimed torpedo, the icy ram would easily stave in the side. Moored powerlessly to Providence Berg, the *Polaris* had no chance to escape. Backing them, this frozen mountain would act as the anvil to the charging iceberg's hammer, ensuring greater damage to the weakened hull.

Buddington and his crew gritted their teeth, gripped the rail, and forced their watering eyes to peer into the blowing snow while they watched their destruction cruising silently closer. One hundred, seventy-five, fifty yards nearer drifted the iceberg. Men prayed and sinners repented as their white destroyer loomed overhead with cold indifference. The icy breath of the iceberg chilled their lungs, the air growing more frigid with each long second that passed.

Twenty yards from the ship, the iceberg struck the underwater beak of Providence Berg. With a grinding rumble, the iceberg turned aside and swept past the astonished men, mere feet from the wooden railing. The submerged tongue of Providence Berg that had tortured the ship's keel for so long had deflected the charging monster and protected the vessel.

Dodging more ice, Buddington moved his ship closer and closer to shore. Two days before Chester and Tyson returned, a thick fog had descended on the bay. Disoriented, Buddington ran the ship aground in eleven and one-half feet of water. As the tide ran out, the ship heeled over until the port-side scuppers slipped underwater. This added more water to the beleaguered bilge and necessitated burning more coal for the steam pumps. Shorthanded, Buddington could not free the ship. Fortunately the tide rose and lifted the ship enough to raise the scuppers out of the sea, but the keel remained firmly wedged into the floor of the bay. As soon as Chester and Tyson arrived, the full crew rowed the remaining anchor out into deeper water, and all hands laid on the capstan to warp the ship free. The anchor bit into the bottom ground, the men strained against the wooden bars protruding from the capstan, and the drum slowly wrenched the ship into the deeper sea, where it refloated.

Unbelievably the *Polaris* had dodged two disasters in close succession, but the near misses wore away at whatever resolve Buddington still had to continue their mission to reach the North Pole. Nothing on earth could compel him to face those floating white mines again.

Grasping for straws, he decided the scientific portion of the expedition could be claimed a great success. Emil Bessel had stocked the hold full of collected rocks, bones, and specimens preserved in those bottles of alcohol that had not been drunk. Pages of scientific readings, measurements of seawater temperature, magnetic flux, and star sightings filled dozens of notebooks that Mauch, Meyer, Bryan, and the good doctor had kept. All that must count for something, Buddington reasoned. He hoped it would help offset their dismal failure to reach the top of the world and the death of Charles Francis Hall.

Washington would appreciate their difficulties, he hoped. In spite of them, Hall had carried the flag higher than any white man had previously done. And there was all that new land named after President Grant, Secretary Robeson, and Senator Sumner.

Drinking heavily now, he announced to Chester and Tyson that there existed "no probability" whatsoever for them to do anything other than help him head home. Realizing how the two boat teams had robbed him of sufficient hands to man the ship, he resolved never to repeat that error. As the men rightly feared, their mission was finished.

Sadly his poorly concealed anxiety only subjected him to more of his sailors' scorn. Arising out of Buddington's patent dread of the floating ice, a growing, open contempt for him developed on the part of his crew. An incident described by Tyson highlighted this disdain.

Shortly after the boat crews returned, Tyson suggested the three watches be assigned to use the hand pumps instead of the steam donkey. Doing so would save burning their dwindling supply of coal yet provide pumping round the clock. While Buddington considered the idea, a sudden rush of fresh seawater flooded into the hold. The amount of this new leakage far exceeded the capacity of the hand pumps, so the steam pumps remained active and the idea of the men's taking turns pumping by hand was abandoned.

The suddenness of the new leak and its timing raised suspicions that someone in the engine room had deliberately opened the seacocks and flooded the bilges. Tyson suggested this idea to Buddington, citing that it was done "so that those in favor of hand pumping 'should have enough of it.' "

Showing uncharacteristic resolve, Buddington marched down to the engine room to see for himself. He arrived outside the engine room only to have the door slammed in his face. Those inside—presumably Emil Schuman; the assistant engineer, Odell; and the two firemen, Campbell and Booth—refused to allow their commanding officer to enter. Adding insult to injury, they also refused to answer his orders to open the door.

Chagrined, Buddington could do nothing but return to the cockpit and hope that the new leak had indeed arisen from a deliberate act of sabotage to gain his concession. When word reached those below decks that the idea of hand pumping had been scrapped, the massive new leak miraculously ceased. This dangerous act of defiance greatly threatened the command and safety of the ship but went unpunished.

Since Charles Francis Hall's suspicious death, discipline and co-hesion of the expedition had weakened and dissolved by degrees over the long winter. Now little remained of the United States North Polar expedition but an unruly, self-serving mob bent on having their own way with no regard for the consequences.

Like grains of sand silently scattered by the wind until the wall they support collapses, minuscule events, affecting both men and matériel, were conspiring to fatally hamstring the *Polaris* expedi-tion. The chain of command had virtually vanished from the crew while irreplaceable losses went largely unappreciated.

Reckless burning of the ship's coal both onboard and in the ob-servatory had squandered the engine's fuel so that only a few days' supply remained. Because the men were too lazy to man the hand pumps, the bunkers held barely enough coal to steam directly south to Disko. Errors and foolishness had reduced their chances of sur-vival and left the expedition with a razor-thin margin for error. Any delay or diversion while steaming—whether from pack ice, gales, or fog—would mean disaster.

The ship's starboard anchor was lost. Already events had demonstrated the fact that a single anchor could not hold the vessel in a strong gale. A lone anchor would drag through the poor hold-ing ground made up of powdered stone known as glacial flour found in the shallow bays. The backbone of the keel was cracked and splintered beyond repair, disposing the vessel to spring ever-increasing leaks when stressed. Here was a ship destined to sink if it did not run aground first. The status of their lifeboats should have concerned all aboard.

But three of the rowed boats had been lost. Half the ship's com-plement of boats was gone. The Heggleman and one stout whale-boat lay twenty miles north, covered in canvas and abandoned. Nothing remained of the other whaleboat but splinters drifting southward. Little was thought of this at the time, but the shortage of whaleboats would soon threaten the lives of all aboard the doomed *Polaris*.

Chapter Nine

RETREAT

And now there came both mist and snow,
*   And it grew wondrous cold:*
And ice, mast-high, came floating by,
*   As green as emerald.*

—SAMUEL TAYLOR COLERIDGE,
"THE RIME OF THE ANCIENT MARINER"

Sensing that the ship might depart at a moment's notice, those men who loved Captain Hall did their best to improve his grave site. Herman Sieman, especially, spent his spare moments tending the mound while he prayed for his former captain's soul. Captain Tyson took the time to rearrange the stones ringing the grave into neat order. The crowbar driven into the frozen earth in the dark of the Arctic winter remained unmoved, but wind and drifting snow had played havoc with the penciled inscription and board Schuman had left.

Realizing his former commander deserved something more, Mr. Chester secured a piece of pine an inch and one-half thick, planed it with loving care, and cut a more fitting inscription into its face:

In Memory of
Charles Francis Hall,
Late commander
U.S. Steamer Polaris, North Pole Expedition
Died
Nov. 8th, 1871—Aged 50 years
I am the resurrection and the life; he that believeth in me,
though he were dead,
yet shall he live.

Later one evening while the waning summer sun watched from over his shoulder, Chester carried his work to the grave and planted it deep enough to withstand the storms. Facedown across the grave lay Schuman's penciled work, while the angled crowbar jutted upright—both untouched, for good reason. The dirt piled over Hall's mortal remains and everything connected with it had become a sort of shrine, not to be disturbed.

As conditions aboard the *Polaris* grew steadily out of control, Hall's forlorn grave presented a pilgrimage site for men to sit and think about what might have been. For all his faults in leadership, their dead commander had possessed the ability to travel and survive in the Arctic. Had Hall lived, no one doubted that things would now be quite different. His presence once instilled confidence, something even the meanest sailor among them longed for at this moment.

At odds with the crew's frequent visits were the actions of the two cocommanders of the disintegrating expedition. Apart from his single failed attempt to photograph the site, Emil Bessel kept well away from the grave, and Buddington never approached it. Perhaps the sea captain already knew that the specter of the dead Hall would haunt him for the rest of his life. Perhaps it was conscience that bothered them both.

In the early hours of July 11, the ice claimed another irreplaceable small craft. Before leaving the Brooklyn Navy Yard, Emil Bessel had ordered a boat built especially for him. Lightweight and flat-bottomed, the craft was affectionately called "the scow" and did useful service ferrying men back and forth from the ship to shore. But it was left tied carelessly to the side of the ship, and the night watch neglected to haul it aboard. One can only wonder if this oversight was deliberate, the result of some insult Bessel had inflicted on a crew member.

Marauding ice discovered the helpless boat, encircled it, and drove it hard against the side of the *Polaris*. In minutes the relentless piles staved in the skiff's sides with a splintering crash, and the ruined scow sank beneath the clear waters. Morning found the remains of the scow swinging in the current from its bowline like a condemned man dangling from the hangman's rope.

Insanely the unexpected came on every twist in the winds and continued to snare the unwary. Freezing weather struck from the southwest, and warmer weather came with gales from the northeast—not at all what they had expected. Tantalizingly the northern winds cleared the harbor and opened broad gaps in the ice blocking Robeson Straits and, more important, Kennedy Channel to the south. But as soon as the ship made ready, the ice pack drifted back to close the channels. Buddington found himself pacing the foredeck in frustration. "As we cannot move now, we must patiently wait what the ice will do with us," he wrote bitterly. "A northeaster would indeed be a blessing."

Seawater found its way into even the most secure lockers. Two barrels of sugar, one of flour, and another of molasses spoiled when the salty water broached their casks.

Chester made a valiant attempt to recover his abandoned canvas boat, with no success. In fact, the effort almost claimed the life of Frederick Meyer. Caught in a sudden snow squall while trekking back, the meteorologist lost his way and spent the night hiding under an overhanging rock for protection. Twenty-eight hours later, the weary Prussian stumbled back to the observatory.

By the sixteenth of July, the plain surrounding the observatory, the ominous overhanging bluff that shadowed it, and the foothills and mountains as far as the eye could see glistened with pure white snow.

While the year before had proved exceedingly mild, fortune and the warm weather turned their faces from the expedition in 1872. The prior year marked the peak of a warm cycle like that used by Scoresby to advance north. Summer ended abruptly, and rain turned to snow. Although it was still the middle of July, the land took on the appearance of the previous September.

Providence Berg, drastically altered from the summer melt and rising water temperatures, became top-heavy and lost its stability. Instead of providing shelter, it threatened to crush the ship. Under pressure from wind, it capsized on the eighteenth of July and rolled over. Giant boulders and rocks the size of houses embedded in the ice boiled to the surface as the iceberg's long-submerged foot burst into view.

All the while Buddington played cat and mouse with the endless armada of ice that entered the bay or streamed southward along the curve of Thank God Harbor. Edging ever closer to shore became a necessary but dangerous defense. Large segments of ice and ice-bergs calved from farther north would run aground in the shallow bay and split apart before they could wreak havoc on the wounded ship.

But seeking the safety of shallower water also risked grounding the ship. All went well whenever the keel struck on a flooding tide. Grounding on a falling tide, however, left the *Polaris* heeled far over with water pouring through the scuppers.

One hour after midnight on the twenty-first, an ear-splitting crack broke the silence. Men tumbled out of their bunks at the noise, which sounded like a cannon shot. On deck they soon dis-covered the cause of the sound. Providence Berg, long their tormen-tor and protector, had split in two. While the two halves still dwarfed the *Polaris*, their separation diminished their ability to screen the ship from the larger icebergs meandering by the mouth of the harbor.

The first of August brought very alarming news. Scarcely enough coal for six days of running at full steam remained. Only under favorable conditions would there be adequate coal to reach Disko. Faced with this grim reality, Buddington instituted the hand pumping that Tyson had long recommended. Three shifts would work the deck pumps for eight to ten minutes each hour to clear the bilges. To prevent a recurrence of the seacock-opening fiasco, the captain made it a point to exempt the two engineers from pumping duty. To cover his concession to the engine room, Buddington also excused the cook and the steward under the guise that the ex-empted persons had no fixed shift.

Indifferent to the ship's plight, the ice in the passage continued to block her line of retreat south. Each day Alvin Odell, the assis-tant engineer, rowed ashore and climbed to the base of Observatory Bluff to scan the horizon for open water. With each visit he piled one rock on another to form a stone pillar. After weeks of fruitless searching, a stone monument ten feet high and six feet square at its base attested to his diligence.

Buddington formulated plans to beach the *Polaris* in the event the ice kept them imprisoned into winter. "As we will be unable to keep the vessel afloat in her present condition during another win-ter, we will be compelled to run her on the beach," he carefully noted in his log. The deepening cold added to his fears. Every night fresh ice formed around the sides of the ship so that the crew awoke to find their vessel encased in ice and the bay iced over. While the thin ice broke apart with the tidal changes, its presence made boating to the shore an added trial.

August 12 dawned to a series of unanticipated events. Hans's wife gave birth to a baby boy. The birth took everyone but the tight-lipped Inuit by surprise. Her loose-fitting parka concealed her condition to the end. True to their custom, when labor contractions began, the two women retired to their cabin to deliver the infant. The lusty cries of a healthy male both startled the sailors and alerted them to the addition of a new member of the crew. Somehow the fact that the birth proceeded without the aid of the physician on board tended to accentuate the strangeness of the Natives. Despite Tookoolito's proficient English and their visit to the queen, the secretive nature of the delivery and the custom of burning the mother's clothing after delivery to ensure the safety of the child only confirmed the sailors' belief that the Natives were civilized merely on the surface. That burning of contaminated clothing and items used in the delivery may have evolved to reduce the risk of puerperal fever surpassed everyone's comprehension.

Even Tyson, who next to Charles Francis Hall held the most sympathetic view of the Inuit, was outraged. Indignantly he wrote:

> These natives have not outgrown some of their savage customs. Like the squaws of our Western Indians and other uncivilized people, the women are left alone in the exigencies of childbirth, and free themselves, like the inferior mammals, by severing the umbilical with their teeth.

Again the possessive attitude of the white man toward the Natives governed his thoughts. "Our Western Indians," he had written. He was not alone in his feelings. The ship's complement usurped the responsibility of naming the newborn themselves rather than letting the parents decide, much as they had named the litters of puppies born on the ship. "Charles Polaris" became the infant's name, combining Captain Hall's Christian name with that of the ship. How the parents felt about saddling their new son with the combined *Inui*, or spirit, of a man who had died under sudden and suspicious conditions, possibly poisoned, and that of a mismanaged and ill-fated ship went unrecorded. Privately they probably gave their son a name with good *Inui*.

The arrival of Charlie Polaris changed the luck of the expedition, at least temporarily. The new father returned from the hillside to report that the ice had opened. Hastily Buddington climbed to the ridge to confirm the report. Still, he could not stand on his own two feet. He needed Captain Tyson's second opinion to cement his own judgment that the ship could break through the thin rime that linked the floating blocks of ice. Enthusiastically Tyson agreed with Buddington: they should try to escape.

Frantic activity followed the order to cast loose. Painfully aware that the fickle nature of the ice might destroy this opportunity, the officers hurried their men. Every second counted. In their haste the men left behind emergency stores that had been moved to the observatory in the event the ship sank. The hitherto undiscovered effect of Providence Berg's splitting apart suddenly became apparent and threatened to delay their urgent departure. Their only remaining anchor, the port one, which they had painfully wrenched free from the seabed, lay trapped under one half of the broken berg. Escape required cutting the shackles to their last anchor and drifting free. Buddington ordered the links cut. More than one seasoned sailor watched with mixed emotions as the chain from their one remaining anchor rattled over the side to slip beneath the snow-flecked surface of the bay. More than ever, their die was cast.

With split stem and leaking hull, the *Polaris* steamed out the opened door of her frozen cage and sallied forth with only ice anchors and ice screws left aboard. In their retreat southward, Buddington and his men would be unable to anchor in the shelter of a shallow bay to wait out a gale. Loss of their ground tackle would force them to grapple to an ice floe or iceberg for moorage whenever they wished to stop.

Again destiny appeared to loosen its grip on the ill-fated expedition only to conspire to draw the ship back into its net. Having escaped one iceberg, the *Polaris* would be forced by circumstances to tie to another one to rest. And this time of year, the available icebergs were rotten mountains prone to capsize, split apart, and turn on any ship foolish enough to be nearby.

Another ominous and disturbing loss marked the ship's departure. Just as the *Polaris* lurched forward, one of the sled dogs named Tiger broke free and jumped over the railing to land on the ice. No amount of coaxing could entice the barking animal to return to the ship. The large Newfoundland was highly regarded as a fine sled dog and was well liked by all the crew. Hearts grew heavy as the men watched their friend and companion shrink into the distance as the ship steamed away. Without food the animal would slowly starve unless a polar bear ate him.

The superstitious among the crew could not help but wonder if the dog could read their future. What terrible ordeal awaited them that would make a Newfoundland prefer an agonizingly slow death to what lay ahead?

They would not have long to wait for their answer.

Threading her way between the floating hummocks and hills, the *Polaris* turned tail on the brooding rise of Observatory Bluff, swung her nose toward the leaden clouds filling the sky to the west, and churned the pewter-colored water with her screw. With a mixed sense of relief and apprehension, Captain Buddington directed the helmsman. He was heading back, a fact that pleased him, but more than a thousand miles of dangerous water lay between them and their home port. Leaving Thank God Harbor exposed him to the dangers of being stranded in the ice that he so greatly feared. All around him the floating ice waited. To deal with his fears, Buddington went below and refilled his tin cup with specimen alcohol.

What Emil Bessel felt as he watched the clapboard shack he called the observatory recede into the watery mist he never recorded. His eyes could not help but notice the solitary mound rising from the level ground near the hut. That lone grave caught his eye whenever he approached his workshop. The image of the frozen crypt wavered constantly in the corner of Bessel's sight, while the specter of the dead commander hovered in the back of his mind.

Fastidious and haughty from the start, the German scientist had withdrawn even further into himself since the death of Captain Hall. His manner and actions had set him apart from the rest at the very beginning of the voyage, and the closeness of the crew, coupled with the lack of proper sanitary conditions, only heightened his alienation.

Imperious as well as aloof, Bessel had openly striven to make himself the overall head of the entire expedition. While he never said so directly, his actions further tagged him as wanting to be the first to reach the North Pole. Only Captain Hall appeared to stand in his way. With the demise of Hall, Bessel believed he had achieved both objectives: he could reach the Pole and direct the expedition. The lion's share of the glory would be his. Of course, the official orders split the command between the German and Captain Buddington, but Bessel expected the drunken sea captain to be happy to follow his directives.

Two things conspired to frustrate Bessel's ambitions, however. Buddington not only hindered any plan to reach the North Pole after Hall died but steadfastly refused to consider any undertaking other than retreating farther from their objective. Second, the Arctic forced a harsh reality on Emil Bessel: he was not physically strong enough to be an Arctic explorer, much less make the trek to the top of the world. Whenever he had tried to act the explorer, snow blindness struck him down. Why he never used the carved, slitlike goggles the Inuit wore for protection is another mystery. Perhaps he considered it beneath him. Perhaps he believed his will would see him through. But his eyes failed him at every turn. To the German, who considered himself superior in every way to Captain Hall, this weakness, which had never bothered the dead commander, must have been particularly galling. In any event even brief exposures to the constant glare of the snow and ice disabled him for weeks at a time.

It must have been a bitter experience for Bessel to hide from the light with his eyes swathed in bandages while men he considered inferior to him trudged about with impunity. In the end he buried himself beneath mountains of scientific measurements and collection specimens, piling those things around him for a barrier. Eventually he became even more withdrawn and brooding. Faced with his failures, Emil Bessel the man ceased to exist and was replaced by the two-dimensional Bessel the scientist. In all the testimony later taken from the crew and all the written journals, little is found that describes his human side.

While the Inuit mother nursed her infant son below decks, the *Polaris* crept cautiously southward, following the twists and turns of the open channels that beckoned. Crozier Island and Franklin Island hove into view like hostile monoliths. Because the ship was without anchors, the two islands offered neither shelter nor comfort. While they passed Franklin Island, a thunderous roar overrode the whine of the wind and rattled off the distant cliffs like the shot of a cannon. The report came from an enormous landslide that greeted them, spilling down the island's rocky side to set the sea boiling amid crashing boulders and tumbling clouds of milky glacial dust.

Passing to the east of Crozier Island, the ship sailed beneath the silvery white face of Cape Constitution. Morton and Hans Christian watched glumly as they passed the point that the two of them had reached by sled in 1854 during Dr. Kane's expedition. Their seamed faces showed little of the excitement they had felt when they had steamed northward past the point less than a year before. For Morton this would be his last journey to the far North. Never again would he share the exhilaration of stepping onto undiscovered land with his old friend Hans.

Two days into their steaming, fog settled across the entire length of Kennedy Channel. Buddington steered the vessel west along Cape Frazer, then back toward the western side of Greenland in his attempt to keep within the open channel. Meyer hastily took a sextant reading before the fog obscured the sun. His calculations placed the ship at 80°1' N latitude.

Weaving his way through the tiny, shifting openings day and night weighed heavily on Buddington. All around him cakes of ice threatened the weakened ship, and the open leads he followed grew narrow and turned without warning. As usual he consoled himself with nips from his pocket flask. By noon of the fifteenth, the captain was considerably drunk.

The wrong order slurred from Buddington's lips turned the ship sharply out of the slender canal and drove the vessel into the bordering ice. Thinner, freshly formed ice might have parted beneath the *Polaris*'s ironclad prow, but Buddington picked the wrong floe to hit. This floating island stretched more than five miles in length and measured many feet in thickness. In an instant the string of two days' worth of good luck that had come with the birth of the Inuit snapped. With a sickening grind, the bow of the ship rode onto the floe. Abruptly the *Polaris* jerked to a halt.

Instantly Buddington ordered the engine into full reverse. The screw beat the water into a greenish froth while the hull painfully wriggled its way off the island. Men held their breath and gripped the handrails while the ship struggled to free herself.

Running the prop in reverse carried a danger of its own. Adjacent blocks of floating ice, drawn in by the suction of the propeller, closed about the screw like wolves on a wounded deer. The blades struck one mound after another. Chunks of ice flew into the air and spattered the stern before littering the foaming sea with ivory chips. The bronze blades bent in the process.

Below decks the engineer Schuman sensed the stress on the screw and signaled frantically to the bridge. Another minute might see the driveshaft snap. Reluctantly Buddington ordered the engine shut down. With a groan the ship settled onto the ice and heeled onto its side, once more resuming its familiar angle.

Two days into their escape, the Arctic ice had recaptured the *Polaris*. More ice gathered around the free side of the ship, packing around the hull. New ice quickly formed between the blocks, sealing the openings until the spidery rime once again entrapped the *Polaris* in an icy cocoon.

Chester barked an order, and men leaped onto the floe to drive ice screws and anchors into the solid surface to keep the ship from rocking to pieces. Within an hour stout lines secured the bow and stern.

Just 120 miles south of the farthest point the *Polaris* had sailed, Arctic ice again ensnared the woeful ship. Slowly the sailors walked along the deck peering down at the ice encasing their home. For all their efforts to escape the clutches of the Arctic, little good had come of it. In fact, they were considerably worse off. Providence Berg, despite splitting apart, had remained grounded on the shallow floor of Thank God Harbor, thereby offering some degree of protection. The floe that presently held them was adrift. Like a flea riding the back of a dog, the *Polaris* no longer controlled its destiny. Worse still, they had burned two more days' worth of their irreplaceable coal and bent their propeller blades.

Paradoxically the ship appeared to be moving *north* at times! While the current generally moved from north to south, strong southerly winds buffeted the pack and pushed the ice floe north, preventing it from drifting down the coast. Not only had the region recaptured the retreating expedition, it appeared to be drawing the ship back into its northern lair.

The grounding on the ice floe reactivated Buddington's worst fears. The very danger he had worked so hard to avoid had come to pass. He and his ship were trapped in the ice fields. If they could not free the *Polaris*, surely starvation and cannibalism awaited them. Visions of Sir Hugh Willoughby's Muscovy Company sailing ship drifting onto the shores of Lapland with its ghastly cargo of frozen corpses probably haunted his dreams. Even though Sir Hugh's catastrophe had occurred three hundred years before, its dreadful image frequented all the recent publications, adding color to a long string of Arctic disasters that led up to Sir John Franklin's. Ironically the *Polaris* expedition would contribute to the tales, and it would not be the last calamity.

Two days passed before the ice resorted to its old trick of nipping the ship's sides. Hummocks piled into the free side of the *Polaris* with sufficient force to raise the keel and increase the angle of heeling. Panic swept the crew, and Buddington prepared to abandon ship. Supplies littered the deck, readily located for heaving onto the ice should the worst happen. Later that evening another onrush of ice battered the ship again. Heeling increased dramatically while the men looked wistfully at open water miles beyond their reach.

A southwest gale added to the men's anxiety and discomfort. Freezing rain pelted the deck and coated every exposed fitting and line with ice. The angled deck became a skating rink, ready to send the unwary crashing into the lifelines. Exposed skin froze to lashings on contact, and strips of skin tore away when the limb pulled free.

Encrusted doors refused to close, blocks froze to their tackle, and icy ratlines proved so treacherous that climbing to the crow's nest risked life and limb. Even so, Chester and Tyson climbed daily to the topmast to search for a way out. The swirling mist and sea fog parted at times to reveal tantalizing glimpses of open water. Always, however, white walls rose in defiance between the ship and their freedom.

Throughout this icy rain, the crew fretted through a deadly game of blindman's bluff. Not a day passed without some monstrous, milky hillock emerging from the freezing mist to bear down on the tethered *Polaris*. With singular purpose one or more would cruise straight for the vessel, threatening to crush it against the frozen expanse at its back. By hauling on the bow and stern lines, the crew could warp the ship fore and aft to evade the onrush. The work was deadly and disheartening. By using blocks and tackle, the capstan, and even raw muscle, the lines would be pulled in to swing the ship away from the path of the charging mountain of ice. Not unlike drawing on strings to turn a child's puppet, the action would pivot the vessel. But this puppet weighed four hundred tons. Around the clock the assaults continued until the sailors strained at their lines with numbed minds as well as hands.

Pressure on the weakened hull continually mounted as the oncoming ice packed tighter and tighter against the exposed flank of the ship. The leaking seams and split boards opened wider as the jaws of the vise inexorably tightened. Again Buddington turned to pumping by the steam donkey. With all hands occupied in moving the ship back and forth along their tightrope, no one could be spared to work the hand pumps on deck.

As the ship drifted back and forth with the floe, the opalescent walls of the Humboldt Glacier shimmered and glistened to the east, guarded by an armada of chalky icebergs passing in review down Smith Sound. Behind this floating wall, the pale lavender and blue mountains of Greenland beckoned like soundless sirens to the helpless crew. On August 25 Joseph Mauch penned words that reflected the prevailing gloom that gripped his shipmates as they watched land pass out of reach: "The ice is opening a few hundred yards from us, but so little that we cannot take advantage of it. The officers are, of course, aware that, ten chances to one, we are lost if we should not be able to reach land."

For the rest of August and most of September, the ice retained its hold on the *Polaris*. No further gales roared up the sound. Instead, fog and freezing drizzle filled the days, alternating with cold, diamond-clear periods during which the hard reflection of the sun off the ice burned everyone's eyes. The absence of stiff winds proved a curse rather than a blessing. Without wind to roil the water, no waves broke the deepening ice, and the swirling current drifted the intact ice pack north and south, east and west. Dead reckoning and celestial sightings noted little progress to the south. Most days the ship moved less than a mile in any direction. Paradoxically the men now prayed for a gale to release them.

Distressingly the sun wearied of sailing aloft as it had during the summer and dipped below the horizon for the first time since April. Taking their cue from the departing warmth, birds and animals fled southward, leaving the stranded ship alone in the ice. Seal sightings grew scarce. By the end of August, the only sign of life seen all day was one ivory gull winging its way south. Buddington's fears of starving grew closer to reality. No longer could the party rely upon the Inuit to provide fresh meat. All that remained were the tinned foodstuffs, and Buddington's calculations raised doubts there would be enough to feed all of them until next April.

Everywhere the region seemed to be settling into the steely grip of the coming winter. The air grew heavy and thick with the cold, and the earthy scents of the land disappeared. Once more the ear-shattering silence of the dreaded Arctic night crept forward to muffle the world.

Unlike the Ancient Mariner's predicament, fresh water was abundant for the trapped men. Melted portions of the glacial ice and snow filled the hollows of the ice pack with pools of fresh water. Daily parties of men crossed the ice to fill their buckets and casks with brackish water to drink and feed to the steam boilers. As the temperature fell and the pools froze, they cut blocks of ice from the icebergs.

More coal vanished in fruitless attempts to break free. One long day of working the hand lines and using the steam engine moved the vessel less than its own length. Nine hundred pounds of coal per day vanished into the firebox of the steam pumps. Chester and Schuman struggled to reduce the constant flow of water from the cracks. Ninety fathoms of chain was fed into the forepeak in an effort to freeze the water in the forward hold in hopes this might slow the influx of seawater.

Tarred sailcloth was fed under the bows and winched tightly against the damaged side. Called "thrumming," the process involved piercing the sailcloth with an awl and feeding short strips of yarn through each of the hundreds of holes. In theory the suction of the leak would draw the yarn into the holes and bind the canvas against the ship's hull. In practice thrumming a sail worked well and had saved many a ship from a watery grave. But that was in warmer waters. Encountering frigid air and icy water, the tarred canvas froze into an inflexible sheet too stiff to closely enfold the damaged hull.

The thud of caulking hammers driving oakum into the cracks rang for days. In the end the leaks proved worse.

Schuman abandoned his attempts to stop the leaks and turned his attention to reducing the coal needed to run the pumps. Besides having a large firebox, the steam donkey labored far in excess of its intended purpose. Originally designed only to transfer water to the engine boilers, the overstressed steam pumps kept the ship afloat by their continuous use, something they had never been built to do. Their breakdowns frayed the crew's nerves and kept Schuman busy with emergency repairs. He settled upon a small boiler designed to aid the combustion nozzles in the engine room. The men brought it on deck and bolted it down. Ingeniously the engineer redirected the small boiler's smokestack through Ebierbing's cabin to provide extra heating for the Inuit while the machine fired.

By the twenty-third of September, Schuman had the little machine working well enough to replace the steam donkey. As he had hoped, it did cut down considerably on the amount of coal needed to do the job. Only 350 pounds of fuel per day emptied the holds of water. However, their respite did not last long. Six days of heavy use burned up the boiler beyond repair. The end of September found the *Polaris* with less than twenty tons of coal left. Forced back to burning close to half a ton of coal a day just to keep from sinking, by November the *Polaris* would be out of coal to fire its engines. Hall had stored enough coal for two and one-half years, but the leaks had drastically altered fuel consumption.

Buddington prepared for the worst. Should the pumps fail or the ship's side be crushed by the ice, the vessel would sink within minutes. Following Captain Hall's lead, he moved stores necessary for survival topside. The storm staysail and gaff-topsails were cut up and sewn into seabags. Bags filled with two tons of coal and loaves of bread joined the growing piles of tinned goods, twenty barrels of pork, and cans of molasses heaped by the guardrails. One remaining whaleboat was lowered onto the ice and the last remaining skiff unlashed from the cabin roof and swung over the side on davits, ready for fast deployment.

Probably to keep Captain Tyson occupied, Buddington bestowed upon him the grandiose but hollow title of "master builder" and ordered him to construct a tent on the ice beside the ship. During the construction, they discovered that the ice surrounding the *Polaris* measured six feet thick. Sinking poles into the ice for support and lashing the crossbeams together, Tyson, Morton, Mauch, Bryan, and Ebierbing built a frame twenty-seven feet long and twenty-five feet wide. The canvas used to house the deck during the winter at Thank God Harbor enclosed the tent. Eight hundred pounds of bread was stacked in canvas bags beside the shelter. Within days of the food transfer, a polar bear approached the camp, probably attracted by the smell. Two rifle shots wounded the animal without bringing it down. Half the crew took out after the fleeing bear, but it escaped. By week's end tracks of three more bears crossed close to the cache of bread.

October ended their two-month respite. Just as the donkey steam pump broke down yet again, new and dramatic events gripped the ice floe and its captive sailing ship. The ice started to move. First, the vast island swung slowly around until the bow of the ship faced directly west. Then a gale struck from the south, creating waves and troughs that crumpled the weaker parts of the ice. Hills and hummocks rose before the men's eyes, accompanied by grinding noises that reverberated throughout the ship. Giant, razor-sharp shards pierced the frozen seascape surrounding them and tumbled over close by. Any one of these frozen knives striking the ship could easily hole the wooden hull beyond all repair.

Resigned to the fate of spending another winter locked in Smith Sound, the crew found themselves propelled backward by the sudden and swift movement of the ice southward. Snowfall accompanied the storm, obscuring any sun sight. Meyer used land bearings to place the *Polaris* at 78°45' N. The next day he reckoned the ship to be 12 miles from Cape Grinnell. They had drifted south another 120 miles in a matter of days.

Spirits rose. Their floating world approached the northern outlet of Baffin Bay. At this rate they would soon drift within reach of help. Once the vessel entered Baffin Bay, it would float with the pack until spring melted the ice. Besides, each mile brought the ship closer to Disko, where a storehouse of coal and food awaited.

But progress came with a price. Pressure increased on the ship's sides, and the vessel protested constantly with nerve-racking creaks and snaps and fresh leaks. Buddington redoubled his preparations to abandon ship. The men piled a total of eighteen hundred pounds of bread about the tent. All items necessary for survival were brought topside and stacked for quick access. Should the ship suffer a fatal blow, the plan was to heave the goods onto the ice. Yet the unstable nature of their surroundings prevented moving the items off the boat until the last moment. To place all their supplies on the ice would be to risk losing everything should the ship break free or the tent be swallowed by a sudden opening in the island. Crates of tinned pemmican, tobacco, and hams rose on the deck in preparation. Piles of musk ox hides joined the jumble until walking about became difficult. Below decks prudent sailors stuffed their belongings into seabags and waited.

Chapter Ten

A DREADFUL NIGHT

The ice was here, the ice was there,
The ice was all around:
It cracked and growled, and roared and howled,
Like noises in a swound. . . .

— SAMUEL TAYLOR COLERIDGE,
"THE RIME OF THE ANCIENT MARINER"

They wouldn't have long to wait. Late in the day on October 15, the sky grew threatening. Dark clouds gathered to the northwest and steadily advanced in a glowering mass of molten lead until the edge of the storm hung over the ship like a black pall. Ominously the wind died down. An oppressive stillness pressed down upon the ship. The nervous banter of the deckhands trailed off until the only sound heard was the creak of the ice-encrusted deck as the men moved warily about.

As if spurred on by the coming gale, the stretch of ice that encompassed the *Polaris*'s world surged forward, dragging the ship along. Out of the icy mists, two ghostly mountains rose directly ahead. Shimmering and sliding silently through the water, these icebergs loomed like twin giants, drawing ever closer to the ship.

Men standing their watch gasped as their drift drew them inexorably toward their doom. The ship was trapped in the floe, and there was no possibility of escape. Within minutes the floe bearing its puny vessel would crash into the frozen giants. If the ship did not hit one of them directly, the pileup of the oncoming ice pack into the icebergs would surely shatter the expanse of ice surrounding them and crush the hull like a paper cup.

Just then the gale struck from the northwest. Snow, mist, and ice crystals swirled about the air. Visibility dropped to mere inches in front of the men's faces, punctuated by fleeting glimpses of the ice and water when the wind scattered the snow.

The ice field swung around with the storm and drove between the two towering mountains. The floe shuddered to a halt upon impact. High-pitched screams emanated from the icebergs as slabs weighing tons sheared from their sides to tumble onto the floe.

Resembling an earthquake opening fissures, the impact buckled the floe and sent spidery cracks racing outward from the point of impact. Close behind these widening fissures, the ice rose and heaved like falling dominoes. The crumpled ridge rushed toward the trapped ship like an ivory tidal wave.

Then it struck the ship. Crumpling, cracking, and twisting, the enormous sheet of frozen water encasing the *Polaris* exploded into fragments. The force lifted the *Polaris* bodily and drove it onto its port side. Shuddering and trembling from the pressure, the vessel wrenched out of its frozen bed and rode up onto the ice. A cleat securing one of the ice anchors pulled free with a sharp crack and vanished over the side with the hawser. Heavy oak timbers groaned and snapped, mostly abaft the beam. The stern section appeared to split in two.

A tortured groan wrenched George Tyson from his deep sleep and caused him to sit bolt upright in his narrow bunk. Flakes of frost from condensed moisture on the walls rained down on him as the ship's sides trembled. The cold flakes stung his face like needles and brought him fully awake.

Groping within the blackness of the cabin, his fingers touched the rough oak walls of the ship, an act of reassurance every mariner performs when frightened. No sounds of rushing water reached his ears; no streams of freezing water met his touch. The solid sides were still intact. Tyson murmured a prayer, and he calmed himself.

Tyson cocked his ear, uncertain of what exactly was happening. As assistant navigator of the expedition, his twenty years sailing the Arctic had prepared him for the creaks and sounds each ship makes as it lives uneasily among the ice. No vessel ever masters the Arctic seas. Rather, the massive bergs and blocks of ice *permit* a ship to exist. Already cracked and leaking, the *Polaris* had plenty of reason to protest the pressure of the ice, but these sounds were different— more intense, more . . . painful.

Tyson blinked in the dark. He must get topside, he realized. A feeble shaft of light marked the forward ladder. Another, lesser moan followed the first, this one issuing from the ribs of the ship itself. It was as if the *Polaris* were being tortured, crying out in pain with each blow to its sides.

Suddenly the vessel lurched violently to port, throwing Tyson from his bunk.

"We are sinking!" The shout came from the deck. Another roll followed close on the cry, and a sharp grinding shook the keel. Above his head running feet thudded across the deck, mixing with the scrape of sliding crates.

A voice he recognized as belonging to Campbell, the fireman, screamed down the hatch: "The ice has driven through the side!"

Instantly Tyson leaped to his feet and bounded up the ladder. A wall of frigid air struck his lungs as he skidded onto the ice-rimmed deck. His bare fingers caught the rigging to keep his balance. The frozen cordage burned like molten iron.

The perpetual gloom of the Arctic winter provided scarcely more light than his darkened room, but he could see the faint outlines of the forecastle rising like a dark wedge into the inky sky. Snow and sleet peppered his face, blinding him at times. Squinting through the mist, he forced his eyelids to remain open. What he managed to see chilled his heart.

Surrounding the ship, ice floes and jumbled pack ice hovered in the blowing snow like ghostly specters. Two monstrous icebergs threatened the ship from both sides. At first Tyson thought the bergs had struck the ship, but a swirl of the snow revealed that not to be the case. The bergs had struck the ice floe instead, he realized.

A body tumbled past Tyson, striking his left leg on the way by. The tilt of the deck had slid the crew against the port railings, clustering them in a bunch like ninepins near the waist of the vessel. Those who could stand peered over the railing. Tyson slipped and skated to them and followed their gaze over the side.

Razor ridges of ice pressed against the ship's sides, compressing the timbers and forcing the *Polaris* upward until the scarred iron and copper sheeting lay exposed to the frigid air. Clusters of barnacles and patches of sea grass, the ship's watery beard, coated the edges of ice that had sheared them from the hull. Ironically, the cracked timbers that had eluded repair rode high above the water.

Quickly Tyson skated to the starboard rail.

Solid ice gripped that side as well. The blowing wind and waves had forced frozen hummocks and knife-sharp *sastrugi* against the floe to which the *Polaris* was moored. Adding to this, the massive weight of the two icebergs leaned against the crumpled edge of the ice field. Thousands of tons of frozen water now pressed against the trapped ship. Between these jaws the *Polaris* was being crushed.

A well-founded vessel, designed for such a contingency, would wriggle free of the closing jaws and rise above the crushing forces. Thus, resting on top of the ice, it would lie safely while the vast pack of ice shifted and moved inexorably north or south with the ocean's current. Now the navy's decision to cut costs by reusing the unsuitably shaped narrow hull of the old *Periwinkle* would threaten the lives of all aboard.

To Tyson's alarm the starboard side of the vessel still lay within the frozen jaws, while the port side obediently rode above the danger. Each gust of wind drew protests from the groaning hull as the ice tightened.

Just then Schuman, the engineer, burst from the aft companionway, shouting in German as he flailed his arms. His feet slipped on the icy deck, and he bowled into the crew clustered by the railing. Tyson grasped the officer by his collar and dragged him to his feet.

"Speak English!" he ordered. "What is it? What's the matter?"

"We're sinking!" Schuman stuttered. "The ice has opened the seams. Many new leaks," he gasped.

A terrified moan arose from the deckhands. Their widened eyes, glowing white even in the darkness, signaled they were close to panic. If the ship sank, all were lost. Not only were there no other ships within hundreds of miles, but the nearest settlements were also hundreds of miles south. Those who made it to an island of ice were doomed to a drawn-out death from frostbite and starvation. With the seawater temperature at 28°F, no man would last longer than fifteen minutes. Anyone who fell into the sea would drown as the cold robbed his muscles of any strength. More than a few minutes in the water so stiffened the small muscles of the hands that a man could not grasp a rescue line.

"The pumps, man," Tyson said as he shook the engineer, "start the pumps!"

Schuman shook his head. "We are pumping, but it does no good. The water is gaining on the pumps. It rushes into the hold. We are lost!"

Tyson released his grip on his fellow officer as a shaft of light flashed in the doorway of the master's cabin. It was Captain Buddington.

Hauling himself along the lifelines, Tyson slid to the sailing master. "The ship is being strongly nipped, sir," he yelled over the howl of the wind. "Schuman says the seams have opened and the pumps cannot keep up."

Buddington stared uncomprehendingly at Tyson. The captain's breath reeked of alcohol. His eyes blinked rapidly while his lips moved, but no words came out. Now more than ever, Tyson wished for the solid, sturdy face of Captain Hall. Unflappable in any emergency, the late captain was sorely needed.

"We are sinking!" Schuman screamed through the blowing snow. "Sinking!"

As if responding to the engineer's cries, the *Polaris* lurched farther to one side and rose by the bow as the ice pack shifted.

Schuman's words and the ship's movement galvanized Buddington. He rushed forward to the crew, waving both arms at the pile of supplies lashed to the center of the deck. Heavier supplies like the bags of coal were stacked forward, while ammunition, rifles, and lighter boxes had been collected aft.

Buddington threw his arms up in the air and yelled: "Throw everything onto the ice!"

Gustavus Lindquist and Peter Johnson spun about at these startling words. Other sailors stopped and cast nervous glances at one another. Had they misunderstood the captain? Was the ship really sinking? During previous threats of swamping, calm orders were issued and goods transferred safely onto the ice until the danger passed. Surely all was not lost?

Buddington answered their unspoken questions. "Work for your lives, boys!" he bellowed.

Panic erupted. Terror-stricken, the crew rushed about cutting the lashings and flinging whatever they snatched over the railings on both sides. Boxes and crates flew into the darkness and the swirling snow. All the while the *Polaris* rose and fell with the rolling ice and roiling waves from the growing storm. The sway of the hull and the force of the storm opened wide gaps in the ice that moments before had encased the ship. Level floors of ice cracked and drew apart like broken china. Other sections tumbled and overturned as the supporting sea roiled beneath its frozen roof. Blinded by their fears as well as the pelting snow, the men worked feverishly and foolishly. Superhuman strength imbued many and galvanized those who saw their impending death.

One man single-handedly pushed a sled through the gangway and hefted it over the side. Not waiting to see where it landed, he rushed aft to help empty the deck of the goods stacked there. Boxes of ammunition, stacks of rifles and revolvers, tins of preserved fruit cascaded off the ship and rained into the darkness.

Over the roar of the wind, Tyson heard a splash. He leaned far over the port railing. To his horror he saw the results of the hurried evacuation.

Most of the supplies were falling into the sea.

The navigator's heart sank as he watched box after box vanish beneath the dark waters or shatter as the roll of the ship against the ice crushed and splintered the crates. Cans and crates bobbed in the open gaps. From the corner of his eye, Tyson saw Joe and Hans, the two Eskimo hunters, slip over the railing onto a crust of solid ice and begin to drag what they could onto the ice floe. The Natives had kept their heads while the "educated and civilized" crew lost theirs.

A crash caught Tyson's attention. The last remaining whaleboat thudded to the ice as the desperate men cut the lines to its davits. It slid back off the ice, coming to rest half in the water. The oars and sails for the boat rattled against its plank sides. Floating against the churning hull, the longboat risked being instantly crushed.

"The provisions are sinking!" Tyson shouted to his befuddled skipper.

"Move them back!" Buddington ordered.

The assistant navigator jumped down and snatched a box from certain doom. He struggled with the whaleboat until more hands joined him. When he looked up, he could see a dozen others working on the ice. He wondered briefly whether Buddington had sent them down or whether the men had come on their own.

Gathering a working party, Tyson followed the Eskimo onto the jumbled ice away from the ship. In their wisdom the Natives were moving their possessions toward the pitched tent, where the ice appeared the thickest.

Aboard the ship Tookoolito watched Hans's wife leading her daughter toward the canvas tent. On her back the woman's newborn son, Charlie Polaris, slept contentedly. Tookoolito watched them vanish in the swirling snow before turning back to the companionway. More of her possessions remained in their cabin. Extra furs, two seal-oil lamps, and her sewing kit were still below. Quickly she gathered these precious things up in her arms.

The simple lamps made by grinding a shallow depression in a flat stone would provide light and heat for her family on the ice. Filled with seal oil and regulated by a braided grass wick, the lamp was all they needed to warm an igloo. New wicks could be fashioned from sea grass stuffed inside her mukluks for insulation. Equally important was her sewing kit. With its bone needles and awls, Tookoolito could fashion new garments and repair torn ones. Those two items, the lamps and the sewing kit, ensured her family's survival. Without them they would be lost.

Coming up the steps, she encountered the oil-smudged face of Alvin Odell, the assistant engineer. The unspoken concern in her dark eyes caught his attention.

Odell stopped and laid his greasy hand on her shoulder. His gaze rested on the articles clutched tightly against her breast. The heavy hand patted her shoulder reassuringly. "Don't worry, little lady," he chuckled. "We've got the leaks under control. We'll have you back on board before long."

Tookoolito followed Odell up the steps to the deck. He spotted Captain Buddington and headed over to him. The Inuit woman looked about at the confusion sweeping the foredeck. Buddington now added to her consternation by ordering her onto the ice.

Through the whistle of the wind, she heard her husband, Ebierbing, call her name. The snow parted to allow her a fleeting glimpse of him beckoning from the ice. Quietly Tookoolito slipped over the side and dropped onto the ice. She would take her chances with her husband, she decided, rather than on this ship with its bad *Inui*.

As she slipped onto the ice floe, Tookoolito carried one other precious thing. Gripped tightly in her arms was also a small wooden box given to her by her dying friend Charles Francis Hall. While Buddington and Bessel had collected all of Hall's papers upon his death, Tookoolito had hidden this small box of letters from them. Honoring Hall's dying wish, she protected and preserved them with her life.

Behind her Bryan and Meyer wrestled with chests filled with the expedition's scientific papers. Over the side Bryan tossed his own personal box with his private letters and notebooks. He and the meteorologist lifted case after case over the railing.

Hours passed unnoticed as the men fished floating crates from the waves, wrestled them onto solid ice, and dragged them toward the center of the floe. In the darkness time had little meaning, especially while the fury of the storm mounted.

A disheartened Tyson finally dragged himself onto the ship to report his progress. What supplies they had salvaged were now clustered around a whaleboat dragged to the most solid part of the floe. He estimated six thousand pounds of canned pemmican had sunk along with many bags of the precious coal. The helter-skelter jettisoning had proved ruinous. The bulk of the ship's emergency provisions littered the ocean floor.

As he reached Buddington, the ship shifted to port again, just as the ice released the starboard side of the *Polaris*. Black open water swirled around the hull.

Both men stared at their reprieve. One side was now free. One jaw of the vise was gone. If the leaks could be contained, the ship would be saved.

"How much water is the vessel making?" Tyson asked anxiously.

Buddington grinned sheepishly and shrugged. "No more than usual," he answered. "When the bow rose, the water in the hold rushed forth. Schuman mistook that for a new leak. But he was mistaken. The vessel is strong." He gave a nervous laugh. Odell's second assessment had calmed his fears. "I guess we're not sinking after all. The engineer's first report was a false alarm."

The navigator studied the pumps. The steady clank of the steam donkey reassured him that it was pumping smoothly. Two men working the hand pump motioned to their hose. Water and air gushed out the nozzle. That pump was sucking air, Tyson realized. The bilge must be almost dry.

The storm permitted them no time at all to rejoice. A stiff gust of wind rattled the rigging and howled through the cross spars and showered them with shards of ice stripped from the fittings. The deck with all its frenzied activity vanished in a blanket of stinging ice crystals and snowflakes. The surrounding ice field groaned with the accompanying storm surge.

"Look." Tyson pointed to new cracks appearing about the ship. "The ice is breaking up even more." The vast floor of ice resumed its rising and falling in sections like waves, with cracks and fissures opening and closing with each shift. The clouds of snow parted to expose additional crates scattered about the port side of the vessel that Tyson and the men had missed.

Buddington's attention shifted to the precious supplies. "Mr. Tyson, get everything back as far as possible on the ice," he ordered.

Tyson nodded wearily and crawled down onto the floe to resume directing his exhausted men. Another hour passed as the men slid and pushed the freight back from the cracking edges. In the whirling snow, visibility was cut to a few inches. The force of the blowing wind stung their faces, and the icy sleet cut the men's eyes whenever they faced into the gale. Half the time they stumbled blindly about while the ground under their feet writhed and turned like a living beast.

Lindquist manhandled an enormous barrel of molasses to the tumble home. Using his back for leverage, he pushed the cask over the side and watched with satisfaction as it crashed onto the ice and rolled away from the edge. Then he headed back into his quarters to check on his seabag. Alarmingly, his bag, containing all his clothing, was missing from his bunk.

Separation of the Polaris *and the floe party (Culver Pictures)*

Back on deck Lindquist spotted his bag lying on the field, bobbing atop a wedge of ice surrounded by twelve feet of floating slush. Someone had thrown it overboard. He started over the side.

Strangely Captain Buddington stopped him.

"I don't see any need for you to go there now," Buddington advised.

Lindquist pointed to his endangered duffle bag. "I'd like to get my clothes bag," he pleaded. Nearly all his belongings were on the ice.

Buddington let his arm drop from the sailor's shoulder. He shrugged. "Very well, go ahead."

Lindquist climbed hand over hand down the taut bowline to the floe. He would quickly regret that move.

Above Lindquist, Meyer struggled to push the last chest of documents through the opening in the railing. Grasping both handles of the chest, Meyer leaned far over the railing to lower it carefully down to the ice.

Without warning the icy plain erupted in a plume of seawater, snow, and ice.

The *Polaris* lurched violently. Meyer's feet shot out from under him while the box swung into the night. The weight of the crate dragged Meyer over the side, and the two plummeted downward. Below, Lindquist dove to one side just as the massive chest crashed beside him, missing his head by inches. The startled sailor glanced over his shoulder just in time to see Mr. Meyer follow the chest onto the ice. The fall knocked the wind out of the meteorologist's lungs, and the dazed Prussian looked up to find himself flat on his back where he least wanted to be—on the ice.

The cataclysm engulfed the entire expanse of ice surrounding the ship. As Tyson clambered about the relocated goods, the ice beneath his feet exploded, flinging him to the ground. He struggled to his knees just in time to see a cloud of snow billowing along the side of the *Polaris*. The cloud rolled the entire length of the ship like exploding gunpowder.

Mooring lines secured to the floe snapped like rifle shots, and the ice anchors ripped loose. The vessel wrenched free of the ice's grip and lurched into the darkness. In an instant it vanished within the swirl of the storm. A second later the ice floe, freed of the ship's weight, tilted precipitously and fractured into a hundred pieces. Inky water bubbled forth from the widening rents.

Through the darkness and swirling snow came the plaintive cry of John Herron, the steward. "Goodbye, *Polaris* . . ."

"Hurry! To the whaleboat, men!" Tyson shouted. To launch their small craft in search of the *Polaris* was impossible. But the longboat would save them from the frigid waters if their floating island disintegrated.

As his crew huddled about the boat, Tyson spotted a dark shape through the blowing snow. He shielded his eyes and looked again. A precious bundle of musk ox hides, essential for warmth, was slipping into a widening fissure in the ice. Tyson stumbled forward and snatched the corner of the disappearing hides just as they threatened to slide into oblivion. He dug his heels into the ice and pulled. The corner of the hides flipped back, exposing two frightened faces.

Shocked, Tyson realized the bundle of hides contained the Eskimo children of Hans and Tookoolito. The Inuit families had combined their offspring and placed them where they thought it was safest. However, no place on the cracking floe remained secure for long.

The navigator tugged desperately as the fissure widened. For a minute it was touch-and-go as to whether the children would slip beneath the black waters. Gradually the furs slid back from the edge with the children still inside, and Tyson bundled them back to the safety of the boat. Tookoolito, working about the whaleboat, stopped when she saw the children. She flashed Tyson a grateful smile as she embraced her child.

One hide remained in the crack. As Tyson looked back, the fissure ground shut with a savage groan. The lone fur vanished like a morsel in a giant's jaws. The navigator shivered. He'd almost been too late.

But there was no rest for the worn-out Tyson. A cry for help drew his attention to his left. Five men stranded on a bobbing raft of ice shouted to him. They had been working close by the *Polaris* when the breakup occurred. Only desperate leaps had saved them from being sucked under as the ship sprang free. Now they huddled together on a frozen chip less than eight feet square. Any movement caused the sliver of ice to tip and bob like a cork. In a minute the wind and waves would capsize their island and throw them to their deaths.

Tyson launched the ship's scow, the small, square-nosed boat that the crew affectionately called the "little donkey." But waves swamped the craft, and the would-be rescuer scrambled back to solid ice, barely escaping a plunge into the deadly sea. Next he tried the second whaleboat, which had broken free of the *Polaris* and beached itself by the water's edge. Rowing by sound as much as sight, Tyson paddled through the frigid veil, guided only by the cries of the stranded men. Anxious minutes passed before he located the men and hauled them off.

More cries for help filtered through the snow and sleet. For three long hours, Tyson added to his boat as he ferried stranded men back to their tiny fort.

When morning came, the storm abruptly quit, departing as suddenly as it had struck. Low-hanging clouds persisted, but the Arctic sun rose on a painfully scoured sky and commenced its skimming along the horizon. Blackness retreated before silky purples and rose colors that bathed the sky, the water, and the shards of ice, coating them in delicate shades of pink and blue. Dark and fearsome mere hours before, the Arctic changed its face to a soothing landscape fit to rival the canvases of the finest impressionists.

Still, things looked bleak for the stranded men. No one knew the fate of their ship. Had the *Polaris* sunk in the storm? If not, were its engines working so it could return to rescue them? Stranded on the floe, hundreds of miles from help, the party's chances were slim.

The cause of the ship's sudden expulsion from its icy cradle glowered over the marooned sailors for anyone with the interest to see. The storm had driven the twin icebergs together like hammer and anvil, crushing the ice field that had held the *Polaris*. No one really cared at that point. Only Tyson remained awake. Natives and sailors alike slept under snow-covered hides and blankets. Everyone but the navigator had accepted their fate and crawled under cover to await the inevitable.

Bone-tired, Tyson counted heads and took stock of their situation. Emerging from their white cocoons, tired faces greeted his count. Ten men from the ship's company and the two Eskimo with their wives and small children, nineteen in all, resided on a circular floe of ice less than several miles around.

Pitiful as their roster was, Tyson realized their residence was far worse. Their domain consisted of a floating island of sharp hills of tumbled ice, more like massive, razor-edged crystals, interspersed with pressure ridges of snow and scattered lakes and ponds of fresh water still melted from the summer sun. Their terra firma was anything but that. Parts of the floe thinned to several inches, insufficient to support a man's weight, while other sections measured more than forty feet thick. Careless wandering would plunge the unwary into freezing water.

They were miles from land, and interwoven barricades of ice prevented their rowing ashore. Unless a dramatic change in the current dispersed the floating islands, they were trapped on a section of drifting ice that might break apart at any moment.

Rescue by their ship remained the most favorable prospect, but Tyson's heart sank as he scanned the ice-strewn horizon. No sign of the *Polaris* existed. The vessel must have sunk in the storm with all aboard, he concluded. They were on their own.

The party had two whaleboats and the nearly useless scow, half filled with water. To feed the nineteen souls, Tyson counted fourteen cans of pemmican, fourteen salted hams, eleven and a half bags of flour, and one can of dried apples. Of the hundreds of pounds of bread, meat, and coal, most had sunk or drifted off.

Unknown to the navigator, the marooned crewmen had taken special pains to salvage their personal belongings at the expense of saving essential gear. Whereas Tyson had only the clothing on his back, most of the crew had their seabags with coffee and chocolate, fresh clothing, and firearms.

As ranking officer, he had no weapons—a distinct disadvantage, he suddenly realized. How could he impose his will over those seamen who had firearms? This detail would devil him in days to come.

Roll call revealed that the navigator's company included Frederick Meyer, the troublesome Prussian meteorologist whose collusion with his fellow Teutonic knight Dr. Bessel back at Disko had aided the undermining of Captain Hall. The unfortunate Meyer, dragged over the side by his crate of papers, represented the only member of the scientific corps. Suffering from the effects of scurvy, which drew his leg up so that only the toe could touch the ground as he hobbled about, Meyer would be of little use other than to take sightings. If the fog and ice mist persisted, sextant readings would be impossible, and Meyer would be of no use at all.

The able-bodied seamen were Fred Jamka, William Lindermann, Peter Johnson, Fred Anthing, and Gustavus Lindquist. J. W. Kruger, now called Robert by the others, completed the list of sailors. Tyson remembered several of these men as being mutinous, among them some who had broken into the ship's stores and drunk the alcohol used for the scientific specimens. None of the sailors had any expertise surviving in the Arctic.

Tired as he was, Tyson had to chuckle at the irony. His command contained most of the ship's seamen. He had the sailors but no ship to sail. Buddington, if he still lived, had only Joseph Mauch, Noah Hayes, Herman Sieman, and Henry Hobby to crew the *Polaris*.

William Jackson, the black cook, and John Herron, the ship's steward, represented the entire galley staff. Tyson had the galley staff without the galley, while Buddington's command was top-heavy with officers and the two scientists. Fate had split the command along the least favorable lines.

On the plus side of Tyson's party stood the stalwart Inuit, Ebierbing and Tookoolito, the faithful husband-and-wife team called "Joe" and "Hanna." Most important, Ebierbing was an excellent pilot. Hans, the other Inuit, was a proven hunter capable of taking seal and even bear from his fragile kayak with either spear or rifle. When the food ran out, the two Inuit men would have to hunt for them all.

Tookoolito and Hans's wife, Merkut, whom the sailors called Christiana, were adept at tending the seal-oil lamps and sewing the needed clothing. Yet even the Inuit's presence had a downside: there were the extra mouths of their children to feed. Tookoolito's adopted daughter, Puney, and Hans's four children—Augustina, Tobias, Succi, and newborn Charlie Polaris—were too young to hunt or fish.

Now that the snow had stopped, Tyson checked his bearings. Six miles to the southeast rose gray, wind-scoured peaks of land, but plates of pancake ice blocked that route except for a narrow channel of open water. The ice floe where they huddled lay jammed between the two towering icebergs. As chips of ice and smaller scrabble flowed past in the current, he realized the two bergs were firmly grounded on the ocean floor with their floe wedged tightly between.

The bite of the wind rising from the northeast caused the navigator to turn his face in that direction. What he saw sent shivers up his spine. Chunks of ice, mixed with broken plates and saucers, converged on the only open lee. The shifting wind was blowing closed the only route of escape from their fragile stand. They must move quickly. If they failed to paddle through the gap before it disappeared, they would be trapped.

"Quickly, men, get up!" Tyson shouted. "Load the boats. We must launch the boats before that opening closes." He pointed to the distant landfall. "We must reach that solid ground."

Overcoming his fatigue, the navigator raced about, kicking and prodding the snow-covered mounds of sleeping men. Try as he might, he could not get them to obey. Instead, the half-frozen sailors stared at him blearily.

"Hungry," Jamka mumbled. An accompanying chorus agreed with him.

Instead of preparing the boats, the men got slowly to their feet and began to search among their kits for food. To a man they ignored Tyson's entreaties.

Soon a score of pitiful fires, started with seal oil, rags, and scraps of wood, flickered uncertainly on the ice. Tinned cans of meat were pried open and used to thaw their frozen contents over the flames. After licking the tins clean, the sailors boiled snow in the cans to make coffee and chocolate. No one offered Tyson a single bite. The hungry navigator could only stand and watch in frustration. Performing his duty had placed him at a terrible disadvantage.

The Inuit, aware of the danger, ate their frozen seal meat while they waited by the boats and watched the greedy sailors. If they disapproved of the selfish behavior, they said nothing. Survival on the ice meant making hard decisions, something the Natives understood. More likely, they agreed, it might come to every man for himself.

Inexorably the pack ice tightened its noose around the open water. The channel to the land narrowed to a thin thread.

By insisting on eating, the men probably saved their lives at the cost of losing their only path to solid ground. Tyson's prowling about the floe all night using his muscles had kept him warm. The wet, tired seamen lying on the ice sank into hypothermia. The thick blanket of snow that covered them had kept them from freezing to death. But without some external warmth, whether a fire or hot food, their body temperatures would continue to slide to deadly lows. Their fumbling, somnambulant actions and slurred speech were symptomatic of this disorder. Their minds had cooled past caring or following orders. Only a primitive instinct directed them to find warm food. Consequently for them it was the right decision.

More than an hour passed while the men boiled more coffee

and tea in the empty tins. Slowly their energy returned. Next they hunted inside their oilskin seabags for a change of dry clothes. While an incredulous Tyson watched, the men changed out of their wet clothing before following his orders. Again no one offered to share his dry articles with the officer.

Well past nine in the morning, the party finally dragged and skidded the boats to the water's edge. Rowing and poling through the slush, the party struck off for the elusive shore. A low fog rolled in from the north as they got farther from their ice island. Tyson struggled to keep his bearings as the sliver of land ahead vanished and reappeared in the mist.

Halfway across, the lee ahead closed completely. Now they were on neither land nor solid ice but caught in a slurry of slush and ice that threatened to swamp them. If they could not break free, they would face the white death every Eskimo afloat feared: trapped in a rime of ice too thick to navigate through yet too thin to walk upon. Only death from starvation or freezing could follow.

Desperately the men rowed for the largest floe they could see. Hacking and chopping through the slush with their oars, they finally reached it. About a hundred yards across, the ice proved thick enough to support the boats. The men pulled the craft onto the floe to keep the whaleboats from freezing solid in the closing ice. Exhausted, the men flopped down in the shelter of the boats.

Just then Tyson spotted the *Polaris*.

Steaming around a point about ten miles north, the ship was under way, apparently undamaged, and making way under sail and steam. Sunlight glowed off her sails, while a dark plume of smoke streamed from her stacks. Black, open water sparkled off the bow of the ship and spread to within a mile of the stranded whaleboats. From there on only pancake ice sealed the difference. With her reinforced prow, the ship could easily smash her way to their rescue.

A signal was needed. The *Polaris* could not help but see them; still, Tyson was taking no chances. Light glaring off the ice and water might mask the party. There was no time for a fire, much less the wood to make a notable blaze. Dragging a sheet of India rubber from the bottom of one boat, Tyson draped it over a mound of ice. His men followed his example.

In minutes an American flag, canvas bags, musk ox hides, and even a pair of red flannel long johns sprouted from poles and oars stuck in the snow. While his men cheered, Tyson watched the *Polaris* through his telescope.

A shiver ran down his spine. The *Polaris* looked like a ghost ship. The decks were clear. No one kept watch in the crow's nest, and the quarterdeck appeared empty. Silently, like the Flying Dutchman, the ship cruised closer with no sign of life aboard.

The *Polaris* steamed on, following the curve of a lump of land that Tyson assumed was Littleton Island. Inexorably the vessel bore down on them. The men jumped and yelled in celebration. They were saved. This night would see them warm and dry on their ship.

When the *Polaris* reached the tip of the island, it turned away. Tyson snapped his glass shut in amazement as the cheers of his men died.

The *Polaris* vanished behind the land and was gone.

Chapter Eleven

MAROONED

We heard a crash, and looking out the window, we saw the ice coming in on us.
—PETER JOHNSON, FIREMAN, TESTIMONY AT THE INQUIRY

The sudden snap of the hawsers and the explosion of the ice propelled the *Polaris* into the mouth of the storm. The lurch that followed those breaking ropes sent Captain Buddington sprawling across the quarterdeck, sliding over the ice-covered planks until he careened into the raised cabin. Even as the ship danced wildly through the clouds of snow, he scrambled to his feet and shouted, "All hands to muster!"

He did not know how many of the crew remained behind on the ice. For a fleeting moment, he feared he might be alone. Quickly he calmed his fears. The engineers at least were still aboard—them and the tiresome Dr. Bessel. Throughout the entire storm, the physician had not stirred from his cabin.

White-faced men raced to his side, and a roll call was hurriedly taken. Anxiously Buddington counted the bodies while he searched each bundled face in recognition. The mad carpenter, Nathan Coffin, grinned lopsidedly at him. Resenting every minute he had to stand in the cold, Emil Bessel glared back sullenly. Beside him stood the gentle Bryan, his face placid as he prepared to meet his Maker. There, too, were the stolid features of old William Morton, the second mate, and Hubbard Chester, the first mate.

Half the crew was missing. Sieman, Hayes, Mauch, and Hobby were the only able hands left to man the ship. Four such men could not handle the sails in a strong blow, Buddington realized. He cursed his bad luck in ordering so many men onto the ice. He cursed Tyson, too, ever the thorn in his side, for having both the whaleboats with him.

The door to the companionway swung open, and four coal-blackened faces gazed up at the group. Schuman, Odell, Booth, and Campbell—all the engineers and firemen were still aboard.

"Schuman?" Buddington asked.

The engineer shook his head, answering the unspoken question that burned in the mind of each and every one. "Water still rising."

"And the engines?"

Schuman wiped an oily hand across his mouth. "The fires are lit in the boilers, but there's not enough steam yet to run the engines. If the water in the bilges reaches the fire plates, it'll put out the fires."

Buddington looked up to watch an iceberg half the length of the ship scrape along the ribs of the vessel. Chips of ice and snow showered onto the deck as the danger floated past. Even with their sails furled, the force of the storm pushed the *Polaris* along on bare poles. With the rudder and screw damaged and no steam, the ship drifted among the floating ice like a lamb among wolves. Without anchors, without ice hawsers, and with no lifeboats, the men were helpless.

Worse than that, they could not even jump onto the ice should the ship sink. The current and blasting wind had cleared their channel of everything but "brash" ice mixed with swiftly passing icebergs. The slush filling the space between would not hold a man's weight. Thick enough to impede swimming, the slush would keep even the strongest swimmer from reaching an iceberg. To the Inuit this was the treacherous *qinuq*, the rotten snow and slush floating on the sea, which could trap an unwary kayak.

Their only hope lay in holding back the flood until enough steam was raised to run the engines and the larger pumps.

Buddington pointed to the hand pumps. "Now, work for your lives, boys," he again exhorted his diminished crew, ironically using the same phrase that had sent most of his men onto the ice. The threat of a watery grave prodded the crew to extraordinary efforts. Pails, cups, and buckets supplemented the hand pumps. An hour passed with the water gaining on the desperate men. A bucket of precious hot water siphoned from the engine boiler melted the ice from the steam donkey. After a few coughing starts, that engine caught and began to pump water overboard.

Men ran about kicking ice that blocked the scuppers and bailing with cooking pots. Officers worked frantically alongside seamen. Anything that could burn was fed into the boilers. Schuman threw broken furniture, repair lumber, and even slabs of seal blubber retrieved from the aft deck into the firebox.

One hour and ten minutes passed in frenzied activity. Seawater reached the door to the engine room, and the ship's rocking set the water to lapping over the doorjamb. An anxious Schuman watched the pressure gauge slowly approach the needed level. With not a minute to spare, he spun the valves and the steam engine hissed into life. The greased piston arms clanked slowly back and forth, picking up steam until the pumps coughed out their trapped air. Salty water gushed over the side as the powerful pump tackled the leaks. Gradually the level in the bilges and holds receded.

The *Polaris* had won another reprieve.

Long after midnight the wind died off. The *Polaris* drifted silently along until its bow nosed into more substantial "pash" ice. This soup of heavy blocks congregated in the still water. With a grinding crunch, the vessel drove into the field and stopped.

The moon broke through the clouds and cast its gibbous light over the depleted survivors. Soaked to the skin with salt water and sweat, the sailors shivered under damp blankets. Unfortunately the seabags of all those remaining aboard had been thrown onto the ice during the storm. Mauch, Hayes, Hobby, and Sieman possessed only the dripping garments on their backs. The officers fared little better. While they had a change of dry clothes, none of their bedding, blankets, or rugs had survived the frantic jettisoning. To keep warm, the officers huddled together in Chester's cabin and awaited the dawn.

The morning of October 16 proved clear and windless. The dazed Chester guessed the ship lay halfway between Littleton Island and Cairn Point and perhaps five miles off the head of land where Dr. Kane had taken refuge. Ironically—through quirks of wind, weather, and tide—the Arctic was herding this doomed expedition toward the exact spot that Kane's failed party had named Lifeboat Cove.

Schuman reported that only a few days' worth of coal remained. That was the final straw for Buddington. He'd had enough of his miserable ship, enough of the frightening ice, and enough of the sea.

Land was in sight, and the way to shore lay open. With the fresh ice encasing the ship measuring less than twelve inches in thickness, Buddington figured the hull and coal would last just long enough to run the *Polaris* ashore and ground it.

For all its valiant service, the *Polaris* would be abandoned.

Had cooler heads prevailed, something different might have resulted. With skill and reduced canvas, the ship could have been sailed to safety. After all, Hudson and Scoresby never had steam-driven vessels. But Buddington had reached the end of his rope. He wanted off his ship. To ensure that goal, he ordered the foresail cut up into bags to hold the remaining coal and loaves of bread.

In defense of Buddington's decision, Schuman found that the sprung planking at the six-foot mark had snapped completely off in the storm. Surprisingly, however, the propeller sustained no further damage, and the rudder still could steer the ship.

The arrival of a fresh wind from the northeast broke the ship free, and Buddington ordered the jib, mainsail, and staysail set. Ignominiously the *Polaris* sailed obediently to her fate and ran aground. When she struck bottom, she swung dejectedly around to lie with her starboard rail facing the beach.

The shallow, sloping bay ran for another four hundred yards before silt and gravel rose out of the powdery water. A shallow beach appeared and vanished at the pleasure of the tide, but solid ground was at hand. Climbing over the piled ice hummocks and wading through the shallow water would bring the men beyond the clutches of the remorseless sea and its grinding battlefields of ice. At the cost of their ship, the remnants of the first United States polar expedition had finally reached the relative safety of the Greenland coast. It was a price that Buddington was willing to pay.

But what of their companions on the ice? The dreadful night had kept all aboard the ship fighting for their lives. Battling the rising water and breaking ice from the standing rigging left no time to look for anyone stranded on the ice floe. The clear, fine morning found the sailors exhausted, but no more so than Tyson's company.

Chester and Hobby claimed they had looked for their ship-mates. Chester climbed to the crow's nest and scanned the horizon with his spyglass. "I was up and down the masthead all day every ten or fifteen minutes," he later testified at the hearing, "until we got to land. I went up there to look for our lost parties, but could not see them at all."

When he spotted something on the ice, Chester thought it might be some of the crates and boxes jettisoned in the dark. Others decided it was black ice or stones and debris, and he never argued the point.

The dark specks he did see about four miles from the ship were most likely Tyson and the others waving their rubber blanket. That was precisely where they were marooned in the middle of Smith Sound. Exactly who decided the sighting was debris was never clarified. Certainly Buddington made no extra effort to send smoke signals or study the observation further. With the exception of Meyer, all the men lost during the night had been a burden to him. Bessel, too, was strangely silent.

Chester noted lamely in the ship's log: "The large floe that our party were on must have stopped to the south of Littleton Island, and very near the east shore of the straits." Other excuses for not seeing their shipmates ranged from the ship's drifting out of sight of the men to the vessel's being hidden by the island.

Many aboard the *Polaris* felt that the men on the ice were better off, as they had all the longboats and most of the supplies. With the whaleboats the stranded crew could reach shore and later sail down the coast, the shipboard sailors reasoned. The crippled *Polaris* could not look for them, so they should search for the *Polaris*, the consensus went. Buddington put their sentiments into words: "As, however, they had the boats, even to the little scow, we were in hopes they would possibly be able yet to make for us." He neglected to mention that he had issued no order for continued efforts to signal the ship's location to the lost men.

All those were simply excuses that begged the true issue. Another, more pervasive thought had wormed its way into the mind of every man standing on the ship's heeling deck, a dark and selfish notion that no one would ever admit to in public: now *it was every man for himself*. They had lost most of their food and gear, their ship was damaged beyond repair, and no rescue was in sight. There was precious little to go around. Freezing and starvation seemed likely. With half the mouths to feed, their chances of surviving suddenly doubled.

It was the ultimate rule of the Arctic: food and fuel are always scarce. Sharing what little you have threatened both donor and recipient. Two weakened individuals would die in the far North where one strong person at least has a chance to survive. The Inuit knew this well and accepted the consequences. Starving villages could not expect help from nearby settlements if it meant endangering that community's resources. A traveling hunter with only enough food for himself would run away from another traveler whom he found starving.

During his earlier searches for the Franklin expedition survivors, Charles Francis Hall encountered two Inuit, Tukeeta and Owwer, who had actually met Francis R. M. Crozier, the captain of HMS *Terror*, and a party of his starving men. To the unfortunate Crozier had fallen the overall command of the surviving 105 men after Sir John Franklin died on June 11, 1847, and the two ships, *Terror* and *Erebus*, were abandoned.

These two Natives with others met the emaciated British near the southwest coast of King William Island. By careful interrogation, Hall pieced together an ugly but heart-wrenching picture. Crozier had approached the party and gestured with his hands to his mouth, repeating the word *seal*. The natives shared some of their seal meat with him and his men. However, somewhere in the one-sided exchange, the sharing threatened the stores of the Natives. Hurriedly they packed up and departed the next morning, despite the pitiful begging and entreating of Crozier, who tried to stop them but was too weak to do so.

The fact that these Inuit had deliberately turned their backs on the starving white men made a lasting impression on Hall. His ideal of the noble Arctic savage vanished in a darkened cloud of disillusionment. Hall penned a bitter pronouncement of their actions in his diary when he learned the full truth of what had happened:

> These 4 families could have saved Crozier's life & that of
> his company had they been so disposed. But no, though

noble Crozier pleaded with them, *they would not stop even a day* to try & catch seals—but early in the morning abandoned what they knew to be a large starving Company of white men.

The whites branded this a callous and selfish act; to the Inuit it was a wise and necessary move.

Blood ties, friendship, or camaraderie all will cause a man to risk his own life for that of another. Military fighting units foster such loyalty, and any combat veteran will tell you that in the grimmest of battles, he really fought for his buddies rather than for his country or high-minded principles. Such closeness would have dictated that the grounded men of the *Polaris* make every possible effort to locate their shipmates.

Regrettably the members of the *Polaris* expedition had no such unity. In reality, they couldn't even call one another shipmates. Divided by nationality, differing loyalties, and conflicting purposes, the crew of the *Polaris* had lost all cohesion. The rigors of the Arctic had reduced them to splintered coteries of men in league with one another.

Were Charles Francis Hall still alive, no doubt greater effort would have been made to retrieve the rest of the crew. Neither Buddington nor Bessel ordered anything more. Sadly none of the crew pressed to continue the search.

So one day's cursory scan of the horizon marked the sum total of all attempts to locate the men separated from the ship during the storm. Tyson and those on the floating ice were left to their own resources.

Strangely the crew did see two blue foxes scampering along the shoreline, which they duly noted in the ship's log. Their actions highlight a pitiful metamorphosis that had overtaken the expedition. Hammered incessantly by the Arctic, the members had lost their initiative, become tentative and timid, and retreated to the passive role of observers. Somehow they must have felt that recording these observations successfully fulfilled their mission and would compensate for their other failures.

The next morning Buddington ordered preparations for leaving the ship. He had slept in Chester's cabin along with Bessel, while

Morton, Bryan, and Mauch retreated to the forecastle. Scraps of clothing and blankets were scrounged from the belongings of Captain Tyson and others not present to protest.

Low tide revealed even more extensive damage to the bow. The entire stem, the curved timber where the bow planks join together, had now completely broken away below the six-foot mark, taking with it the iron sheeting and cross planks. Of the scant pieces of lumber left, several planks on the port side were bent sharply back. Such extensive damage should have rapidly sunk the *Polaris*. Only the insistence of Captain Hall that the bow be double-planked and backed with a watertight bulkhead had saved their lives. Neither Buddington nor Bessel gave the dead man that credit. "I called the officer's attention to it," Buddington noted in his journal, "who only wondered she had kept afloat so long."

Slowly the crew dismantled the dying steamship. Being rigged as a fore topsail schooner, the ship had two yards, two booms, gaffs, and two topmasts. Pole by pole the rigging was cut down and laid on the deck. To a sailor this duty must have been painful to perform, akin to disassembling one's home or dissecting a favorite pet. Wading ashore at low tide, the crew carried the spars ashore along with the yards of canvas sail.

Again the sense that Buddington had washed his hands of his long-suffering ship pervades the scene. Until its removal, the standing and running rigging of the *Polaris* remained sufficient to sail the ship southward. The engines still worked, and the rudder and screw could provide some assistance. With the beached ship fully exposing the damage to the keel, repairs were possible. And the ship's carpenter, Nathan Coffin, mad as he was, could have made those repairs.

Perhaps in forsaking his vessel, Buddington relied upon Arctic history. Parry, Kane, and Hayes had all abandoned their ships and survived to tell about it. Odds favored those explorers who had retreated in the spring, hugging the coastline until they encountered a passing whaler or reached native villagers willing to transport them to the closest white settlement.

Unlike Buddington and his crew, those survivors had their small boats. The fourteen men stacking timber, canvas, and sail bags filled with coal and bread on the beach had no means of transportation other than their feet. The dogs and sleds drifted on the ice with Tyson's group. Travel overland by foot was suicidal. No party could push or carry enough supplies by hand to survive. Sir John Franklin's expedition had proved that conclusively. Scott's Antarctic failure reconfirmed that grim fact years later.

Exactly what Buddington's plans for the future were are unclear. Enough timber existed for Coffin to build a lifeboat, even cabins on the shore. Being near Lifeboat Cove, he remembered rumors of an iron boat abandoned there by Dr. Hayes. Hayes and his men had mentioned it on their return ten years earlier. It is likely Buddington hoped that a tardy whaler might cross their path before the whaling season ended or expected that the United States Navy would come looking for them when the expedition failed to return. For the moment being on solid ground was enough for him.

The nineteenth of October dawned clear and tranquil, as so often happens following a storm. The northeast winds scoured the skies of all clouds and blew the obstructing ice from the straits. Standing on the shore Sieman and Hayes marveled at the irony. The sea before them lay clear of the ice pack as far as the eye could see. Dark water sparkled to the horizon southward and westward. Sadly there was nothing they could do about it. Reluctantly the men returned to their tasks of stacking and piling the meager collection of crates and boxes that constituted their winter supplies.

Then the yelp of barking dogs reached their ears.

Excitement gripped the working party. It had to be Tyson! Tyson with all the extra food and supplies. The sailors rushed about seeking to pinpoint the sounds echoing off the low foothills. Several men waded into the water and scanned the ocean for a floating island bearing Tyson's group into their cove. Only an empty sea greeted them. Other men rushed along the southern rim of their harbor, expecting to see their separated companions trudging along the beach.

Those who looked inland spotted tiny figures approaching from the east. Since the sixteenth the sun had skipped along the horizon well below the Greenland mountains. With the low winter's light glaring across the snow, the backlighting transmuted the approaching party into ghostly, shimmering images.

Slowly the shadows fused into two figures driving a sled.

Chapter Twelve

ADRIFT

The fear of death has long ago been starved and frozen out of me; but if I perish, I hope that some of this company will be saved to tell the truth of the doings on the Polaris. *Those who have baffled and spoiled this expedition ought not to escape. They cannot escape their God!*
—CAPT. GEORGE TYSON, ON THE ICE, 1873

As he watched the *Polaris* slip behind the island, hope and despair struck Tyson in the pit of his stomach like a fist. Why did they not come? Surely someone had seen them. He could clearly make out the deck and the vacant crow's nest, so anyone looking for them had to see the black rubber blanket flapping in the wind. The vessel was making way under power and sail—which boded both well and ill for the men on the floe.

Long moments passed while Tyson wrestled with his misgivings. He sank to the ground while the crew returned to their blankets and cooking fires. The wind picked up again and tore at the canvas laid across the ice hummocks for shelter. His mind turned to saving the canvas from being ripped apart by the rising wind.

Poles for the supply cache he had been building when the storm struck still lay on the far side of their ice floe, so Tyson persuaded two men to retrieve them.

Half an hour later, the two returned to report they had spotted the *Polaris* again. Elated, the navigator jogged to the farthest point of the ice cake and pulled open his spyglass. The *Polaris* was indeed there, lying in the shelter of the island. *And she was tied up.*

No smoke issued from her stack, and all the sails were furled. Facing as she was into the wind, Tyson assumed she was tied to the surrounding ice, although he could not make out any ice hawsers. The uneasiness returned. She could not be disabled, he thought. She was steaming when he last saw her. Don't they intend to come over? he asked himself.

As he pondered his question, the ice beneath his feet began to move.

Tyson looked about. The ivory hills and tumbled landscape shifted before his eyes. Their floe had broken loose. The rising wind had dislodged the crumpled floe and wrenched it free from its wedged position between the two grounded icebergs.

They were drifting away from the tethered *Polaris*.

Ice and slush accumulated within the channel separating the ship from the moving floe, but the whaleboats could cross the opening if they hurried. Already larger slabs drifted threateningly closer to the dark gap of water.

Tyson raced back and exhorted the men. "We must start immediately," he shouted over the rising wind. To his astonishment, his words fell on unheeding ears. Instead of jumping to the task, the men stumbled about like automatons, collecting every scrap and article of their clothing as if they were precious jewels. Faced with the choice of speed or parting with their possessions, the crew opted to collect their scattered goods.

While Tyson ranted and raved for them to leave their trash, the men slowly packed one boat with everything that once littered their base. Naturally pushing and dragging the overloaded craft across the broken ice proved arduous and painfully slow. Exasperated, Tyson rushed ahead of the grumbling and muttering crew, leading the Inuit and the cook to the launching site.

Before he had stumbled two hundred yards, a blizzard struck, and the erstwhile leader vanished in a shroud of swirling ice and snow. Tyson backtracked to find only Jackson following his footprints. The Inuit had retreated. When the cook realized that he alone followed Tyson, he, too, fled back to the struggling boat party.

At long last the boat reached the far edge of the ice floe. Frightened by the wind-whipped strait with its churning slabs of ice, the men hesitated to enter their overloaded whaleboat. Tyson put his shoulder to the craft, launching it before he jumped inside. The rest clambered in, following their worldly belongings into the jaws of danger.

While the craft bobbed along the ice, Tyson ordered out oars. To his consternation, only three oars appeared. *And no rudder!*

In their misguided zeal to save their belongings, no one had shipped the tiller, sails, or the rest of the oars. Sourly Tyson wondered if the omissions were deliberate, as the men clearly were reluctant to leave the ice floe.

What followed was folly. Without sufficient oars and with no tiller, the vessel made no headway in the turbulent seas. The wind rose to gale force and easily tossed the whaleboat about before blowing it back against the icy island. Nothing could be gained by further effort, Tyson realized. "We shall all have to suffer much for such obstinacy," he cried out to the unheeding wind.

Pulling the boat back onto the ice sapped the last of their strength. Night was falling as the party flopped exhausted onto the edge of the floe.

"We have to drag the boat back where she was," Tyson ordered. Distressingly no one had the energy. Leaving the loaded boat, the party retreated to the higher center of their migrating home.

Tyson crawled under a scrap of canvas and rolled himself in a musk ox hide. Chewing a piece of frozen meat, he fell fast asleep. He had been on his feet for forty-eight hours without rest.

While he slumbered, the storm descended with full force upon the bay. Waves and fetch roiled the pack ice, and wind piled drifts of snow against the jumbled hummocks. Too exhausted to dream, Tyson slept on, unaware of the changes raging about him. A piercing cry from the Inuit jostled Tyson to his senses.

Bolting to his feet, he screwed his mittened hands into his eyelids to wipe away the frost that had glued them shut. The wavering Arctic twilight greeted him. He'd slept the entire night, he suddenly realized.

Focusing his eyes, Tyson followed the outstretched arm of Ebierbing, and his heart jumped into his throat. The storm had broken their floe into pieces. Salt water lapped at the edge of their island of ice less than 75 feet away! The one on which Tyson and the seamen slept measured less than 150 yards across.

Worse, the loaded whaleboat with the bulk of their provisions and the pole tent drifted silently away on the other slice of their is-land. Urgently Tyson roused the sleeping sailors. Confused, tired, and fearful, the men could only stand and stare at the growing separation. Finally the lead of frigid water widened beyond any hope of jumping the gap, and Tyson slumped helplessly onto the snow to watch the current catch the other piece and swirl it into the mists.

The effects of the storm continued to hammer their tiny king-dom. The heavy seas, running under the bite of the wind, chipped away relentlessly at the edges of the diminishing plate. As he watched inch after inch of ice break off, Tyson could only pray: "God grant that we may have enough to stand upon." Laconically he realized the *Polaris* could sail right up to the stranded men if it ever sighted them.

For two more days, the tempest raged while Tyson's hungry party huddled around their flimsy camp. Strangely, spotted seals bobbed nonchalantly in the heaving waters. For these marine ani-mals, the storm and the breaking ice pack were simply part of their normal day.

Now the hunting skills of Ebierbing would prove crucial. Most of their food had drifted away in the other boat. The seals could provide not only food but also oil for cooking and to keep them warm. Cautiously he slid his kayak into the water and paddled toward the unsuspecting animals. Using his barbed-tipped bone spear instead of his rifle so as not to alarm the creatures, he caught one seal on each day. He might have taken more, but the cheering and rushing about of the grateful sailors prompted the other seals to dive out of sight.

While Ebierbing hunted, Tookoolito and Merkut dutifully un-packed their seal-oil lamps and set up camp. When Ebierbing re-turned with his kill, the ice floe took on the appearance of a slaughterhouse. Blood streaked the snow as cubes of seal meat and blubber were divided among the party. The hungry men wolfed down the slices of raw meat. Nothing was wasted. Congealed blood from the kill was collected in a tin pot, mixed with snow, and cooked into a thin soup over one of the stone lamps. The blubber was diced and squeezed to coax its release of precious oil for the lamps. With that meager meal in their bellies, the men retreated to their robes to await their fate.

Two days later Ebierbing cried, "I see the boat!"

Tyson swung his telescope where the Inuit pointed. He spotted the whaleboat holding their supplies lying on the ice at the extreme end of the ice pack. The perversity of the winds and currents had reunited the divided portions of the original floe and returned the errant boat to the far side of the ice. Tyson and the Native, along with six sled dogs, hurried to retrieve the craft before the plates drifted apart again. Rocking against each other as they were, it was only a matter of minutes before this would happen. Hitching the dogs to the boat, the two men managed to slide it across to their side. Now the party was reunited with the sum of their food and furnishings.

Over the next day, their tiny domain drifted tantalizingly close to the shore of Greenland, to the east, close enough to tempt Tyson to consider making a dash for land. But the young ice would neither support a man's weight nor allow them to use their boats. While the captain pondered his dilemma, the wind blew their raft back westward toward Ellesmere Island. Playing with the floating base like a cat plays with a mouse, the sea batted them back and forth until it finally tired of the game and abandoned the insignificant sliver of ice holding nineteen souls in the very middle of the strait.

Faced with the facts that they could not reach land and that their minuscule oasis of ice would hardly withstand another gale, Tyson decided to move camp to a larger island abutting their plate. Hitching the teams of dogs, Tyson and the Inuit pulled one whaleboat after the other over to firmer ice.

Just as they completed this task, the gap between their islands started to widen. The Eskimo's two kayaks still remained on the smaller floe. None of the worn-out sailors responded to Tyson's plea to save those useful craft. When Ebierbing risked his life by jumping the gap to save his boat, the cook, Jackson, and Lindermann followed. Despite their efforts, they could save only one kayak. Now they were down to a single kayak, essential for hunting seals, and two whaleboats. Soon even that number would change.

Ironically all their efforts had returned them to the original section of the ice floe where Tyson had first built his pole tent beside the *Polaris*. For all their risks and pains, they were back where they started and much worse off, for land was far beyond reach.

Still, the two whaleboats were intact, and they had retrieved two compasses, twenty-seven cans of preserved meat, and eight hundred pounds of bread.

Stoically the Inuit realized that this place was to be home for some time. The men commenced building better shelter. Ebierbing excelled at this task. Using his long-bladed knife to cut blocks of snow, he set about creating igloos. Hard packed by the wind, the snow shaped readily under the Inuit's skilled hands. First, he leveled the floor before building a raised platform opposite the future entrance. This elevated portion served as the sleeping quarters, designed to catch the rising heat from the seal-oil lamp. Then, cutting blocks as he went, Ebierbing built the spiraling walls up around himself, carefully shaping, carving, and sloping each successive layer until an arched roof enclosed the entire structure.

A low, tunneled entrance completed the building. Inside, bodies would sleep packed tightly together like sardines in a tin. Scarcely large enough for a man to stand in the very center, the structures were designed for survival rather than luxury. Heat from the stone lamp and body warmth would keep the interior just above freezing regardless of the subzero temperatures raging outside.

Working quickly, Hans and Ebierbing constructed an entire village, building an igloo for each of the Inuit families, a half-igloo for Tyson and Meyer, and a larger branched structure for the crew, which had a storehouse and cooking room attached by tunneled corridors.

Without a stone lamp of their own, the crewmen adapted a tin pemmican can and a strip of twisted canvas for the wick. Tyson and Meyer managed the delicate task of keeping their lamp lit without difficulty. The crew did not. Half the time they set the entire tin of seal oil ablaze, and the other half they managed to smoke themselves out of their dwelling.

In frustration they did an extremely foolish and dangerous thing: they broke apart one of the whaleboats and used it for firewood. Again the ugly lack of discipline endangered them all. Since Tyson had never formally commanded the crew, and since he had no firearms while they did, he could do little to stop the piecemeal cannibalizing of the boat for fuel.

In his journal Tyson noted his helplessness: "This is bad business, but I cannot stop them, situated as I am, without any other authority than such as they choose to concede to me. It will not do to thwart them too much, even for their own benefit."

Now a single kayak and one whaleboat remained for the party of nineteen.

Doing his simple arithmetic, he noted the problems a single boat presented: "These boats are not designed to carry more than six or eight men, and yet I foresee that all this company may have yet to get into the one boat to save our lives, for the ice is very treacherous." He was to prove unerringly prophetic.

More calculating revealed another alarming fact: Their island was locked in the center of the massive Greenland ice pack. Drifting erratically southward at a snail's pace, the pack kept them centered in the middle of Smith Sound and eventually Baffin Bay while preventing their reaching the shore. It would be a good six months before the spring breakup released their island to drift ashore or enabled them to row to land. Neither could they expect rescue by another sailing ship before spring. No whaling vessels would venture this far north in search of whales before April or May.

Despite the twenty pounds of chocolate, canned hams, dried apples, tinned meat and pemmican, dividing that amount of food by nineteen mouths revealed a shocking conclusion: there was simply not enough to feed them all for the six months it would take for spring breakup to free the ice. Captain Buddington's relief, expressed after the death of Captain Hall, that they would not starve to death on the ice was proving premature—at least for this fraction of the crew.

Friction reared its ugly head almost immediately. Tyson quarreled with Meyer over their location. Meyer placed their last sighting of the *Polaris* close to Northumberland Island. "I ought to know," the Prussian sniffed when Tyson questioned the sighting, "for I took observations only a day or two before."

Tyson disagreed. "Of course he ought to know, and of course he *ought* to be right," the maritime navigator griped over the landsman Meyer's reckoning. "But my recollection is that Northumberland Island is larger than the one the *Polaris* steamed behind." That island had to be Littleton, he judged. Both islands arise in Smith Sound where it narrows into Smith Passage, but Littleton Island is considerably north of the other island.

Next someone stole the remaining chocolate. After four servings the entire twenty pounds vanished. What canned meat or bread was also purloined was impossible to tell from the disorganized piles. While Tyson and Meyer took pains to measure out the daily rations of eleven ounces per person, no practical way existed to place a guard on the supplies. The subzero weather prevented anyone's standing watch. Grumbling increased as the navigator tightened the daily allotment. Stealing and hoarding rose, offsetting his restrictions and defeating his efforts.

Alarmingly the seals disappeared with the departing sun. As the temperature fell, open leads of water froze over, and the animals no longer sunned themselves on top of the ice. Choosing to spend all of their time in the relatively warmer water, the seals could be found only when they surfaced at breathing holes to gulp fresh air before diving again. No white man in the group could spot the two-inch airholes amid the jumbled and tossed *sastrugi*.

Finding a breathing hole was just the beginning. Seals cleverly scattered their openings randomly across the ice and visited them irregularly. Just locating a breathing spot was no guarantee that a seal would stick its nose through it. Only an Inuit hunter had the patience to sit silent and unmoving beside a seal hole for the thirty-six to forty-eight hours it usually took for the animal to show.

If he was lucky enough to be at the right hole at the right time, the hunter had to quickly strike the seal in the center of its rounded head with his spear. The barbed point of the spear would penetrate the thin skull and keep the creature from sinking while the man furiously enlarged the hole. Only then could the prey be pulled onto the ice.

That left two men, Hans and Ebierbing, to hunt for them all. Both men excelled at this sort of thing. Disturbingly, the bad joss of the whole expedition appeared to divide itself to follow the men on the ice as well as Captain Buddington and the ship. Good hunting failed to favor the Inuit's tireless efforts. Three weeks passed without a single catch. Belts were cinched tighter as the rations grew slimmer. "May the great and good God have mercy on us, and send us seals, or I fear we must perish," Tyson scribbled in his journal.

With little seal oil remaining, the meat rations were eaten frozen. Reserving the precious oil for heating the igloos, Tyson even cut back on using it to melt ice for fresh water. Men turned to eating snow.

The dogs, too, suffered, starving faster than the crewmen. By the end of the month, the crew shot five dogs and ate them. After that the daily meal consisted of dried biscuit, usually one and one-half crackers per person.

By the first of November, the weather cleared enough for Tyson to make out Cary Island some twelve miles southeast. If they could reach it, they would have solid land beneath their feet. In desperation Tyson ordered a run for the distant shore with the remaining dogs. Leaving early in the morning with their heavily loaded sled, the entire group pushed across the roughened surface in the dim twilight. The thickened ice easily supported their progress for several miles.

As they were crossing a crevasse roofed over with windblown snow, the ice bridge collapsed under the weight of the sled. Only the frantic scrambling of the men saved the sled and all their possessions from the gaping maw with its waiting dark waters. Even then, half the crew had to leap back to rejoin the rest. Discouraged, Tyson wrote: "Fate, it seems, does not mean that we shall either get back to the *Polaris*, or even reach the shore. Here we are, and here, it seems, we are doomed to stay."

As if to punish this escape attempt, the Arctic hurled a fierce storm at the stranded group. Only the rapid building of new igloos saved them all from freezing. Days of howling winds and whiteout conditions in which one could scarcely see the hand in front of one's face precluded any further efforts to reach land. Trapped inside his snow hut, Tyson collapsed from lack of food and sheer exhaustion. "The weather is so bad no one pretends to leave the hut," he wrote. "We are all prisoners."

Miraculously Ebierbing continued to hunt in the worst conditions. On the sixth of November, he returned with one spotted seal and in the process almost lost his life. Stumbling about in the storm, Kruger spotted a white creature climbing stealthily over the hummocks and readied his pistol to shoot the approaching polar bear. Waiting in ambush, the sailor drew a bead on the white fur.

Just as Kruger's finger tightened on the trigger, the face of Ebierbing hovered above the pistol sights. Shaken, the seaman quickly lowered his revolver. The snow-dusted fur parka of the Inuit caused Kruger to mistake him for an ice bear. Only fortune had prevented Kruger from killing the one man capable of keeping them all supplied with food.

One small spotted seal did not go far. Tyson and the others eagerly drank the warm blood and consumed the entire animal, devouring the raw meat "skin, hair, and all." Still, the dark days melded into equally dark nights to the hungry cries of Puney and the other Inuit children. Weak from hunger, the adults trembled as they moved listlessly about the camp.

Again parties unknown raided the meager supplies of bread. "The bread has disappeared very fast lately," Tyson scribbled in alarm. "We have only eight bags left."

On the twenty-second, Ebierbing took another seal. Reserving part of the animal for Thanksgiving, the crew passed about a can of dried apples to mark the occasion. Starving as they were, images of food incessantly occupied their thoughts on that occasion. Few found any reason to give thanks.

Tyson assuaged the gnawing hunger in his belly by warming a few strips of frozen seal entrails over a guttering lamp before he gobbled them down.

"No doubt many of my friends who read this will exclaim, 'I would rather die than eat such stuff!' " he penciled in his journal. "You think so, no doubt; but people can't die when they want to; and when one is in full life and vigor, and only suffering from hunger, he don't want to die. Neither would you," he added philosophically.

Hardship only widened the gulf between the various factions instead of fostering cohesion. Old loyalties, already formed aboard the *Polaris* and never submerged very deeply, resurfaced with a vengeance. The instrument of hunger hammered the wedge of discontent deeper into the marooned group.

Meyer and Tyson, essentially the only officers, grated on each other's nerves worse than when they were aboard ship and refused to support each other. The German crew reverted to speaking only their native tongue. Tyson moved in with Ebierbing and Tookoolito, where he could at least understand them when they spoke English. The navigator complained that in the men's hut, only German was spoken and he could understand not a single word of it.

Responding in kind, the Germans lined the floor of their igloo with canvas yet refused to help drag similar tent scraps to Tyson's hut. Only the two Scandinavians, Lindquist and Johnson, and the cook and the steward helped Tyson to floor his igloo.

Darkly Tyson worried about his lack of firearms. Still puzzled by Buddington's arming of the crew after Hall's death, the navigator lamented that he had neither rifle nor pistol while every other member of the crew had both. Sourly he blamed his commitment to duty for his "unpleasant situation." "While I was looking after the ship's property," he wrote, "the men secured their guns and pistols." Had he selfishly gathered his possessions and armed himself the night of separation as the crew did, he told himself, he would be far better off. "I am the worst off of all," he bemoaned, "for I have neither gun nor pistol of my own, and can only make a shot by borrowing of Joe. This is a disadvantage in other respects; the men know it; they are all armed, and I am not."

Craftily Tyson tried to inveigle a firearm out of Ebierbing, but the savvy Inuit refused to part with any of his weapons. "Joe," the navigator scribbled in his diary, "has both a shot-gun and a pistol; but he didn't seem to care to give either up, and I will not force him to."

Deepening cold layered atop the oppressive darkness that December brought. The Arctic winter swallowed any distinction between day and night. Mocking the prolonged starvation of those clustered on the drifting ice, the skies overhead unleashed a spectacular show of lights. Streamers of blue and violet danced and coiled across the heavens, unfolding their beauty to anyone with the energy to appreciate it.

A form of rheumatism struck down Hans at the very time his

hunting skills were most needed. Ebierbing doubled his efforts with no success. Without light the seals spent only scant minutes with their noses pressed to their breathing holes before diving away. Without seals no polar bears appeared. Without bears no foxes followed to scavenge scraps from their kills. The delicate food chain shifted brutally into reverse. Absolutely nothing edible inhabited the stranded men's domain.

"The darkness is on us," Tyson wrote heavily. While the navigator gave vent to his blackest thoughts in his notebooks, Meyer limited his writing to sterile notations like "colder today; wind blowing from the southwest."

Rations now were reduced to a few ounces. Food occupied the waking thoughts of all. Insidiously their starvation worked to perpetuate itself. Lack of the proper nutrients robbed them of the energy needed to drag their boat and supplies to safety if the opportunity to reach land had presented itself. The white men huddled listlessly inside their igloos and dreamed of feasts long past.

Other thoughts, far more foul and unspeakable, crept along the corners of the hungry men's minds, ideas that surpassed the limits of humanity.

One day Ebierbing handed his coveted revolver to the startled Tyson. Looking over his shoulder at the sullen sailors watching them, Ebierbing placed his pistol firmly into Tyson's hands as his eyes drifted back to the Inuit families sitting outside their igloo. Ebierbing's gaze rested on the children playing in the snow. Then the Inuit looked back at the seamen.

"I don't like the look out of the men's eyes," Ebierbing whispered darkly.

A cold shiver shot down Tyson's spine as he fingered the pistol. *He thinks they will first kill and eat Hans and his family,* the navigator thought. *And then he knows Hannah's, Puney's, and his turn will be next!*

Cannibalism? The very idea jarred the captain. Tyson looked at Tookoolito. The fear and worry in her eyes confirmed that she felt as her husband did. The Inuit sensed that the sailors, driven by the pains of hunger, would eat them.

They had good cause to worry. The cracked long bones and

knife marks on the skulls of the Franklin expedition's skeletons told of cannibalism. Inuit all along the coast knew of this. If the ordered British would resort to eating their own, what could be expected from this lawless bunch? A tender young child would make their starving mouths water. Even the solid John Herron wrote in his diary: "The only thing that troubles us is hunger; that is very severe. We feel sometimes as though we could eat each other."

Added to this was the general feeling among the party that the Inuit were less than human. The Natives' strange customs, lack of bathing, and habit of eating their meat raw fostered that perception. On more than one occasion, the Inuit's cabins aboard the *Polaris* had had to be cleaned and deloused by the crew when the smell and offal inside grew too much even for the rank seamen. It was all relative, however. The sailors themselves were no paragons of cleanliness. But seeing the Natives turn their rooms into what the white men considered a pigsty contributed to the seamen's view that the Inuit were animals.

Tyson slipped the revolver into his pocket and nodded to his friend. An unspoken bond was established between them. In exchange for the pistol, the captain would guard the Inuit with his life. Later Tyson scribbled in his diary, "God forbid that any of this company should be tempted to such a crime! However, I have the pistol now, and it will go hard with any one who harms even the smallest child on this God-made raft."

From a practical standpoint, eating the Natives would deprive the men of their only effective hunters. Tyson recognized this. While he doesn't mention it in his diary, most likely he circulated among the crew and expressed that idea. He wrote:

> Setting aside the crime of cannibalism—for if it is God's will that we should die by starvation, why, let us die like men, not like brutes, tearing each other to pieces—it would be the worst possible policy to kill the poor natives. They are our best, and some may say only, hunters; no white man can catch a seal like an Eskimo, who has practiced all his life. It would indeed be "killing the goose which lays the golden egg."

Fortunately two things averted such an unthinkable event. First, Hans recovered, adding his strength to the opposition once more. Second, he caught a fox, which the men devoured down to the last bone. For the time being, the thoughts of eating the Inuit receded.

Looking for ways to divert their thoughts from food, the Germans seized upon the reward given the crew of the *Hansa* who had experienced a similar situation. For surviving their drift on the ice, their government awarded each man a gift of one thousand talers. Animated by their greed, the Teutonic contingent swaggered about the ice with their rifles and pistols and boasted that Congress would likely double their pay. The sailors forgot that they had no control over their destiny. No one would collect a cent if they never returned.

Christmas arrived with strong winds raking the ice floe. Even though it meant using the last of their ham and dried apples, the event called for some sort of celebration. "Our Christmas dinner was gorgeous," Tyson wrote. "We each had a small piece of frozen ham, two whole biscuits of hard bread, a few mouthfuls of dried apples, and also a few swallows of seal's blood!"

John Herron, the steward, had balked at eating sealskin on the first of December because "the hair is too thick, and we have no means of getting it off." By Christmas hunger had erased his doubts about eating anything. Of the banquet, he wrote, "We had soup made from a pound of seal blood, which we had saved for a month." After adding that to their mulligan stew, he remarked, "the whole was boiled to a thick soup, which, I think, was the sweetest meat I ever ate."

With that feast went the last of the apples and the one surviving canned ham. Taking stock of their remaining food, Meyer and Tyson found six bags of dried bread and nine cans of pemmican. The cold and darkness continually conspired to thwart the Inuit's search for game. With the open leads sealed under thin ice, neither man could paddle the one kayak far in search of seals, nor could they spot the dark heads, for there was no open water. By the end of December, Tyson's hunger forced him to gnaw on cooked scraps of dried sealskin that Tookoolito had saved for repairing their clothes. Even the strips of seal blubber that had been burned dry of all their residual oil in the stone lamps were fished out of the sooty bowls and wolfed down.

By this time the daily intake of those on the ice was, at best guess, less than five hundred calories. Nazi nutritionists calculated that their slave laborers would need a minimum of eight hundred calories a day to perform useful labor for a period of four to six months before they starved to death. While the men on the ice floe reduced their activity whenever possible, the weather was also considerably colder for them, requiring more calories to keep warm.

So, like the unfortunate captives of the Third Reich, the company of the *Polaris* was also starving. Their symptoms included listlessness, weakness, and constant thoughts of food as their shrunken stomachs groaned and knotted in emptiness. Their hair, nails, and teeth became brittle as the body dissolved itself in search of essential nutrients. Scurvy attacked them all, loosening their teeth and causing their feet to swell. Stocky individuals with more muscle and body fat would last longer than the thin ones, but all suffered from lack of vitamin C.

To make matters worse, Nature conspired to starve them over prolonged periods before tossing a few mouthfuls of food at them just when they were on the verge of collapse. Then the agonizing cycle repeated itself. Tyson and his party were experiencing firsthand Buddington's fears of starving on the ice.

On the twenty-eighth, a lead opened in the ice. Hans shot a seal, which sank before they could retrieve it. The next day Ebierbing shot another Greenland seal, and anxious moments followed as the men raced to launch the kayak while the dying animal drifted away. Fortune, however, smiled that day, and the animal was caught and dragged ashore.

What followed was an orgy of gruesome proportions. The entire skin, with its blubber so vital for the lamps, was stripped off. Then the carcass was rolled onto its back, and the abdomen carefully opened to retain all the blood inside the cavity. The clotted blood was swallowed whole, while cupfuls of the steaming blood were drunk before it cooled. Liver, brain, heart, and meat disappeared uncooked into the shrunken stomachs of the nineteen people. In deference to the Inuit custom, the eyeballs were given to the youngest in the party, baby Charlie Polaris. Even the entrails were wiped clean on the snow and set aside for later.

Normally sinew and strips of skin would be saved for harness, rope, and clothing, but not that day. The men even ate the membranes the Inuit saved for covering the windows in their igloos. What good was having windows when the transparent tissue would ease the hunger pains that racked the men's stomachs? they reasoned.

New Year's dinner brought the usual watery soup made by floating a minute square of dried pemmican in a cup of warm water. Some men sarcastically referred to the broth as "pemmican tea." This night the seal intestine added a second course. Tyson dined on two feet of frozen gut with relish. Smacking his lips, he scribbled, "and I only wish we had plenty of that, but we have not."

Persistently the ice erased its openings and sealed the watery leads. Hunger preoccupied everyone's thoughts, entertaining their dreams along with every waking moment. Pilfering of the food supplies resumed. "The provisions are disappearing very fast—faster than the distribution of rations will account for," the navigator noted. With tongue in cheek, he added, "there must be some leak." Yet little could be done to prevent it. The thin clothing and weakened state of all precluded posting a watch. Anyone left outside for long would freeze to death.

With hunger came hallucinations and fanciful thoughts. Having satisfied themselves that their suffering would reap them great financial rewards from Washington, the men fantasized that they could reach shore and walk overland to Disko. Despite Tyson's warnings that the ice floe was drifting inexorably west, several of the crew insisted that a run to the east would get them ashore. Their delusions infected Ebierbing, who considered making the trek with his family. Certainly if anyone could do it, the Inuit stood the best chance.

Shaken by his stalwart Inuit's admission, Tyson worried even more about the stronger men splitting apart from the company, taking the last of the food, and making a dash to the east. Among the enfeebled party, a handful of men stood out as far healthier and stronger than the rest. They acted as ringleaders, and Tyson judged these sailors to be the thieves who had pilfered the stores. How else could they have retained their energy and strength when all the rest crawled feebly about for want of nourishment? he reasoned.

Without a doubt, if the group divided, everyone would be lost, Tyson argued. Even the fittest among them lacked the strength to cover the distance. And it was suicidal to try to reach land by going east. No one could carry enough to survive. The dogs were all eaten, and the unruly men had burned the sled for fuel. The last remaining whaleboat was far too heavy to drag any distance, and it was needed intact in case their floating base should break apart. If there were those who doubted this would eventually happen, they had only to listen to the growing grinding and creaking that arose from the ice beneath their feet.

Moreover, Disko was still a long way off, not only to the south but to the east. Meyer's last sextant sighting had placed them at 72°N, near the middle of Davis Strait and far to the west of the shores of Greenland. The party on the ice floe had drifted to a spot more than three hundred miles from their point of separation from the *Polaris* and nearly six hundred miles south of the lonely mound of shale and stones that covered the half-buried coffin of their late leader, Charles Francis Hall.

Chapter Thirteen

ON THE BEACH

It would be very desirable indeed if the men could acquire the taste for Greenland food; since all experience has shown the large use of oil and fat meats is the true secret of life in these frozen countries.
—SIR JOHN ROSS, 1832

The condition of those men lining the shore beside the dying *Polaris* was little better than that of George Tyson's group, nor would their lives improve. Unlike their compatriots, they had reached land, but that was all. The cold, darkness, and famine extended their fingers across both ground and water.

Buddington, Chester, and Bessel crowded together on the shore as the sled approached. The rest of the crew rushed to the edge of the ice and waved their hands wildly. Loping across the snow, the dog team and its riders came on, advancing with measured pace, until the bone-tipped runners of the sled flashed in the reflected light. The cries of joy died in the men's throats, and disappointment filled their hearts.

The new arrivals were Inuit.

Through sign language the Natives indicated they had smelled smoke from the ship's fires and followed their noses overland to the cove. They were from the village of Etah, they said. By chance both Inuit, Miouk and Awahtok, had lived with Dr. Kane during his last polar expedition. In fact, the two men recognized the aging Morton and remembered a few words of English. Since fate and the currents had driven the *Polaris* close to Life Boat Cove, where Kane's ship died, the coincidence is not too remarkable.

The bundle of steel knives stacked amid the ship's stores attracted the Inuit's attention. A metal knife was far superior to the bone devices fashioned by the Inuit and impossible to obtain except in trade from the white man. Since they had little food, the two men offered their services in unloading the ship. In exchange for a shiny new knife, each Inuit would help move supplies from the *Polaris* to the safety of land.

Over the next four days, the Inuit worked hard ferrying goods from the sinking *Polaris* to the beach. The lighter sleds with their bone runners proved invaluable in crossing the crevasses and twisting paths among the piled ice. Coffin had built a heavy sled with its iron-edged runners to carry the whaleboats. Without sled dogs it proved next to useless. Even sawing the ponderous sledge in half did no good. The divided parts were still too heavy to use.

On the shore overlooking the bay, Chester erected the framework for the company's house. The salvaged spars and scraps of lumber became the ridgepole and rafters. With the help of Sieman and Booth, the first mate raised a structure twenty-two feet by sixteen feet. When they ran out of sufficient wood to roof the house, Chester stretched two of the ship's sails over the rafters.

While in the act of transferring his possessions ashore, Dr. Bessel broke through the ice on two occasions. To avoid frostbite, the doctor had to suffer the humiliation of crouching beside the ship's stove like a boy with wet pants while the men continued working. It must have especially galled that educated man that all his training went for naught on the ice, and he could not emulate the skill of the two illiterate savages, who jumped nimbly from floe to floe with effortless agility.

Whenever the German scientist left the security of his observatory or the ship, the Arctic dealt with him harshly. Clearly one of the causes of friction between the late Captain Hall and Bessel arose from the physician's attempts to take over the exploratory part of the expedition. Bitterly he refused to admit that for all his degrees, he did not qualify as an Arctic explorer. His stiff neck brought him nothing but the grief and pain of snow blindness and frostbite.

After all that could be salvaged was transported ashore, Miouk and Awahtok sledded happily away with their shiny knives tucked in the sealskin scabbards swinging from their necks. Before they left, the two Inuit discovered the collection of iron-tipped harpoons and whaling lances from the ship. To the Inuit this was a treasure, indeed. They resolved to return as soon as possible.

The crew of the *Polaris* settled in to take stock of their new home. While they possessed most of the Sharps rifles, the officers found that the metallic cartridges for the heavy rifles resided with the long-lost Tyson company—as did the heavy keg of black powder. Both had been tossed onto the ice during the night the two groups were separated. Among all the men, counting the powder in their flasks, they could muster only eight pounds of powder and a handful of Sharps cartridges found in their pockets.

Only six tons of coal remained, but piles of scrap wood—stripped from the decking, bunkers, bulkheads, and cabins—ensured that they would not freeze anytime soon. Clothing remained the other critical shortage. Most of the seabags had been thrown off the ship in their panic.

If Buddington had planned on receiving help from the village of Etah, he was sorely mistaken. The people of that place were starving and in desperation quickly fastened upon the white men with their weapons of shiny stone as their salvation. Within one day of leaving, Miouk and Awahtok were back with five more dog teams and four friends—all eager to work for a metal knife. With their help, the heavy galley stove was transported ashore and tiers of bunks built inside the *Polaris* hut. When a crack widened in the ice between the supply depot and the rudimentary cabin, the Inuit unloaded their sleds and carried the cargo over the six-foot gap. For their efforts the crew showered their newfound laborers with spoons, buttons, nails, and other metal objects that the Natives readily fashioned into useful tools. All the while the Natives kept their eyes on the metal harpoons.

Freed up to improve his handiwork, Mr. Chester enlarged the living quarters, adding a galley and attaching a storehouse at right angles to the side wall.

On October 24 Schuman and Odell both agreed that burning their limited coal to keep the pumps going was foolish. Without fanfare they extinguished the fireboxes. Like a dying man taken off his respirator, the USS *Polaris* sank slowly under the weight of the rising water in her hold. Struggling to the end, the ship heeled onto one side and refused to die. Stripped of masts and rigging, gutted of her inner walls, the ship fought to retain her dignity as she lay on her side. Only the blackened and twisted smokestack jutting from the center of the barren hulk gave mute testimony to the once-proud silhouette of the American steamer.

Within a week the rest of the population of Etah arrived via sleds—nine men, three women, and eight children. Feeding these extra mouths sorely taxed Buddington's supplies. Other than the ubiquitous dry biscuit and their salted sections of blubber, there was little enough to go around. Numerous forays in search of fresh game yielded little. Several shots were fired at fleeing caribou, without success. From day to day a fox was shot and added to the cooking pot. How far a scrawny blue fox went in feeding the camp of thirty-eight people can only be imagined.

Throughout the months of November and December, blue foxes, white foxes, and the occasional unwary raven would supply the camp's only fresh meat. Since the usually skittish foxes approached the site only because they, too, were starving, their sparse frames carried little worth eating. For some reason the men of Etah found no seals.

Monotony and fatigue settled over the land base. Morosely the men watched the *Polaris* settle deeper and deeper into the silt of the bay. To those with the gift of insight, the gutted hulk stood as a daily reminder of the expedition's failure.

Excitement rose one day when a man was spotted running across the horizon. From the runner's gait, Buddington and Chester declared it was a white man. Surely he must be one of their separated shipmates, they judged. Morton and a half dozen sailors took off after the distant runner. Only Morton reached him. Disappointedly he returned to announce that the man was an Inuit crossing the ice field in search of food.

For some unknown reason, the Inuit loved to visit the big house, where they would sprawl about on the floor sleeping and disrupting the sailors' movements. Disagreement arose, and the Natives would leave, returning to their hardscrabble settlement. But within a few days, a new group would arrive. And so it went, men and women coming and going on a daily basis. Perhaps the Inuit were stealing bits and pieces from the *Polaris* camp, but Buddington makes no mention of any theft. One main reason the Inuit kept returning was to beg ship's bread from the camp. While the white men's situation was desperate, that of the people of Etah was far worse. Like the starving men with George Tyson, the villagers of Etah were eating their sled dogs.

One hope burned brightly in Captain Buddington's mind. When Dr. Kane had abandoned his camp at Life Boat Cove, he left behind an iron-plated scow and a sizable keg of black powder. Mr. Morton's recollection matched that report. Here in an ironic twist of fate lay the solution to Buddington's two most vexing problems. With plenty of weapons, they were sorely short of powder, and a sturdy boat would go a long way in carrying the crew down south when the ice broke up. Since the bay where they had run the ship aground was close to Kane's old camp, the captain proposed a party to find the needed objects.

Chester, Hayes, Coffin, and Dr. Bessel mounted a search party. Armed with picks and shovels, the four men followed the contour of the land until they reached the site of the earlier expedition. Days of digging about in the snow and driving an iron rod through the wind-hardened crust failed to find any trace of the boat or the powder. Disheartened, the company trudged back.

About the same time the men were searching in vain for Kane's things, an Eskimo family arrived at the camp. Tattoos streaking the woman's face marked her as belonging to Inuit from Ellesmere Island, across Smith Sound. Tattooing was common practice among these "western" Inuit but not usual among the "eastern" Inuit of Greenland. Her husband also carried a bow and arrows, weapons the Greenland Inuit did not use. The man called himself Etookajeu. When his name tripped the seamen's tongues, they promptly renamed him "Jimmy." His wife, Evallu, like Tookoolito, possessed a gift for learning English and soon was conversing freely with Captain Buddington.

Her story confirmed his theory that she had come from the western side of the sound. Five years ago she and a large party had crossed the open water in an *oomiak* along with five kayaks. Of the families that came across, she and her husband and children were all who remained. But what she also told him drove a stake into the heart of any further attempt to find Kane's iron boat.

In their traveling along the coast, Evallu's group had landed near Life Boat Cove and stumbled across the observatory Dr. Hayes had built farther inland. They also found the iron scow and the powder. While the Ellesmere Island Inuit recognized the metal scow as akin to their large *oomiak*, the nature of the black powder eluded them, as their village had not seen any white men at that time.

Anguish clouded Buddington's face as the woman related that the boat they found was useless and far from seaworthy, with the gunnels staved in and the sides full of holes. The Inuit, ever grateful for windfalls, appropriated the wood and canvas from the sails, mast, and oars. The woman told of her people's sleeping inside the observatory and heating the place with their usual stone seal-oil lamps. Tragically one night an open flame was placed too close to the keg, and the black powder exploded, killing five Natives, including the father of her husband, Jimmy.

The Ellesmere Inuit took the deaths in their party as a bad omen in this new land and paddled back to their homeland with the doctor's oars and canvas. Evallu and her husband remained behind and eventually joined the village of Etah. What remained of Dr. Kane's scow was scattered over the eastern slopes of Ellesmere Island in possession of the migrating Inuit.

There would be neither a fortuitous iron boat nor a keg of black powder to make his task lighter, Buddington realized. He also came to the disheartening conclusion that the Inuit would not be able to feed them as he had hoped. It would be a long and hard winter with little to eat. He was no longer on the floating ice, he realized, but the danger of starving was just as great on the land.

With the Natives of dubious help, the crew's survival hung on the sailors' shooting fresh game—a task made all the more difficult by the fact that they possessed so little powder. Every shot at an animal must count. Yet the ravens and bony foxes the men caught hardly fit the bill. Already evidence of scurvy reared its ugly head among the castaways. Booth, pressed into service as a steward, lay confined to his bunk with swollen feet and ankles.

Christmas and New Year's arrived at the base camp with little cause for celebration. The salvaged coal, burned all too freely in the stoves, diminished at an alarming rate. Buddington tried to save fuel by abandoning use of the cast-iron galley stove without much success. The cooking pots turned out to be too large to use on the smaller secondary stove. Finally rations were reduced to one meal a day.

Although they were standing on solid ground, the plight of the men ashore was just as grim as that of their shipmates drifting miles to the south on the ice floe. No mention is made of celebrating either Christmas or the end of a dreadful year. Apparently Buddington and his men did not even have one can of dried apples to open for their special dinner, as Tyson's group had.

On the twentieth of January, the stove swallowed the last lump of coal, and Buddington faced a hard decision. Every scrap of wood he burned meant one less piece he could use to build boats to carry his men southward after breakup. The pile of wood scraps stacked beside the house lasted a mere seven days.

The hand of the Arctic winter bore down heavily on the desolate cove, adding to the crew's discomfort. The only signs of light consisted of scattered ribbons of violet and purple fluttering briefly behind the sable mountains. Without the warming rays of the sun, heat fled the country. All the while the thermometer stayed well below zero. Plummeting as low as 42° below zero, the pitch-black days averaged minus 28°. Without a source of warmth, hunger would no longer be a problem. A man would freeze to death before he starved.

Increasingly fuel proved just as critical as food. To make matters worse, Buddington's group had fallen into the trap of conventional thinking. They had built a traditional-style house out of wood and canvas, whereas snow igloos would have been wiser. Larger, more open, and poorly insulated, the walled tent lost heat readily to the subzero air. Heating the building required burning their precious fuel in large quantities, whereas the Inuit way could heat a cramped igloo with a single seal-oil lamp.

Like Saturn eating his children, the *Polaris* expedition cannibalized the *Polaris*. Wood from the wheelhouse provided two additional days of warmth. During this process, Chester and Buddington watched their men with eagle eyes. No wood considered useful in the construction of their lifeboats was burned. The carpenter collected every brass screw and nail from the dismantling for future use. Hungry and cold as the men were, even the dullest among them realized that a lifeboat was their last and only hope.

February saw the bowsprit, masts, and riggings thrown into the insatiable stove. The hatch to the forecastle had been moved ashore to provide a level platform for Bessel's transit. That, too, found its way into the furnace.

By the end of the month, Buddington counted fifty-one different Inuit coming and going from the camp. During crowded periods the bodies strewn about the canvas floor challenged even the most sure-footed sailor.

Eventually the men's tolerance toward the Inuit began to pay dividends. Evallu repaired the sailors' clothing, and Jim hunted for his newfound friends. Slowly, steadily, the other visitors brought a trickle of fresh meat to trade for odds and ends. Although scarce, the slices of walrus and hare kept the seamen's scurvy at bay, limiting the signs to a few loose teeth, open sores, and swollen ankles.

On the first of March, Awahtah, an ancient Inuit, spotted a polar bear crossing the ice not far from the wreck of the *Polaris*. With his four-foot-long bone-tipped spear in hand, Awahtah took off after the bear. Cracking his whip over the heads of his sled dogs, the hunter and his team vanished into the blowing snow. Three days passed without a sign of the old man. All that time a gale piled drifts against the tent that forced the men to dig out their only entrance.

On the fourth day Awahtah returned to camp with the dead bear riding in his sled basket. When Awahtah took off his sealskin parka, Chester's mouth dropped at the sight of the terrible scars from previous bear encounters covering the old man's back. Obviously the elderly hunter had learned his lessons the hard way.

March saw the sun once again peeking over the powder-blue mountains that rimmed the east like a broken saw blade. Just that added amount of daylight spurred the mate, Chester, to lay plans for their rowboats. With the help of Coffin and Booth, he organized the lumber he had faithfully protected from the woodstove and piled it by the house.

The promise of spring and the Arctic twilight galvanized Dr.

Bessel into action. Over the past six months, the doctor's star had ascended with the death of Captain Hall only to crash precipitously as the Arctic foiled his every attempt at being a polar explorer. Even his battling with Captain Buddington over the man's drinking and the issue of who ultimately controlled the expedition receded into the background following the storm of October 15. The sudden loss of half the crew and the subsequent grounding of the *Polaris* focused all attention on staying alive after that date.

What happened to Buddington's drinking during this time is unclear. He may simply have run out of specimen alcohol to drink, or he may have become more surreptitious about raiding the scientific supplies. Happily for the captain, those who hated him and had kept a record of his drinking were floating miles away on the pack ice, so there is no mention of his being drunk in the camp.

In either case Bessel suddenly lacked the adversary he sorely needed. Without an opponent, the physician retreated into a mind-numbing morass of measurements and magnetic observations. The fledgling rays of the sun, however, rekindled the German's dreams of becoming a world-renowned explorer.

Exploring the Humboldt Glacier fired his imagination. Once there he planned to sled across the frozen Smith Sound and explore Hayes Sound. Studying those areas would fit the bill nicely. The fact that more than one hundred miles of rugged terrain lay between the camp and the Humboldt Glacier failed to faze him. Neither did the miserable history of his previous attempts at being an Arctic traveler.

Immediately Bessel laid plans for his journey. Buddington, perhaps happy at the prospect of being rid of his old nemesis, did nothing to discourage the trip. Maybe the wily captain figured the effort might salvage some of the ruined expedition's honor. Certainly, if nothing else, it would get Bessel out of his hair.

Two sleds and ten sled dogs were purchased at astronomical prices with metal harpoon heads, metal carpenter tools, and the ever precious bits of food. The harsh winter had forced the Inuit to eat all but a few of their dogs. Those that remained were their most prized animals, and they were reluctant to part with any of them. Bessel's timing was poor. In a few months, new litters of puppies would replenish the teams, but Bessel could not wait.

On the thirteenth of April, Emil Bessel, graduate of Jena and Heidelberg, embarked. In preparing for the journey, he made the same ignorant mistakes that had dogged his other trips. First, he overloaded both his sleds. Filling one to the brim with provisions for a month and a half, he then packed the second sledge with "all necessary instruments."

Second, he chose Jim as one driver and Arrowtah, a one-legged Inuit, as the other driver.

As a child, Arrowtah had crushed his leg under a boulder. His mother had been forced to amputate the limb six inches below the knee, and the surgeon of the passing whaler *North Star* had built a wooden leg for the boy in 1850. Dr. Hayes in his travels had repaired the artificial limb. Currently Arrowtah limped around the camp on one he had "fitted with an ankle-joint of his own manufacture," according to Admiral Davis's later description.

Besides his disability's being unsuitable for a rigorous passage over *sastrugi* and ice hummocks, which would tax a two-legged person, Arrowtah's motivations differed greatly from Bessel's. Whereas the good doctor wanted to explore the western side of the sound, Arrowtah hoped to find a wife. Since he was a widower and none of the women along the eastern coast "exactly suited him," again according to Davis, he looked upon Bessel's expedition as an excellent opportunity to find a new mate. Finding a new partner necessitated Arrowtah's traveling to other Inuit villages across the sound. Such villages tended to be more southerly, where game and climate were more favorable.

Whether Bessel understood the man's goals before they left is unknown. Mixing the Prussian's haughty and abrasive attitude with the passive-aggressive defenses of the Inuit could only lead to problems.

Needless to say, within five days Bessel was back in camp, complaining about Arrowtah's insubordination. When Bessel and his two drivers had attempted to cross Rensselaer Bay at the southeastern edge of Smith Sound, they found the unexpected—open water. Detouring first east, then north, and finally northeast, they struggled to circumvent the open sea. However, at every turn sharp-sided hummocks of crumpled pack ice presented formidable if not impassable barriers. Bessel tried cajoling and finally threatening, but the wary Natives refused to drive their sleds into those tumbled dragon's teeth. The doctor took their reluctance for insubordination and laziness, even cowardice. To the Inuit, understanding that the icy ridges would break their sled runners and exhaust them to no good purpose was simply common sense. So they balked. The sudden onset of a storm forced the three men to spend an entire day in a hastily built snow cave. The evil weather only confirmed the Inuit's suspicions that making this trip was a bad idea.

Under a black cloud and an equally gloomy sky, Bessel returned. Looking for a replacement for Arrowtah, he enlisted the help of a man called Ewinokshua, whom Captain Buddington had nicknamed Sharkey. The offer of a long-bladed metal knife so useful in cutting snow blocks for igloos convinced Sharkey to join the team. By mutual consent Arrowtah opted out, as he positively refused to try again, and Bessel would have nothing more to do with him.

Once more Emil Bessel rode forth to conquer the far North. On April 22 he and his new team drove their sleds out of camp. The twilight was cold, clear, and silent. The heavy air carried the soft crunch of the sled dogs' feet and the creak of the sled bindings long after the blue-gray expanse had swallowed the two sleds.

Nine hours later they returned, this time with a badly broken sled runner. When they reached Cape Inglefield, endless rows of jagged *sastrugi* had greeted the party. To Sharkey and even Jim, the way was impassable.

Ingrained in the hunters was the concept of conserving their energy along with their lives, and both men quickly realized they would beat themselves to death in the crossing. Yet Bessel remained adamant. He would not be denied a second crossing. He ranted and railed.

Confronted with this dilemma, the Inuit resorted to an old trick that worked well whenever white men obstinately refused their sound advice. Without Bessel's seeing him, Sharkey purposefully rocked one of his sled's runners over a sharp edge and broke it in two. Now there was no question, they would have to return.

Back at camp even Jim lost heart and refused a third attempt. In fact, none of the Inuit would go with Bessel. The acerbic doctor had alienated them all. Undeterred, the physician convinced the weak-willed Buddington to let him try with only Henry Hobby. Secretly Bessel planned on replenishing his food from the goods left at Thank God Harbor and recruiting new dog drivers from the Natives he expected to meet there. Those suppositions were risky. It never occurred to him that Thank God Harbor was a summer camp for the Inuit, and none would be there. Bessel even offered Hobby two hundred dollars as incentive. Fortunately, the sailor had the good sense to refuse, and the doctor's plans fell through.

Four days later a violent storm hammered the coastline. With the howling wind came another sound, one added atop the clash of the tempest. It seemed to arise from the ground itself, and the men felt it vibrate through the soles of their boots. A low rumbling and grinding shook the ice and reverberated against the watching foothills. The growling ice lifted and rolled like free water under the blows of storm swell punching its underbelly. Before the men's eyes, the vast basin of blue-and-white ice rose and fell, breaking apart with ear-splitting groans. Frozen parapets plunged beneath the leaden sea while spewing foam and froth into the air to freeze. White-walled castles and cities climbed above the floor, only to topple or sink minutes later. All about them the landscape changed and reformed as the sea broke apart the crust that had covered it for so long.

By the end of the day, most of the bay was open, dotted with bobbing and rolling slabs of ice. Breakup had come.

Chester and Coffin laid the keels of both lifeboats on the nineteenth of April. With breakup, work on the boats rose to a feverish pitch. Patched-together scraps of cotton sheet and linen towels would serve as sails for the vessels. Buddington opted for a triangular spritsail, while Chester chose an easy-to-set square sail.

As the builders worked, illness claimed the lives of several Inuit. Most died following a brief but intense inflammation of their lungs. Miouk, one of the first to reach the stranded white men when they came ashore, paid the ultimate price for his discovery. During that time Buddington and Chester also developed respiratory symptoms but recovered rapidly. Most likely the white men had traded, along with their metal knives, pneumococcal pneumonia and tuberculosis with the Natives. Without previous exposure and acquired immunity to these respiratory illnesses, the infected Inuit died quickly.

The Inuit buried their dead in the traditional way, pulling the dead man in his sled up to the top of a bluff. There they placed him in a hole in the snow, sitting upright and facing west with his spear by his side and his sled laid over him. As a sign of mourning, the Native men placed a twist of dried sea grass in their right nostrils, while the women placed a similar amount in their left. To the sailors' horror, the widow of the buried man smothered her youngest child, who was barely six months old. Without a man to hunt for her, food would be hard to come by for the new widow. Whether the woman killed her child to spare it the agony of starvation or to make herself more marriageable was never explained to the startled crew.

May almost claimed the life of Mr. Bryan. While the chastened Bessel puttered close to the camp, Bryan embarked on a sled journey to Rensselaer Harbor with Jim. Since the harbor was the site of Dr. Kane's winter camp, it had the most carefully established meridian measurement along the entire coastline. Bryan intended to use that spot to measure its difference from the *Polaris* camp.

The Arctic played no favorites, and Bryan encountered the same icy teeth that had frustrated Bessel's attempts. However, the amiable chaplain followed his guide's advice and reached Kane's abandoned camp. Searching about, the men found the copper bolt soldered into the crack of a rock that marked Kane's observatory. Nothing else of value remained save a few scraps of wood and iron and shards of broken crockery and glass. Bryan found the graves of two men named Baker and Schubert, members of Kane's expedition. Already, the land was erasing their presence. Wind and weather had almost scoured the white paint lettering their gravestones.

After building an igloo, Bryan did something that nearly cost him his life. He sent Jim back with the sled and kept one dog to pack his gear. Ever obliging, the young man understood that his contract with Jim only included staying one night. The onset of a storm prevented him from taking his sightings that day, so he would have to remain another twenty-four hours to complete his readings. Not wanting to "impose upon the good-natured Eskimo," Bryan insisted that the man return while he waited for clear weather to take his readings. Over Jim's objections, Bryan prevailed, and the Inuit left for the base camp.

Alone, Bryan took his readings and then compounded his error by doing two more foolish things. He ate breakfast and gave all the rest of his provisions to his dog. Then he assembled his gear and tried to strap it to the animal. It proved too heavy for the dog. So instead of lightening the pack, Bryan decided to carry it himself.

Off he trudged, retracing the route back to the *Polaris* camp. With each step the pack grew heavier and heavier. After twenty hours of stumbling across the broken plain, the chaplain abandoned his pack and veered onto the smoother ice covering the inlet.

Exhausted and now hungry, Bryan slipped into a snow-covered crevasse. As he fell, his outstretched arms caught the edges of the crack and saved him from disappearing forever beneath the surface. Soaked from the armpits down, Bryan lurched on with the dog trotting alongside. Without food his strength began to fail, and his situation grew more desperate with each passing hour.

Ahead on the ice, a dark object caught his eye. The dog caught a whiff of something to eat just as the chaplain recognized that the thing was a piece of seal meat. A footrace ensued, which the animal easily won. But Bryan's hunger pangs overcame his love for animals. When he reached the slab of blubber, he beat off the dog before it could swallow the meat whole.

Then Bryan discovered why the normally frugal Inuit had discarded that piece of meat on the ice. It was gamy. The seal that had been killed was a male deep into rut and so rank and strong-tasting that even the Natives refused to eat it. Still, food was food, and Bryan was in no position to be picky. Holding his ravenous dog at bay, he hacked the greasy slab to pieces. Beating back waves of nausea, the young man swallowed chunk after chunk of the pungent blubber until he could stomach no more. The dog wolfed down the rest.

The meat restored his energy, but each ensuing belch reminded him of his offensive meal.

Eight and a half hours later, Bryan stumbled into camp. He had walked the sixty miles back to camp in three days and paid dearly for his mistakes. Snow blindness struck immediately. For two days he could see nothing while his damaged eyelids locked shut and tears constantly flooded down his face. The skin of that face blistered and peeled from frostbite and sloughed off entirely. Wet as

Bryan's feet and legs were, the heat of friction from his boots and leggings probably saved the man from developing frostbite of his lower limbs. Days passed before he healed.

While Bryan recuperated, Coffin and Chester painted the boats, dismantled the empty storehouse, and burned its wood for fuel. On the twenty-seventh of May, Coffin hammered the last nail in place. The two boats were done.

An orgy of killing followed as the sailors gathered fresh meat for their escape. With the warm weather, the birds and seals had returned, and parties of sailors hunted them around the clock. Auks, dovekies, and hares packed every spare corner of the boats. The Inuit helpfully supplied fresh seal meat and snared auks with long-handled nets. Even as the Natives worked to help the white men, evidence of the differences between the two cultures continued to unfold.

On a brief trip to Port Foulke, the recovered Mr. Bryan discovered the grave of August Sonntag, the astronomer of Dr. Kane's ill-fated second expedition. In earlier days William Morton and Hans had traveled with the late Sonntag. To Bryan's dismay, their Native friends had dug up the body and scattered the bones about. The cleric collected and reburied the polished skull and bones and replaced the headstone. Later he learned that the Inuit had desecrated the grave for the wood from the coffin.

On the thirtieth the dying *Polaris* made one last attempt to remain with her crew. An offshore wind sheared away the crust of ice riming the beach, and the half-sunken ship drifted free. Wallowing steeply on her port side and groaning out her death rattles, the ship floated two hundred yards south before running aground. That would be as close as the *Polaris* would ever come to returning to home port. The ship had given her all. The Arctic had set its claws into the doomed ship and resolutely refused to let go. When high tide rolled in, two feet of water covered the upper decks.

Indifferent to the fate of the vessel he never had loved, Captain Buddington ordered the boats dragged to the shoreline and loaded the next day. Each man was restricted to eight pounds of personal gear, and the boat crews were selected. Buddington chose Coffin to man the tiller of his boat and selected Morton, Odell, Hayes, and Mauch for his crew. For good measure, he placed the Reverend

Bryan in the bow. The first mate, Chester, commanded the second craft and got all those people who vexed the captain. Emil Bessel steered for Chester as the stroke, and Schuman, Booth, Campbell, and Hobby pulled the oars. Again, like a lucky figurehead, Buddington selected the pious Herman Sieman to ride in the bow of Chester's boat.

According to Buddington, the books about the Arctic that Charles Francis Hall had loved so well were packed in his sea chest along with two of the *Polaris*'s logbooks the following day and dragged a quarter mile from the camp. There—along with two boxed chronometers, the pendulum, and the transit—they were buried in a stone cache. As an afterthought, Buddington included a letter detailing the directions and the plans of the two lifeboats in case a whaling vessel might stumble upon the marker.

On the third of June 1873, while a predawn pink glow illuminated the open bay as far as the eye could penetrate the sea mist, the men launched their two boats. The Inuit lined the shore and watched silently. By two-thirty in the morning, the sailors had poled their way past the brash ice and set their sails. This half of the *Polaris* expedition was once more heading south.

Chapter Fourteen

SLOW STARVATION

I sometimes fear it will be impossible to save this party of disobedient and lawless men. I know not how this business will end; but, unless there is some change, I fear in a disastrous manner.
—CAPT. GEORGE TYSON, ON THE ICE, 1873

If the winter months were hard on Buddington and the men at Life Boat Cove, life on the floating ice during those months was far worse for Tyson's group. Throughout January his band fractured further and further apart. The Germans camped sullenly in their igloo, disdaining any work other than what directly benefited them. Besides the Inuit, only John Herron, an Englishman, and Jackson, the black cook, sided with Tyson.

The long process of starvation did not help. Almost three weeks passed before Ebierbing shot a seal. To the dismay of the Natives and Tyson, the crew snatched the animal away from the hunter and dragged it into their igloo. In minutes nothing much was left. Angrily the captain scratched in his journal:

They have divided the seal to suit themselves, and I hope they are now satisfied; but it does seem hard on the natives, who have hunted day after day, in cold and storm, while these men lay idle on their backs, or sit playing cards in the shelter of their huts, mainly built by these same natives whom they thus wrong.

The crew returned his animosity in kind. One day Robert Kruger barged into the navigator's igloo and swore at him, threatening to beat the captain senseless. No fight erupted. But Tyson fingered Ebierbing's pistol during the tirade, perhaps recalling the event that had led Hall to shoot one of his sailors on his second trip to the North.

The seamen's dislike for their navigator-turned-leader also took the form of indirect acts of aggression. All of Tyson's worldly possessions resided in a small seabag that had been tossed over the side during the fearful storm that separated the crew. In it were a few shirts, several pairs of stockings, a vest, underpants, and one pair of heavy pants. One day it disappeared, probably stolen or dropped through a crack into the sea.

From then on the hapless commander had nothing else to wear. Working and sleeping in the same oil- and blood-soaked clothing often made his stomach churn.

Despondent and depressed, Tyson extended his quarrels to everyone, especially Frederick Meyer, who obviously headed the German hierarchy. "The German Count," as the men referred to Meyer, clearly vied with Tyson for overall command of the drifting rabble. The curse of the *Polaris* continued to haunt even those separated from her. Instead of working together, they fought. On a chip of dissolving ice, the officers of the *Polaris* still engaged in a struggle for control, much like two lice battling for ownership of the hide of a dead dog that was drifting over a waterfall.

"If Meyer had not been on board the *Polaris*, these foreigners would probably have behaved better," Tyson grumbled, "for then they would not have any one to mislead them about our position."

Of Meyer's navigation, he wrote:

There has been, I suspect, an error of sixty or seventy miles in Mr. Meyer's brain as to the latitude from the start. Mr. Meyer, who is the fountain of all knowledge for his German brethren, places us within a few miles of the land, and that on the east coast.

In that criticism he was justified. Their ice floe was miles from land, farther than any of them could travel. If the men believed Meyer's faulty readings and started for land, a real danger would arise.

Eventually Tyson grumbled about even Hans, blaming him for the failures of previous polar explorations. When the Inuit's actions spooked a bear the two were stalking, Tyson's spleen spilled over. "This Hans acts like a fool sometimes. He is the same Hans who deserted Dr. Kane, and the same who was the cause of Dr. Hayes losing two good men on his expedition."

The epidemic of criticism even touched the normally taciturn Ebierbing. One day the hunter cried indignantly to Tyson, "They talk about Eskimo being dirty and stinking, but sailors are worse than Eskimo."

They all chewed on scraps of sealskin, drank melted snow, and savored a half ounce of dried bread per day until the first part of February. Then the Hans whom Tyson had maligned captured a seal by using his ingenuity. A young seal poked his head through fresh ice that had formed over a section of open water. Immediately Ebierbing shot the animal. But reaching it before it sank posed a challenge. The ice surrounding it was too thin to support a man.

Jumping into the kayak, Hans hopped the craft across the thin ice by using his paddle while simultaneously lurching his body forward inside the frail craft. Pole-vaulting along, he reached the seal, attached a line to it, and bounced back without breaking through the frozen surface. Divided among the nineteen, it yielded one small piece for each.

The only bright event was the return of the sun, reappearing after eighty-three days of total darkness. The golden thread rimming the east so inspired John Herron that he lit his pipe and smoked the last of his precious tobacco as he sat outside his snow hut and enjoyed the glow. And with the light, the birds returned.

Hundreds of tiny Arctic dovekies soon darted and swooped over the ice. Similar in size to a sparrow, one or two of the stubby black-and-white birds, at four ounces apiece, hardly satisfied a growling stomach. And because Ebierbing and Hans had no way of making the long-handled basket snares the Inuit usually employed to catch the birds, each one had to be shot down, wasting powder and shot. The ghostly white shapes of narwhals appeared for the first time as the whales migrated north, shimmering below the surface like ivory blades. The carcass of one narwhal would feed the crew for weeks. Ebierbing shot one, but the dying animal sank before he could reach it.

As March arrived, the situation looked bleaker than usual. Blubber for the stone lamps was nearly gone. Tookoolito had saved two small pieces, which would see her through the next two days. Hans had only one. Then there would be neither heat nor light.

Miraculously Ebierbing spotted a dark mound on the floe. It was a bladder-nosed seal, called an *oogjook* by the Natives, far larger than the usual spotted seals. He shot it, and the nine-foot-long animal not only supplied a hearty meal but furnished thirty gallons of oil for the essential lamps. Another orgy ensued as the starving sailors tore into the raw flesh with fingers and knives. Blood spattered the snow and smeared their hands and faces until the men looked subhuman. Part of the skin was boiled to soften it to eat. Long past caring, the men drank the greasy water after swallowing the skin. Ebierbing shrugged and remarked stoically, "Anything is good that don't poison you."

"You mustn't eat the liver, steward," Tyson warned Herron.

"Why?"

"Because it's poisonous."

The gaunt Englishman wiped his gory hands across his matted beard. He glanced at his shipmate. "Oh, damn the odds. We'll eat it. Won't we, Fred?"

Despite more warnings from Tyson, half the men gorged themselves on the seal's liver. Arctic seals and polar bears concentrate vitamin A in their livers to such a high level that it is toxic to humans. Poisoned by their meal, these men suffered cramps and diarrhea for a week, while the skin of their faces, hands, and chests blistered and then sloughed off.

Only Herron admitted his mistake. "Oh, Captain," he complained as he peeled the skin from his hands, "that *oogjook* liver played the devil with me."

Tyson showed little sympathy. "Well, you know I told you not to eat it."

Herron nodded wisely. "That's so, and I'll bet I eat no more of it . . . or bear's liver either." Then the gnawing inside his stomach caused him to reconsider. "Unless . . . yes, we might get a young bear." He looked hopefully at Tyson. "And then, perhaps, the liver would be good."

The navigator shook his head while the stricken man studied his shedding skin.

"No," Herron decided firmly, "I'll be damned if I trust it. No more liver for me."

With the warming trend came renewed storms and the added danger that the thinning ice might break beneath their feet. As gales pounded their island, more than one night passed with the frightened men dressed and standing beside their sole boat while their floor buckled and groaned and the crack of ice splitting apart filled the air like artillery fire. Nervously the returning Inuit reported encountering *imarnirsaq*, openings clear through the old ice, not just cracks in the young, thin ice. Breakup lay around the corner. Their turning, unstable world was about to become an even more precarious anchorage.

And while birds and seals returned with increasing frequency, so did the bad weather. Amid hail and blowing snow, hunting proved impossible. So it went, weeks of agonizing hunger punctuated with brief periods of frenzied feeding on a single seal or a handful of scrawny fowl arriving just as the men were at the point of death by starvation. To a starving person, a sudden feast can be just as devastating as the hunger. Physically the body has made drastic adjustments to the lack of nutrients. The stomach has reduced in size, the alimentary tract has slowed to more efficiently extract what little food passes through, and all resources are focused on maintaining the vital functions at their lowest levels still consistent with life. The sudden ingestion of fat-laden, energy-intensive food like seal meat disrupts these adjustments. Cramps, bloating, and diarrhea follow as the food shocks the digestive system into overdrive. Lower-than-normal protein levels in the bloodstream make the person susceptible to fluid leaking out of the blood vessels into the surrounding tissues. An unexpected load of salt and protein greatly exacerbates this swelling.

So the erratic arrival of food to those enduring their trial on the ice proved just as unbearable as their periods of hunger. The food did little to relieve them of their pains and cramps and only ensured that they would be alive to suffer another day of their ordeal. This cruel game of cat and mouse with death continued throughout February and March. Just when they had reached the end of their rope, fate tossed them a bone with no assurance that another one would follow. The psychological toll must have been terrible.

Spinning and drifting on the ice, everything was either hunter or hunted. Sometimes the tables turned unexpectedly. One night near the end of March, Ebierbing stuck his head out of his igloo. A sound near the kayak had caught his attention. There, ten feet away, a polar bear stood chewing on strips of sealskin saved for the lamps. Long since eaten by their masters, no dogs remained to give the alarm.

One rifle and a shotgun rested against the outside of the igloo. Ebierbing's rifle lay inside his kayak, behind the bear. Leaving their firearms out in the cold kept the metal from "sweating" in the warmer interior and rusting into a useless hunk of scrap, as everything was coated with salt spray from the wind-whipped spume.

Quickly the Inuit awakened Tyson. As the two men crept forward to retrieve the rifles, the navigator knocked over the shotgun. The bear spotted them and charged. Tyson snatched the rifle, dropped to his knee, and pulled the trigger. Nothing happened. Big-game hunters say the loudest and most frightening sound is the unexpected silence that follows a hammer's dropping on a useless cartridge. Tyson jerked the trigger three more times, but the heavy Sharps rifle failed to fire. Tumbling backward into the igloo, the shaken navigator hurriedly retrieved a handful of cartridges, reloaded, and poked his rifle down the dark tunnel. A white blur filled the opening. This time the rifle fired, hitting the bear at point-blank range. The bullet struck the animal in the heart and passed out the opposite side.

The bear provided a much-needed day's worth of food. Wisely no one touched the poisonous liver this time.

More than four months on the drifting ice had reduced the men to shambling, filthy, and haggard skeletons. The malicious touches of scurvy loosened all their teeth and covered their bodies with dirty, putrid scabs. One evening while her father, Ebierbing, divided a scrap of frozen hide with his hammer, Puney studied Tyson's gaunt frame with her serious eyes and remarked with a child's honesty and gravity, "You are nothing but bone!"

Her statement was only a slight exaggeration. Their stores of fat long since used up, their energy depleted, and their exertions minimal, their bodies began to feed on whatever tissue they could. Loss of muscle hampered even the strongest. Moving the light kayak about, normally a one-man task, took three to four men, and that exertion left them exhausted and out of breath.

While their ordeal wore away at their bodies, it took an even greater toll on their clothing, mainly a motley mix of wool, fur, and canvas. Since the men were wearing their shipboard clothing when ordered over the side, they did not have the full set of furs and mukluks normally worn during a sledding operation. Only the Inuit possessed their efficient Arctic wear. Razor-sharp ice cut and tore at their coats and leggings, wearing the fabric thin and making holes through which the relentless wind passed with ease. Tookoolito did her best to mend the rents. But food took precedence over clothing. Since the starving men ate every scrap of animal skin, nothing was left to use as patches.

Slowly, hour by hour, the Arctic was erasing these interloping humans from its surface, wearing them away into gray, transparent shadows of themselves. In time there would be nothing left. And all the while their environment tormented them.

Ice, fog, and blowing snow blinded the men as the winds rocked their island. The floor of each igloo trembled and bucked incessantly. Blocks of ice tumbled and crashed along the perimeter of their camp. All around the rifle shots of cracking ice startled them while a wall of impenetrable white prevented the anxious party from seeing their danger. As night fell, a sable curtain replaced the milky wall that enclosed them, yet the disruptions continued, robbing the exhausted sailors of sleep. The situation caused Tyson to remark, "If man has ever suffered on earth the torments of wretched souls condemned to the 'ice hell' of the great Italian poet, Dante, I think I have felt it here."

April Fool's Day unleashed a cruel trick on the party. Tyson had just written in his notebook: "We have been the 'fools of fortune' now for five months and a half." As the fog lifted, an even more alarming sight greeted him. Their home for five and one-half months dissolved. Wind and current had detached their minuscule raft of ice from the rest of the ice pack. Some twenty miles of ice-choked waves separated their home from the relative security of the drifting pack.

There was nothing left to do but launch the boat and row for the drifting mountains of ice.

Now the folly of burning their second boat for firewood returned to plague them. Cramming nineteen souls into a whaleboat designed to carry eight left no room for their provisions. The boat wallowed and shipped water with each wave. Icy seas lapped over the gunnels, drenching the tightly packed occupants and threatening to swamp the craft. In desperation Tyson threw their meat from a recent kill over the side, nearly one hundred pounds of it, and most of their spare clothing. Loss of this precious food must have come especially hard. Hundreds of rounds of metallic cartridges were abandoned before they even launched the boat. Ignoring pleas of the men to jettison the box, Tyson and Tookoolito preserved Captain Hall's writing desk.

To the rhythmic cries of the frightened Inuit children, the sailors poled and rowed as best they could. Arms, heads, legs, and backs blocked each pull on the oars. By midday, the spent rowers reached the closest slab of ice. For all their efforts, the thick sections of the Greenland pack remained farther away. Exhausted, the sailors pitched their canvas tent and crawled inside. The Inuit slept in the boat.

For the next three days, Tyson and his party played a deadly game of chess with the water and ice. Rowing whenever they could and poling when they could not paddle, they threaded their craft among the razor edges of the brash ice. Whenever the ice closed around them, they landed at the largest floe and waited for another opportunity. Sea foam and waves soaked their clothing, which froze into sheets as stiff as iron. Once an edge of ice holed their boat and caused them to bail for their lives. When things looked darkest, as Tyson noted in his diary three days later, "[some] of the men, by their expressions, seemed to intimate that they would not have hesitated to throw over the women and children to save their own lives."

Finally they reached a substantial piece of ice and made camp.

Ebierbing built an igloo, and the spent party fell asleep. Herron found himself too cold to sleep and spent the time stomping around their tiny island to keep his feet from freezing.

At five in the morning on the fifth of April, a gale struck. Buffeted by the winds, their sanctuary broke apart. The startled inhabitants rolled out of the igloo just as the crack widened, and the ice house drifted away. The storm rose in ferocity and continued.

Hastily Ebierbing built another hut. The next day the ice split directly under the igloo, cutting it in half. Now too little real estate remained for Ebierbing to build another igloo. Without options the men pitched their tent and took turns hiding from the storm. Few slept.

Their isle of respite now became their trap. Piece by piece it broke apart under the storm's pounding. Yet taking to the boat would have been suicidal, for the steep waves and fierce wind would have sunk the overloaded craft.

On the third day of the storm, the ice split between the tent and the boat. The piece bearing the kayak and the boat shot off with only Mr. Meyer aboard. In desperation the meteorologist launched the kayak toward the two Inuit, who scrambled to the frothing edge of their slab. The wind blew the light craft beyond their reach.

While Tyson watched helplessly, Ebierbing and Hans performed a perilous ballet, vaulting and springing from one chip of bobbing ice to another. Each jump brought them closer to the hapless Meyer, but each leap also threatened to plunge them into the roiling water. Using their paddles and spears, the Natives approached close enough to Meyer to catch a rope he tossed to them. Then they pulled themselves to his side.

Now more than half a mile away, the three men and the boat drifted off as darkness fell.

Morning found the three elements of the group triangulated— the kayak, the main party, and Meyer's group separated by equal amounts of water. Unfortunately neither the sickened Meyer nor the Inuit had the strength to launch the whaleboat.

Taking his cue from the Inuit's ice dance, Tyson grabbed a stick and hopped onto the rocking plates that filled the gap. Kruger followed him. Slipping and sliding, they eventually made it across.

Even then, the five men could not budge the boat. One by one the rest of the crew crossed over the bar. All but two swallowed their fear and traversed the shifting stepping-stones. The boat was launched and the kayak retrieved before they returned. Once more united, the men pitched their tent, and Ebierbing built his third igloo in twenty-four hours.

Frederick Meyer had suffered terribly from his ordeal. Already nearly dead of starvation, he fell into the water during the rescue and stopped breathing. Hans and Ebierbing applied their primitive form of artificial respiration—with good results. By vigorously rubbing Meyer's chest and face with snow and pulling his arms up and down, they restored his breathing and his consciousness. They had saved his life. But his toes had frozen solid.

The storm passed, but its effects lingered for another day. Fetch and wind generated huge breaking waves that battered the limited expanse of the campsite. While an uncaring sun set in a cloudless sky, waves broke over the camp and washed the men out of their tent and the Natives from their igloo. The cold beauty of the evening contrasted with the desperate struggle taking place on the ice. What little everyone possessed was loaded into the boat along with the children. The night passed with the adults standing beside the boat as frigid water lapped at their ankles. Without a dry place to light their lamps, no food was thawed, and no ice could be melted for water. Morning found the party worn out, hungry, and thirsty.

By the twelfth their pitiful island had wedged itself between two icebergs. While their position presented the possibility of being capsized and crushed at a moment's notice, the lofty white peaks did provide some shelter from the wind and waves. Along with this respite came the realization that they were again captives of the meandering ice pack.

By April 15 a sun sighting placed their position at 54°58' N. They had drifted twelve hundred miles—past Disko, past Upernavik, and even past Cape Farewell at the southern tip of Greenland. While the current kept them frustratingly far from the coast of Greenland, it dragged them southward toward the Labrador coast. Now each mile they drifted south increased the possibility of spotting a whaling ship.

But starvation threatened them first. Only two pounds of pemmican and bread remained. As before, someone raided the supplies and ate most of them. All around hundreds of birds flew in flocks, heading northward to their nesting grounds. Skittish and familiar with the habits of men, these birds stayed well beyond rifle shot. All the hungry men could do was watch them swoop and dive.

That dangerous look returned to the men's eyes. Tyson recognized it. "This hunger is disturbing their brains," he scribbled with his pencil stub. "I can not but fear that they contemplate crime. After what we have gone through, I hope this company may be preserved from any fatal wrong. This party must not disgrace humanity by cannibalism."

A single seal put off the unthinkable—at least for a few more days. Every scrap of the animal vanished down their blistered throats except for its gallbladder. Cruelly Tyson amused himself by watching the near-dead Meyer gleaning picked-over bones from the ice. With his bony hands encased in oversize deer-hide gloves, the feeble man struggled to pick up the scraps. Hampered by the gloves and his cold-numbed fingers, time after time Meyer found his gloves empty. Yet each effort of grasping for the bones nearly caused the meteorologist to fall over.

The night of April 20, a cry of alarm pierced the night. Instantly an icy wave of seawater swept over the piece of ice, inundating the camp. As the men struggled to their feet, the wave washed away whatever was not secured. The sea swallowed pipes, socks, shirts, gloves, and the essential oil lamps.

Wave after wave followed. Battered at five-minute intervals, the crew loaded the women and children into the boat just as a monstrous wave ripped the tent loose and carried it off along with blankets and reindeer robes. In that instant all their bedding was lost.

Shouting over the roar of the wind, Tyson ordered his men to stand by the boat. Wide-eyed and trembling, they all obeyed. "Hold on, men!" he cried. "Bear down! Put on all your weight!"

"Aye, aye, sir," came the frightened response.

Each wave lifted and rocked the boat, threatening to wash it off the ice and into the churning maelstrom. Sailor after sailor threw his body across the thwarts to keep the whaleboat from lifting free.

For twelve hours they struggled. Blocks and slabs of ice borne by the waves slammed into the legs and feet of the desperate men. Each blow spun its victim and upset his balance. Chunks of ice the size of dressers tumbled the men like ninepins. Their hands and mittens now frozen to the sides of the craft perversely helped them keep hold as they dropped. One fall meant death, swept away into the roiling tempest. Luckily the crew worked together. Helping hands snatched those who slipped before they slid from sight.

And with each wave, the boat leaped forward, closer to the edge of the ice.

While the men weakened, the storm showed no signs of relenting. By morning the two Inuit women tumbled onto the ice to help hold the boat in place. At seven in the morning, the fury abated.

Tyson spotted a better piece of ice close by and ordered the boat launched. Jackson fell overboard in the attempt, but hands snatched his jacket and pulled the shivering cook aboard. On reaching the new site, the last morsels of dried bread were divided. The crew was split into two watches, which allowed half to sleep in the boat at one time.

Tyson took stock of their situation. It was hopeless. All were soaked and covered with bruises. There was no more food, no shelter except the boat, no dry clothing, and no means of starting a fire.

In their darkest hour, the captain found reason to hope. *We cannot have been saved through such a night to be starved now,* he thought. *God will send us some food.*

As Tyson and his party chewed on strips of their clothing to assuage their hunger, Ebierbing climbed a crest of their frozen world and scanned the jumbled horizon. Three times he ventured to the top to look for food without success.

On his fourth attempt, a slight movement caught his eye. A patch of ivory moved along the blazing white hummocks. It was a bear. Ambling toward the smell of something he could eat, the animal was coming to them.

Ebierbing and Hans ran for their rifles. The anxious sailors flopped down onto the ice and did their best to resemble sleeping seals while the bear approached. As the men held their breath, two shots rang out and the bear skidded onto his nose.

The animal was starving just as they were. Its stomach was empty, and its hide hung loosely over a bony frame. None of the usual layers of insulating fat remained beneath its skin. The bear had meant to eat them. Instead, it became food itself. Its warm blood and stringy meat revived the men, especially the semicomatose Meyer.

But the respite was short-lived. Another gale descended upon the straits. In a recurring theme, the wind and waves ate away at their new home until the group was forced to take to their boat once more. For the next three days, they spent more time in their leaking craft than on ice floes. The warming weather favored rotten ice, and the storm shattered most of the weakened pack ice.

Now a different situation threatened. Little remained of the level places where they could land. Only sharp-faced icebergs that split and capsized incessantly shared the stormy straits with a slurry of slush and brash ice. There was no place suitable to repair their boat. Besides, they had no materials with which to repair it. There was nothing left for them to do but bail the sinking boat and dodge the walls of ice that thundered past.

At four-thirty in the afternoon of April 28, just when their hopes had sunk the lowest, Ebierbing's sharp eyes spotted a smudge of smoke rising from the horizon.

"A steamer! A steamer!" a hoarse voice croaked.

Instantly Tyson hoisted the American flag. Men shouted and waved. The boat rocked perilously while the crew tried everything to get the ship's attention. Through his telescope Tyson made out the steam sealer working its way through the ice on a southwest course.

Pulling with their last ounce of energy, the crew rowed toward the ship. But fog and ice blocked their way. The steamer vanished from sight. Sobbing from despair as well as exhaustion, the men slumped over their oars. Darkness settled over the small boat just as Tyson found a piece of ice barely large enough to land. Lighting scraps of their oil-soaked clothing, they set watch fires in hopes the steamer would see them.

Morning found another steamer approximately eight miles off. Hurriedly they launched their boat and paddled for it. An hour of hard rowing saw them gaining on the idling ship. Another hour found their tiny boat blocked by pancake ice. Clambering onto the highest point of a floating cake, those with guns fired them into the air.

The steamer changed course, heading directly for them. Almost delirious with joy, the men fired three rounds. A report of three shots echoed back. Was it a response from the ship or merely the echoes off the icebergs?

To their dismay, the vessel veered off, weaving first south, then north and west. Tyson and his men shouted, with no result, until their throats cracked. The captain watched in amazement as the ship zigzagged along the horizon. The vessel was threading its way around the ice. "Strange," he wondered out loud. "I should think any sailing ship, much more a steamer, could get through with ease."

Helpless, the men watched in frustration as hours slipped away while the steamer came no closer than five miles from them. Even more depressing, another ship steamed into sight just as the sun set. Night found the castaways huddled on another sliver of ice, bracketed by unseeing sealing ships. Hans caught a baby seal sleeping on the other side of their base, so the depressed party had a little to eat.

As he settled into his night watch, Tyson felt warmer air waft past his windburned cheek. The puff of warm air sent a chill through him. Warm air could mean only one thing: fog! The next day would see thick fog, and that would make their discovery more difficult.

As morning broke on the last day in April, Tyson had just closed his eyes when the lookout cried out, "There's a steamer! There's a steamer!"

Shimmering through the fog like the ghostly image of the Flying Dutchman loomed a ship.

Everyone jumped up and fired their rifles. Tyson tied the flag to the top of their mast and joined the others in shouting. Hans launched the kayak and paddled furiously toward the ship. With its funnel billowing sooty smoke between its two masts, the ship was less than a quarter mile off. Still, fog rolled about the ship and hid it from view.

Hans reached the ship and waved his arms as his kayak

thudded into the side of the steamer. She was the steam barkentine *Tigress*, out of Conception Bay, Newfoundland. Curious men lined the rails to look down at him.

All the while as he paddled, Hans shouted out, "American steamer! American steamer!" Knowing only a few words in English, he could not say more.

Men aboard the steamer looked down in amazement. Where had this Native come from? He was in the middle of the straits. And what did he want? The *Tigress* was no "American steamer."

The fog parted just as Hans pointed at the people on the floe.

Instantly the captain shouted orders. The ship slowed and turned toward the marooned party. Three sealing boats splashed into the water, and their crews rowed for the patch of floating ice.

When he saw the change of course, Tyson doffed his threadbare Russian cap and gave three cheers. His men followed suit. Tears flooded his eyes when three hearty cheers resounded from the steamer. As she hove into sight, he saw a hundred men lining her forecastle, rigging, and topgallant mast, waving and cheering at their rescue.

Not waiting for their rescuers, Tyson and his group abandoned their dented cooking pot and launched their own boat. Boat hooks caught the battered craft as it reached the *Tigress*.

The rescued party climbed shakily aboard. Curious seamen crowded around them. The dirty, haggard group looked less than human. One boatload of sailors from the *Tigress* had peered into the beat-up tin pot to see what the rescued had been eating. The greasy loop of seal intestine spoke eloquently of their dire straits.

"How long have you been on the ice?" Captain Isaac Bartlett of the *Tigress* asked.

"Since the 15th of last October," Tyson answered.

A murmur of disbelief rippled through the surrounding seamen. It was now the end of April. One wide-eyed sailor blurted out, *"Was you on it day and night?"*

In spite of his exhaustion, Captain Tyson chuckled.

After 195 days drifting in the northern seas, Captain George Tyson and the eighteen members of the *Polaris* Expedition had survived their hardship on the ice. Frozen water and an overloaded whaleboat had been their only home for nearly seven months. The

Tigress snatched them from the jaws of the sea just off the coast of Grady Harbor, Labrador, at latitude 53°35' N. In the process they had floated more than eighteen hundred miles.

Their trial by ice was over. If they thought they were done with ordeals, they were mistaken. Their trial by the United States Navy would soon begin.

Chapter Fifteen

THE INQUEST

Unshaven since I know not when, dirty, dressed in rags of wild beasts instead of the tatters of civilization, and starved to the very bones, our gaunt and grim looks, when contrasted with those of the well-dressed and well-fed men around us, made us all feel, I believe for the first time, what we really were, as well as what we seemed to others.
—SIR JOHN ROSS, 1832

News of the disaster and the rescue reached Washington before the salvaged party did. Two days after the rescue, the *Tigress* rendezvoused with another sealer, the *Walrus.* While Captain Bartlett lingered in the Arctic waters to hunt seals for a few more days, Captain DeLange of the *Walrus* sped southward to Newfoundland with the news.

Mr. Molloy, the United States consul in St. John's, immediately telegraphed the American secretary of state. The following week, after being battered by a severe storm, Bartlett limped into Bay Roberts, thirty-five miles north of St. John's, to unload his cargo.

After half a year of starving and subsisting on raw seal meat, the *Polaris* people found that their sudden return to "civilized" food was taking its toll. Everyone, including the Inuit, suffered from diarrhea, migrating muscle pain, sore throats, and swelling of their faces and feet. The swelling resulted from the lowered protein content in the crew's blood. Suddenly faced with a high level of nutrients, their lymphatic systems were overwhelmed. That combined with the damage to the blood vessels from scurvy enabled the fluid and protein to simply leak into the tissues instead of being returned to the vascular system as it normally would have been. Muscle aches and sore throats most probably came from the reintroduction of the isolated band to the host of viruses that plague civilized men. Frederick Meyer's frozen hands and feet blistered and required continued treatment.

Two days later the swollen-faced Tyson and his crew were surprised by the sudden arrival of Molloy. By then the entire coast of Newfoundland buzzed with rumors, speculation, gossip, and disbelief. So-called Arctic experts labeled their story a fraud, asserting that no one could have survived on the ice as they had.

And the blacker side of the expedition bubbled forth to tarnish the gleam of their survival. Tyson's sailors shared the crowded forecastle with the men of the *Tigress* and talked freely of their ordeal. Tyson vented his spleen to Isaac Bartlett, the master of the *Tigress*. Tales of Buddington's drinking and the mysterious death of Captain Hall spread like wildfire. When Molloy met them, Washington and New York hummed as well. Why had they failed to reach the North Pole? Had Hall been poisoned? Why had the *Polaris* not returned to pick up the shipmates who had become separated? Everyone wanted to know.

Molloy questioned the party, gathered their statements, and gave Tyson sixteen dollars to divide among the crew. If this was a sign of things to come, it rudely shattered the Germans' dreams of being handsomely rewarded for their travail on the ice. Furthermore, the nature of Molloy's questions put the crew on their guard. While the people of St. John's cheered them wherever they went, the breeze from Washington blew considerably colder.

Within two days of receiving Molloy's telegraphed report, the United States Navy steamer *Frolic* charged out of New York, making full steam to St. John's. On the seventeenth of May, Navy Secretary Robeson reported to President Grant on "the matter of the disaster to the United States exploring expedition toward the North Pole." Since Grant read the newspapers, he undoubtedly was quite familiar with the rumors.

Those rumors reaching Washington were not good, and Robeson and all involved moved quickly to protect their interests. No one could deny that something had gone terribly amiss. The strange death of Charles Francis Hall, who had embodied the heart and soul of the expedition, troubled everyone. No one forgot the fact that President Grant looked favorably upon Hall and had given his personal blessing to the expedition. The *Polaris* disaster touched even the president. In his report to Grant, Robeson wrote:

> As was obviously proper, in view of the prompt and responsible action which might be required, that the Government should, as soon as possible, be in possession of the fullest and most reliable information upon all the circumstances of the case, the *Frolic* was ordered to bring directly to Washington all the persons having personal knowledge on the subject.

Robeson at long last linked Tyson into the chain of command that had eluded him. His telegraph placed Tyson in charge of the crew and the Inuit until they reached Washington. Correcting that oversight came far too late.

If the Navy Department had hoped Molloy would cooperate in keeping the crew isolated, it was disappointed. After all, the State Department's hands were clean in this matter. Molloy made no effort to insulate the survivors.

Throngs of people visited the Inuit. As a result, all the Natives contracted severe colds, and their children suffered from the cakes and candies fed to them. Citizens took up collections for the crew. Tyson dined with the governor of St. John's and freely expressed his view of the treachery that had swamped their expedition. *Harper's Illustrated Weekly* arranged to photograph the castaways. Its dark lithograph of the somber-faced survivors clustered around their battered boat appeared on the front page under the heading THE COMPANY WHO WERE ON THE ICE-DRIFT WITH CAPTAIN TYSON, adding fuel to the speculations.

Washington quickly wanted control of the loose tongues. The *Frolic* steamed into St. John's on May 27, loaded the survivors, collected their diaries and Hall's writing desk, and hastily departed the next day. The ship sailed directly to the nation's capital, arriving at the Washington Navy Yard at precisely 1:15 P.M. on June 5, 1873. Its commander had to apologize for slowing down when he encountered ice.

If the survivors had expected a heroes' welcome, they were

sorely mistaken. Their return differed greatly from their departure. No one was allowed to disembark. No crowds thronged the wharves, no bands played, and no flags waved. No press was allowed aboard. These members of the *Polaris* expedition, having escaped their icy prison in the far North, found themselves captives of their own government.

At four o'clock that same day, George Tyson appeared as the first witness before a hastily drawn board of inquiry. Tyson was haggard and thin, his face tanned and hardened like leather from months of exposure to the wind, cold, and sun. Transferred from his virtual prison ship, the rescued captain was taken aboard the USS *Tallapoosa* for questioning. Besides Secretary Robeson, the board consisted of Admiral Goldsborough and Commodore Reynolds, representing the navy. Since Frederick Meyer belonged to the signal corps, the army insisted that Capt. Henry Howgate of the signal corps sit on the board. Prof. Spencer F. Baird represented the National Academy of Sciences and the Smithsonian. It was these two august bodies that had carefully chosen Emil Bessel. The reputations of the navy, the army, and the scientific community hung in the balance, and each entity wanted to ensure that it was not made the scapegoat for this fiasco.

If Tyson realized that Commander Schoonmaker, the captain of the *Frolic*, was sizing him up during the voyage, the navigator made no mention of it. But Schoonmaker reported in private to the board before it saw Tyson. When asked by Robeson about his report, the commander responded more like a warden involved in a prisoner transfer than a rescuer.

"I found these people in charge of the consulate St. Johns. I received them on the 27th of May. *I had no trouble with any of them.* They are all well-behaved, orderly people; and all seem to be good men." Schoonmaker went on to provide his assessment of Tyson: "Captain Tyson seems to be very intelligent; I have seen him more than any of the rest; I have had him with me in the cabin. He has made a very favorable impression on me." Surprisingly Schoonmaker's response implied that his mission was more than it appeared. Besides being a warden, the captain had obviously been asked to make a judgment of the character of his passengers. No doubt all of the survivors were on their best behavior.

If the board had thought Tyson would dispel the evil rumors under oath, he surprised them. The forty-four-year-old Tyson lost no time in venting his spleen once more. In the first minutes of his testimony, he named Buddington as the cause the ship had not got farther north. Referring to Hall, Chester, and himself, he said, "Our decision was to go north, but it was overruled by Captain Buddington." For good measure, he added, "Captain Buddington, with an oath, said he would be damned if she should move from here." The astonished secretary for the inquiry duly recorded each bitter statement.

Buddington's drinking came to light, as did the suspicious nature of Captain Hall's death. Tyson spoke of Hall's fear that he'd been poisoned. Now the specter of murder raised its ugly head, and Tyson's testimony pointed to two likely suspects: Captain Buddington and Dr. Bessel. This revelation especially shocked Professor Baird. He had helped select the German scientist.

"How did Captain Hall and the doctor get along?" the panel asked.

"Not very well."

Tyson also gave them a motive for Buddington: "Before his death there had been some little difficulty between Captain Buddington and himself. Captain Hall was about suspending Captain Buddington from duty. . . ."

A second whole day of testimony revealed the fiasco that had put Tyson and half the crew on the ice. The angry navigator took great pains to describe how the *Polaris* had steamed close to them before turning away. Without their prompting he also detailed the deplorable existence he and his party had suffered after being left. His statements drew questioning looks from the board.

A third, equally worrisome detail emerged while Tyson talked. What had become of the expedition's records? Both Meyer's and Bryan's scientific records had been tossed onto the ice and lost. Not only did the expedition fail to reach the North Pole, but the majority of its scientific measurements lay at the bottom of the sea.

And there was the matter of Captain Hall's journals and records. Other than the writing box that his faithful Inuit had carried throughout their drift on the ice, the leader's documents had disappeared. Tyson intimated that they were destroyed on purpose because they implicated someone.

"Was there no public examination of his papers in the presence of the officers? Were they not certified and sealed up?" the board asked incredulously.

"No, sir."

"Did anybody suggest that the papers should be sealed up?"

"I did myself; that they should be sealed, boxed, and screwed down, and suggested it to Captain Buddington."

"What did he say?" Robeson leaned forward, resting on his elbows.

Tyson shrugged. "He did not make any remark whatever, or merely his usual 'Damn his papers.' "

The board pressed cautiously onward. "While [Captain Hall] was delirious did Captain Buddington get him to burn up some papers?"

Tyson nodded. "He told me he was glad the papers were burned, because they were much against him; and he got him to burn them."

The line of questioning drifted back to Hall's demise. "Have you any opinion of your own as to the cause of his death?" Tyson was asked.

"I thought at the time that the man came to his death naturally; it has been talked on board ship that it was foul; but I have no proof of it, and I could not say much about it." Then Tyson dropped a bombshell.

"There were those that rejoiced in his death."

The panel looked at each other. "Who rejoiced in his death?"

"Captain Buddington."

"Did anyone else?"

"I thought it relieved some of the scientific party of some anxiety. They did not mourn him, at least. I know Captain Buddington so expressed himself, that he was relieved of a great load by the death of Captain Hall."

After two days of questioning Tyson, the panel turned to the next officer, Frederick Meyer of the scientific corps. But an easy confirmation of Tyson's accusations was not forthcoming. Without realizing it, the board was reopening dark chapters in each of the survivors' lives, chapters that contained failures in their character that the men wished to keep hidden. As the panel probed, each person remained silent as to his failures and did his best to avoid incrimination. Tyson's testimony would have to stand on its own merits where it criticized his fellow castaways. They would grudgingly confirm the navigator's tale of Hall's bizarre death and confirm their abandonment by the *Polaris*. For their own actions on the ice, the men spun a convoluted picture as obscure as the gray ice fog that had covered their floating island.

Meyer, always the Prussian officer, did his best to present a dry, impersonal account, emphasizing his findings and measurements. But probing by the committee confirmed the strange death of Hall with his "blue vapors" and the dying man's accusations against Dr. Bessel, Buddington, and Mr. Chester.

"Captain Hall called me to his bedside and said that he knew that some persons on board the ship intended to kill him, and he wanted me to stand by his side," Meyer revealed, adding that he was around the captain because he shared the same cabin.

"Did you at any time hear him accuse anyone of an intention to murder him?" the board asked.

"Yes, sir. When I was about the cabin I could hear him. Some persons might be attending to him, sitting by his side, and he would be talking pleasantly, and all of a sudden he would say: 'What is this; what is this blue smoke; and what is that there, all blue?' He thought it was poisonous vapors, he said."

The panel persisted, searching for a name. "Did you ever hear him accuse anyone to other people? When one was sitting by him would he speak of other people?"

Perhaps trying to protect a fellow German, Meyer sought to shift Hall's suspicions mainly to Buddington and Chester. "Yes, sir. He would accuse other people, and ask the protection of the man sitting by his side. He accused Mr. Chester and Captain Buddington—those were the two principal ones—and Dr. Bessel."

Here Meyer planted the idea that the delirious Hall had accused whoever was absent, certainly the sign of a deranged mind to which the panel could point.

"When talking with Chester, for instance, would he accuse anyone else?" the board asked.

"Yes, sir; he would accuse Captain Buddington."

But a disturbing fact emerged. In his torment Hall had never asked for Bessel to protect him. "When talking to him, did you hear him accuse anybody else, and ask the doctor to stand by him?" Meyer was asked.

"I do not remember that I heard him appeal to the doctor to stand by him," Meyer admitted.

Meyer confirmed that Bessel had hovered about Hall during his illness. When asked if Bessel had provided regular treatment to his patient, Meyer replied, "He gave him a great many; hypodermic injections of quinine, I believe, for one." The meteorologist's statement conflicts with the careful record Bessel kept of his treatment. In that record the doctor mentions giving only several injections.

On another subject, Meyer was not shy about discussing Buddington's addiction to alcohol.

"Did you ever know of Captain Buddington's being drunk on board ship?" he was asked.

"Yes, sir; he was drunk most always while we were going to the southward. I do not remember whether he was drunk when we got beset with this last floe. There was only alcohol on board, and he would brew beverages out of the alcohol."

Meyer's statements revealed two new things. First, the crafty Dr. Bessel had not added his own papers to the boxes that Meyer threw onto the ice, keeping them on board during the frenzy. If the *Polaris* still survived, hope remained that Bessel's diaries and measurements did, too. Second, Buddington had possession of Hall's papers at the time Meyer fell overboard. That raised obvious but unspoken questions: Had Bessel and Buddington special information that the ship was in less danger than they pretended? Had they protected their own records while attempting to destroy other incriminating material?

"I have seen the outside of the papers many times, and have seen Captain Buddington looking at them," Meyer continued, referring to Hall's documents. "He had them in a large tin box. I was on board about five minutes before the ice broke. Then I saw

Captain Hall's papers in the cabin; so that they are, very likely, on board. I did not see the journal. The tin box was standing on the table and the papers were lying alongside of it."

Had Buddington been reading the papers just before he ordered Tyson, the Inuit, and those of the crew he disliked over the side? Was there something in Hall's letters that made him choose those men? The panel had to ask.

"At the time when you were separated from the ship had you any idea that the separation was any other than purely accidental?"

Meyer pondered the question that had vexed him while he suffered on the ice. "My idea was at the commencement that it was accidental," he started. Then his doubts poured forth. "But, I thought they neglected to pick us up, for it was possible to do so. The ice was not sufficient to keep them from picking us up. We expected them to come, and did not give up the hope until we saw that we were drifting off, and they did not come. . . ."

As if embarrassed by his outburst, Meyer lapsed into a rambling dialogue. While the stenographer's pen raced along, trying to keep up in shorthand, the Prussian discussed the weather, the shrimp, the types of driftwood found on the beaches, and every aspect of his scientific studies in a disjointed manner. Realizing the panel considered him a suspect, Meyer made it clear that he had no quarrel with Hall. As he closed his testimony, he threw more light on the reasons the expedition had failed: "I believe that a party might have gone much farther north by establishing a sub-base of supplies at Newman's Bay, and this would have been done but for the unpleasant relations existing between Captain Buddington and Dr. Bessel."

Next came the Inuit. Why the board departed from examining the crew and chose the Natives is unclear. As was their custom, the Inuit's words were direct and to the point. Tookoolito with her better grasp of English helped Hans with his answers. Their close association with Hall during his sudden illness cast more suspicion on the cup of coffee.

" 'Now, Joe, did you drink bad coffee?' he asked me," Ebierbing responded when asked about Hall's words. Tookoolito also spoke of the strange-tasting drink. "He said the coffee made him sick. Too sweet for him. . . . 'It made me sick and to vomit,' " she said, quoting the late captain. Both husband and wife confirmed their dead friend's fears he was being poisoned.

Tookoolito also cast further light on Captain Hall's papers. "He said to take care of the papers; get them home, and give them to the Secretary." Robeson straightened at that revelation. Tookoolito turned back to the other man who had asked the question. "If anything had happened to the Secretary, to give them to someone else. After his death I told Captain Buddington of this charge several times. He said he would give them to me by and by."

The men of the panel looked at one another, then changed the line of questioning. To their surprise, Tookoolito revealed Buddington's unusual action during the night of October 15. The captain had ordered her onto the ice even after she told him one of the firemen had assured her the ship was in no danger.

"I asked the fireman who was pumping how the ship was," she said. "He said the ship was all right. Was not tipped at the time. He was pumping close to my door. He said, 'You need not carry anything more out, you will come aboard all right tonight.' I stayed down in cabin a few minutes. Captain Buddington told me to go on ice, and to take my things with me."

Tookoolito paused for effect. "I told him that fireman said ship all right. He replied, 'Never you mind; take little girl and go on ice.' " She raised her eyes to look directly at Admiral Goldsborough. In a voice barely a whisper, she said, "In a few minutes ship went."

Ebierbing ended his interview with a poignant tribute to his dead friend and an implied criticism of those who had assumed command after Hall's death. When asked if he wanted to resume his quest for the North Pole, he shook his head. "I would not like to; Captain Hall, my friend. With a man like him I would go back."

John Herron, the steward, was questioned next. While born in Liverpool, the thirty-one-year-old pointed out that he was a citizen of the United States. Herron could speak only from his personal knowledge. Being in the galley, he'd overheard Bessel's confrontation with Captain Hall over Frederick Meyer's duties and had served Hall the questionable coffee. Defensively Herron explained carefully that he had not made the coffee. Making the coffee was the sole responsibility of the cook. Also Herron had not kept track of the tin cup after he brought it to Hall. He could not recall how many hands had touched the cup. Other than confirming Buddington's drinking habits, the steward offered little that was new.

One by one the board called the able-bodied seamen, all young and foreign. Each man gave guarded replies. Well aware of Tyson's hostility toward them, they did their best to appear bland and cooperative. John Kruger reminded the panel that he was called Robert, praised Captain Hall, and made no mention of his threatening Tyson while on the ice.

Fred Jamka, another German, related overhearing Buddington tell Henry Hobby, "Well, Henry, there is a stone off my heart," and explaining when asked why that was, "Why, Captain Hall is dead." Jamka also had seen Buddington drunk many times. Jamka spoke of the night of the separation, painting Captain Buddington's actions in an even more questionable light. While Buddington had no qualms about ordering certain of his crew onto the ice with supplies, he seemed reluctant to lower the lifeboats.

"We started to transport the provisions farther from the ship," Jamka related, "and thought it rather careless to be on the ice without boats. I sang out to Captain Buddington to lower the boats. *I sang out for a dozen times.* By and by he answered, and lowered the aft and then the forward boat, and we pulled them to our side."

The two naval officers shifted in their chairs. If the *Polaris* were in danger of sinking, any sensible commander would have lowered the lifeboats to keep them from being lost with the ship.

"All at once we heard a crack under the boat," Jamka continued. "At the same time the vessel's stern swung off. All at once the lines slacked, and off the ship went. Captain Buddington sang out, 'Take care of the boats, and I will take care of the ship.' " Like all who had gone before him, Jamka saw no reason the *Polaris* had not returned to rescue them.

Gustavus Lindquist, the native of Sweden, refused to say if any of the officers had been drunk. "I am no judge whether a man has got liquor or not," he said flatly. He kept his testimony factual and added only one personal impression. Tellingly he admitted, "There was good discipline while Captain Hall lived, but we put discipline along with him in his grave."

Peter Johnson, the Dane, and Frederick Anthing, the Russian

born along the Prussian border, had little more to add. Both Lindquist and Anthing remembered Buddington's shouting for them to "work for their lives" as the storm struck. Why the *Polaris* had not seen them and picked them up puzzled them all. The consensus of the crew was that the *Polaris* was still intact with the remainder of her crew, waiting to be rescued.

William Jackson, the cook, came last. Wary of being implicated in anything, he added little. "Did you ever see any stealing of provisions?" he was asked.

"No, sir."

"Did the man who had charge of the provisions give Captain Tyson his share?"

"Nobody, that I know of, refused to do as Captain Tyson told them."

Faced with conflicting reports, the panel turned to the journals kept on the ice. If the members of the board hoped to find written comments that backed Tyson's recriminations, they were sorely disappointed. Frederick Meyer's diary started on October 15 with comments and narratives of the party's situation. But within two weeks it had degenerated into sparse notations of wind directions and air temperatures. Reading the contracting notations, one can easily imagine the starving Meyer withdrawing deeper and deeper into his inner mind.

John Herron's diary painted a graphic picture of the suffering and terror that gripped the party as they floated helplessly amid a white hell. Nothing in Herron's writing, however, confirmed Tyson's tales of insubordination, mutiny, and thoughts of cannibalism. Had the steward wisely excluded documenting that damning behavior, had he been a party to it, or had Tyson's imagination played tricks on him during their dreadful journey? The panel could only wonder.

Two journals belonging to William Morton, the second mate, and Herman Sieman had been tossed onto the ice and accompanied the drifting men. Of the men who remained aboard the *Polaris*, the sturdy Morton and the pious Sieman would be most likely to incriminate any lawbreakers. Had their journals been tossed onto the ice in an attempt to destroy them? Again, the panel could only wonder.

Just one page of Morton's notes survived. Strangely that page describes Dr. Bessel pronouncing Captain Hall's sudden illness as fatal just two days after the man got sick. "Captain Hall seriously ill," Morton wrote, "and Dr. Bessel has no hopes of him. He told Chester and myself so."

Hastily the board of inquiry had Sieman's journal translated from its original German. The devout Sieman filled his pages with prayers and lines of guilt for his sinfulness. He carefully documented Buddington's gradual elimination of religious services aboard the ship. One interesting fact emerged from the water-stained pages. Sieman had dearly wanted to watch over Captain Hall during the first episode of his illness. But Buddington denied his request. Was Buddington trying to protect Hall from being proselytized by the overzealous Sieman, or was the skipper isolating his commander from loyal men? The journal gave no clue as to motive. Only Sieman's disappointment came through.

After six days of grueling testimony, the board of inquiry was no closer to the truth. Its report was printed and submitted to President Grant under a cover letter by Secretary Robeson.

The United States' first exploration to discover the North Pole had failed in every way, and Robeson immediately distanced himself from its shortcomings. Too many questions remained unanswered. There were too many shadowy accusations, and too many people were demanding answers. Charles Francis Hall had died mysteriously, the North Pole had not been reached, half the crew had been abandoned on the ice, the fate of the *Polaris* was undetermined, and the conduct of the officers and men left much to be desired. Ever the consummate bureaucrat, Robeson attempted to deflect any blame away from himself.

"This report is made directly to yourself, *as the person under whose orders the expedition was organized,* and I have myself signed it, concurring as I do in all the statements and conclusions," the secretary wrote to the president.

In some of the testimony as given will be found some statements of facts, and several strong expressions of feeling on the part of some of the witnesses against the officer remaining in command of the ship after the death of Captain Hall.

These I feel great reluctance to publish while the person referred to is absent in the discharge of dangerous and responsible duty; but I am constrained to believe that it is better for him, and will be more satisfactory to his friends, as well as to the friends of those still on board of the Polaris, that they should be published as given, rather than that their suppression should be made the foundation of sensational and alarming reports in no degree justified by the real facts.

It must, however, be clearly understood that in permitting this publication the Department neither makes nor declares any judgment against Mr. Buddington, who is still absent in the midst of dangers, and has had no opportunity for defense or explanation.

Then Robeson laid into Buddington with a damning paragraph:

The facts show that though he was perhaps wanting in enthusiasm for the grand objects of the expedition, and at times grossly lax in discipline, and though he differed in judgment from others as to the possibility, safety, and propriety of taking the ship farther north, yet he is an experienced and careful navigator, and when not affected by liquor, of which there remained none on board at the time of the separation, a competent and safe commander.

Obviously no question remained in the minds of the board of inquiry as to who was to be the scapegoat for a poorly planned and disorganized expedition.

With the fate of the *Polaris* still up in the air, the navy mobilized a relief force with surprising speed. The cries of the newspaper editorialists, the general population, and politicians to rescue the stranded explorers hastened their efforts. A three-masted steamship, the USS *Juniata*, embarked for Greenland on the twenty-fourth of June with seventy tons of coal and extra lumber. This time the navy was taking no chances. Everyone aboard was regular navy, officers and crew. The one exception was Capt. James O. Budding-ton, the uncle of Sidney O. Buddington. Employed as the ice pilot, the uncle might have sailed in an attempt to rescue the family name as well as his nephew.

Racing from Holsteinsborg to Disko and then on to Upernavik, Commander D.L. Braine of the *Juniata* gathered sled dogs and seal-skins for the relief column. At Disko, Karrup Smith, the Danish dis-trict inspector, related Captain Hall's fears of never returning from the expedition as he turned over Hall's manuscript of his search for Sir John Franklin. Ironically now both Hall's and Franklin's bones would reside forever in the Arctic.

With everything set to go, Braine's expedition ground to a halt. None of the Inuit would guide their sleds. The superstitious Inuit sensed that bad joss followed anything associated with the *Polaris*.

In frustration Braine anchored in Upernavik. The steam launch was lowered, filled with food and two months of coal for its boil-ers, and christened the *Little Juniata*. Lieutenant George Washing-ton DeLong, James Buddington, and eight volunteers steamed off on August 2. For nine days they sailed along the Greenland coast of Baffin Bay, searching and poking into suitable coves for signs of the rest of the *Polaris* expedition. Ice and heavy fog blocked fur-ther passage north off Cape York, so the *Little Juniata* returned empty-handed.

After receiving Secretary Robeson's troubling report, President Grant brought the power of his office to bear on the matter. Eyes were looking at him, and he wanted the matter of the *Polaris*'s sur-vival resolved—and quickly. Grant met personally with Joseph Henry, president of the National Academy of Sciences; Spencer Baird; Professor Newcomb, of the Naval Observatory; and Profes-sor Hilgarde, of the Coastal Survey Office. The scientists felt that the testimony proved the *Polaris* was still seaworthy, and they as-sured Grant that the missing half of the crew still had a good chance of being alive. The president's consulting with these men, each a member of the National Academy of Sciences, with no naval representatives present sent a message to the Navy Department:

Grant was unhappy with their performance and was prepared to go outside the regular channels to resolve this matter.

Suddenly red tape dissolved. Secretary Robeson found sixty thousand dollars to purchase the sturdy little *Tigress*, which had rescued Tyson. Built in 1871, the 350-ton vessel was especially designed for sealing in Arctic waters and had the widely flaring hull that the *Polaris* fatally lacked.

With an iron-braced frame, buttressed with heavy beams, and carrying half-inch iron plating along the forward twelve feet of the three-foot-thick bow, the *Tigress* was exactly the vessel the *Polaris* should have been. After her boilers had been converted to burn anthracite coal and her quarters modified, the newly acquired naval steamer sailed from the Brooklyn Navy Yard.

Learning from their mistakes, the navy filled the ship with commissioned officers and men. George Tyson volunteered his expertise and was named ice master, with the rank of acting lieutenant. Ebierbing accompanied Tyson. Hans and his family sailed as far as Disko before returning to their village on the coast.

Under the glare of publicity, many of the crewmen from the ice floe bravely volunteered to return with the rescue effort. In the three months since their rescue, all had fully recuperated and were fit to ship aboard a rescue mission for their comrades. However, when the *Tigress* left, most failed to show up. Only Gustavus Lindquist, William Lindermann, and Robert Kruger sailed. Interestingly the rest of the German seamen slipped into the shadows. History has swallowed them.

Frank Y. Commagere, the noted correspondent of the *New York Herald* who was covering the story, attempted to join the relief effort but was refused. The navy was leery of what it might find, even if half the rumors were untrue. Undaunted, Commagere enlisted in the navy as an ordinary seaman and shipped aboard. When Commander Greer, the captain, discovered who Commagere was, long after the *Tigress* was too far north to turn back, he grudgingly promoted the reporter to yeoman in recognition of his ingenuity. Greer also got back at the *Herald* reporter by quartering him in the forward deckhouse with Hans and his family, whose lack of hygiene offended the noses of all the officers and men.

Ever mindful of the closing window of summer, Greer made all speed to Upernavik, rendezvousing with the *Juniata* on August 10. Two days later the *Tigress* found the *Little Juniata* and learned the distressing news that no trace of the *Polaris* or Buddington had been found.

Greer then drove the *Tigress* up the coast, past Cape York to Northumberland Island. Since their abandonment on the ice, a battle had raged between Frederick Meyer and George Tyson as to their exact location when separated from the *Polaris*. While Meyer steadfastly swore they were off Northumberland Island and based all his calculations on that notion, Tyson believed just as adamantly that the island they saw on the horizon was Littleton. Now Tyson had the satisfaction of seeing that he was right. Northumberland held no signs of the *Polaris* or its remaining crew.

Doggedly Greer sailed close by Cape Parry, Cape Alexander, and Hartstene Bay looking for survivors among the rugged outcroppings of the Greenland coast.

As the *Tigress* approached Littleton Island, Tyson and his former companions shouted out in recognition. The ragged peaks of Littleton and its smaller island, McGary, remained etched in their minds. Greer dropped anchor and lowered a boat.

While they pulled for shore, the sounds of human voices drifted across the waters from the land. "Silence!" Greer ordered. Scanning the rocky coast, Greer shouted, "I see their house! Two tents, and human figures are on the mainland near Littleton Island!"

As the excited rescuers waded ashore, their hearts sank into their rubber boots. The figures were Inuit. Running to meet them were natives wearing scraps of clothing discarded by Buddington and his men. Tyson recognized a half-rotted hawser belonging to the *Polaris* tied to a rock by the shore. The frayed end of the line floated loosely in the churning surf.

Through Ebierbing and Tyson, Greer learned from the chief that Captain Buddington's group had built two boats and set sail "about the time when the ducks begin to hatch." Greer bristled when the village leader informed him that Buddington had made him a present of the *Polaris* before the men left. The ship was a commissioned naval vessel and belonged to the United States.

To the great distress of the new owner, however, the *Polaris* had attempted to follow her crew. Breaking loose during a gale, the ship drifted a mile and a half after her men before sinking. Now she belonged completely to the Arctic, like Charles Francis Hall, and that cold territory had no intention of giving her up. When Greer rowed to the spot where the ship had foundered, he found her grave marked by two icebergs that had grounded on the sunken vessel.

Examining the wooden and canvas house that remained proved unsettling. While the wooden bunks, galley, and carpenter's bench remained intact, the floor was strewn with stores and broken instruments. The naval officers along with Tyson gasped at the disorder. Rigging, bags of potatoes, corn, tea, pork, and meal covered the floor, interspersed with broken compasses and medical supplies. The ship's bell lay beside a pile of broken firearms. As Tyson bitterly noted, "There is one thing certain; these men did not suffer from the want of food or fuel, as discarded provisions were lying scattered all among the rocks, and, of course, the natives had eaten all they wanted in the interval besides."

This wanton destruction cannot be blamed on the Inuit. No Native would destroy a coveted rifle or pistol, and anything metal, such as the instruments, would be kept for trade. The frenzied destruction bore the stamp of frustrated men venting their rage on their own things as they departed a camp that might have been unbearable to them.

Shaking his head, Greer walked among the mess, collecting torn books and manuscripts and broken instruments. Not only was this deliberate destruction of government property, but maintaining records of the expedition and its scientific findings was one of the highest priorities of the mission, next only to reaching the North Pole. Examining the mutilated papers aboard the *Tigress*, Tyson and Greer found many pages missing from the logs. The defacing of the logs and journals was carefully done, something entirely different from the random scattering of the supplies. All references to the death of Captain Hall were torn out. "I had an opportunity last evening," Tyson wrote in another journal he had started on boarding the *Tigress*, "of looking over the mutilated diaries and journals left in the deserted hut off Littleton Island. Not one but has the leaves cut out relating to Captain Hall's death." In fact, no mention of the separation of Tyson's group on the night of October 15 existed either.

It appeared as if someone had taken great pains to systematically eliminate any notation of those two events. Tellingly, on one scrap of torn paper, Tyson found the written words *"Captain Hall's papers thrown overboard today."*

As Greer's men searched further, no evidence of the ship's scientific papers could be found. The captain decided to return at once. No survivors were at the winter site.

Leaving the ruined camp astern, Commander Greer next steered the *Tigress* across the straits and hunted down the eastern side of Baffin Island, just in case the currents had carried Buddington's boats to the west, as they had Tyson's ice floe. As Greer and Tyson traced the coastline to the east, the *Juniata* left Upernavik and resumed combing the western side of the bay. By running both sides of the bay, they hoped to find Buddington and his men.

One night as the *Juniata* steamed through the dark waters far from the *Tigress*, the horizon ahead exploded with signal rockets and flashing lights. The *Juniata* hove to and prepared to meet the oncoming vessel. It was the *Cabot*, a swift steamer, hired by the U.S. consul Molloy, bearing the news that the rest of the *Polaris* survivors had finally been found. Hurriedly the captain of the *Cabot* related the events surrounding the rescue of the remaining group from the *Polaris* debacle.

On June 3 the Scottish whaler the *Ravenscraig*, out of Dundee, had spotted Buddington's two boats beached on an ice floe. Their flag waving atop one of the boat's masts clearly marked them as white men in distress. The watch in the crow's nest first thought the men on the ice were whalers from another Scottish vessel. But those on the ice were waving hats, and all the Scots wore woolen caps. Someone suggested that the group they watched might be survivors of the *Polaris*, and a rescue party was hurriedly formed. As the ice beset the *Ravenscraig*, a party of eighteen volunteers trekked over the ice to rescue the exhausted men.

Due to shortage of space, half the rescued crew was transferred to another whaler, the *Arctic*. On July 17 the *Ravenscraig* crossed paths with a steamer, the *Intrepid*, and transferred Bryan, Booth, and Mauch to that ship. The remnants of the *Polaris*'s crew sailed about in these three ships while the whalers continued their hunt. By August 10 the *Arctic* filled her hold with whale oil; picked up Buddington, Morton, Odell, and Coffin from the *Ravenscraig*; and sailed for home, arriving there on September 19.

The three men aboard the *Intrepid* were transferred to another whaler, the *Eric*, on September 13. After a stormy and prolonged voyage, the last of the *Polaris* survivors stepped ashore in Dundee, Scotland, on October 22, 1873.

More than three months after the rescue of Buddington's group, a weary Charles Tyson arrived in St. John's aboard the *Tigress* on October 16, to watch the harbor pilot climb aboard. The first words out of the pilot's mouth were, "The *Polaris* party is safe."

After two years, the last of the *Polaris* expedition had finally escaped from the grasp of the Arctic. Miraculously, only one man—their leader, Charles Francis Hall—had died.

Chapter Sixteen

THE WHITEWASH

The Polar field is a great testing ground. Those who pass through the winters of darkness and days of trial above the circle of ice know better than others the weaknesses of human nature and their own insufficiencies.
—ANTHONY FIALA, 1905

On September 19, 1873, a telegram from William Reid, the United States vice consul to Great Britain, via the new transatlantic cable, broke the news that Buddington had been found. That day the New York papers, including the *Herald*, spread the word to the anxious people of New York. "The Dundee whaling-steamer *Arctic* had arrived at Dundee, having on board Captain Buddington and the remainder of the *Polaris* crew," read the quote from the telegram. Better than the best mystery novel of the time, the events of the *Polaris* expedition had captivated the public's attention and fueled its desire for more of the sordid facts.

Little more was known save the fact that Captain Allen of the *Ravenscraig* had divided the crew and transferred them to two other ships. All of the rescued men landed at Dundee aboard the *Arctic* except Chaplain Bryan, Joseph Mauch, and John Booth. These last three men reached Scotland aboard the whaling vessel *Intrepid* some days later. While the separation was undoubtedly prompted by limited space aboard the *Arctic*, why those three men were chosen is unclear. Perhaps the guilt-ridden Bryan could no longer stay with the others.

Although telegrams flew back and forth between England and the United States, not one of them came from Emil Bessel. Bessel sent no messages to Professors Henry, Baird, or any of those at the Smithsonian who had sponsored him. Curiously Bessel chose to send his telegram to Professor Petermann in Germany and not to his family or friends in Germany or to any friends he had in the United States. Why? Was the Prussian physician informing the German government of news that it had hoped to hear? That the United States expedition had failed? If anything, the doctor's actions signify that his loyalties were still to the fatherland rather than to America in general or to those who had appointed him in particular.

While the public clamored for more details, the board of inquiry dragged its heels, hoping the controversy would quiet down. Six days passed before Buddington and the ten men in his group caught a steamship from London to New York. They arrived in New York on October 4. There the navy tug *Catalpa* conveyed them to the waiting USS *Tallapoosa*. Unlike Tyson's party, who had been whisked before the board, the second group was allowed one whole week to prepare for questioning.

Mr. Bryan, perhaps recognized by all involved as an innocent, was permitted two additional weeks to travel abroad before returning home. Mauch and Booth waited for him, so the three men were not questioned until the day before Christmas. Their testimony would be taken more as an afterthought, appended to the report to become a mere footnote. Consciously or unconsciously Bryan had moved to separate himself from his shipmates.

Once more the board of inquiry met aboard the *Tallapoosa*. Significantly this time the board was smaller. Admiral Goldsborough extracted himself from the proceedings, as did Spencer Baird. Both men sensed that nothing good lay ahead. Keeping the Smithsonian and the rest of the navy at arm's length suited their purpose. Robeson, Reynolds, and Howgate plodded on. While these men desperately wished to close the book on this unhappy matter, the spreading rumors prevented them from doing so. Whispers of mutiny and murder persisted.

Captain Buddington came first. Tyson had labeled Buddington as disruptive: "I must say that he was a disorganizer from the very commencement."

Well aware of Tyson's damning testimony, Buddington approached the board with a mixture of bluster, denial, and anger. Immediately he attacked the credibility of George Tyson, his most vociferous critic:

Captain Tyson. He is a man that was rather useless aboard, and complained bitterly about the management generally. He did not appear to be satisfied with anything that was done. I would consult him on the subject and he would perhaps agree to it, and then afterward would say that he thought it was no use to do anything of that kind; that he knew it was of no use. He generally acted that way. I got so that after a while I did not pay much attention to him.

Portraying Tyson as a malcontent weakened the navigator's charges but only stirred the muddy waters. Rightly worried that he would be blamed for the failure to reach the North Pole, especially after Hall's death, Buddington denied having opposed Hall's desire to sail farther north when the ice once more cleared:

No conversation occurred in which Chester and Tyson expressed a desire to go north while I expressed a disinclination to do so. I never so expressed myself. I have seen that report printed in the papers, but it is not correct. No man in the ship would ever so express himself to Captain Hall and get along with him.

Lamely, Buddington added, "I did my very best to get the ship north. I never said anything about never going further north."

Chester and Tyson said otherwise. Someone was lying. As the first mate and Tyson had little love for each other, it appears the liar was Buddington.

On the defensive from the start, Buddington slowly came to realize that he would escape the tribunal without punishment but his career was ruined. Gradually he lost his animation and slipped into mumbled, lethargic answers.

Yes, he "did not see any chance to get north" of Repulse Harbor, and no, "no formal survey of the ship was held" before he abandoned her. To the officers of the panel, failure to carefully document the problems of the *Polaris* before abandoning her was unthinkable. A survey in which the other officers and the ship's carpenter examined the damage to the ship, including its weaknesses as well as its strengths, would have determined whether the vessel was still sound. Now they had only Buddington's word on the matter. Unlike the tradition in which a captain goes down with his ship, Buddington appeared to have lost his will to fight the ice and a leaking hull and chosen to "go from his ship" rather than risk going down with it.

On the matter of his drinking, Buddington admitted to only two episodes, including the one when Dr. Bessel had caught him.

"I went to the aft hatch to get something to drink," he admitted. Referring to Bessel's trap, he continued matter-of-factly, "He was down there at the time and made some remarks about it." Trying to gauge the response of the secretary, Buddington shrugged and added, "I just took him by the collar and told him to mind his own business."

The captain underestimated Robeson's reaction. "Was not the alcohol put on board for scientific purposes?"

"Yes, sir," Buddington answered sullenly.

"What did you drink it for?"

Buddington tried for sympathy. "I was sick and down-hearted, and had a bad cold, and I wanted some stimulant." When he saw the frown on Commodore Reynolds's face, the whaling captain waffled. "That is, I thought I did."

The frown deepened. "I do not suppose I really did," Buddington finally admitted.

But he refused to admit that the problem was chronic. When asked if he was "in the habit of drinking alcohol," he lied. "I make it a practice to drink but very little."

Ringing in the ears of the panel was Frederick Jamka's statement that "Captain Buddington was drunk very often" and the words of John Herron that "Captain Buddington if he drinks at all must get drunk."

Inch by inch Buddington retreated, confirming the picture

painted by the ice floe survivors of his undermining Hall's authority at every opportunity and his vehement opposition to pressing farther north while Hall had lived and even after he died. While Buddington never disobeyed a direct order, his opposition hamstrung the pliable Hall's efforts.

Buddington admitted growling at Noah Hayes to "save all those shavings and put them in a barrel." While Hayes looked on openmouthed, Buddington continued his diatribe against Hall's orders to save any combustible scraps, taking the opportunity to jab at Hall's enthusiasm for sledding to the North Pole. Referring to the scraps, Buddington snapped, "They will do for the devilish fools on the sledge-journey."

Of course, Hall overheard. Studying his clasped hands closely, Buddington admitted to the panel, "It was the worse thing I could have said in his case, as he was very much in favor of sledge-journeys. . . ."

As to the nature of Captain Hall's death, Buddington confirmed the man's fears of poisoning but remained strangely vague for one who had spent much time watching Hall die. His recollection of Hall's words to him the afternoon before his death raised more questions about the mysterious relapse. "I shall be in to breakfast with you in the morning, and Mr. Chester and Mr. Morton need not sit up with me at night," Buddington recalled his commander saying. "I am as well as I ever was."

Buddington's recounting of Hall's sudden relapse that night is chilling:

He was sitting in the berth, with his feet hanging over, his head going one way and the other, and the eyes very glassy, and looking like a corpse—frightful to look at. He wanted to know how they would spell "murder." He spelled it several different ways, and kept on for some time. At last he straightened up and looked around, and recognized who they were, and looked at the doctor. He says, "Doctor, I know everything that's going on; you can't fool me," and he called for some water. He undertook to swallow the water, but he couldn't. He heaved it up. They persuaded him to lie down, and he did so, breathing very hard.

About the captain's papers, Buddington was even more evasive. He insisted that Joseph Mauch had charge of Hall's papers. "The clerk had charge of them and stored them in a box ... a large japanned tin box." According to Buddington, Tookoolito held the keys to the box. "The key was among a lot of keys. I think Hannah had the whole of them. She had control of the keys and about everything Captain Hall had." To suggest that the officers of the *Polaris* expedition would entrust an Inuit woman with important journals and logs that were official records is incredible.

Contradicting Meyer's testimony that the papers had been on Buddington's desk the night of the separation, the captain insisted that the box was thrown onto the ice. He did, however, reveal that Hall's letter criticizing him had been burned:

> At one time during his sickness we were having a talk together about one thing and another. He said he had written a letter to me and took it out, and he thought I had better not see it; but if I insisted, he would show it to me. I told him it didn't make any odds. He then said he thought it ought to be burned, as he did not approve of it, and he held it to the candle and burned it.

Tyson's previous testimony was quite different. Referring to Buddington's conversation with him about the burning, the navigator told the panel: "He told me he was glad the papers were burned, because they were much against him; and he got him to burn them."

Had Buddington influenced the dying Hall to do that? Did he burn the letter himself? Was he responsible for cutting the pages referring to Hall's death and the abandonment of Tyson's party out of the discarded journals and logs? The committee would never ask, and it would never learn the answers to those questions.

The confused structure of command now hamstrung the committee as it had Charles Francis Hall. Buddington had surely been insubordinate and weak, but he was a hired whaling captain, not a commissioned officer. The navy could not court-martial him. The scientific advisory panel had no hold over him either. At worst they might sue him for failing to uphold his sailing contract. But even that was doubtful.

One can almost feel the somber realization seeping into the minds of the hearing officers. Every stone they overturned revealed another ugly fact. And all the findings pointed to one dismal conclusion: there were no heroes and no glory to be found from the *Polaris* expedition. To a man the examiners must have realized that their best course was to close this proceeding down as quietly and as quickly as possible. Putting a lid on the rotten events would keep the stench from spreading to the panel and would allow the whole affair to slip from the public's view.

The whaling captain stepped down. Now it was the turn of the others to tell their side of this murky tale.

As the crew testified one by one, they fleshed out the details of an expedition in serious trouble from the start. No one escaped unscathed except perhaps for Chaplain Bryan. But even he found himself lacking.

If the panel had intended to hang Buddington over his drinking, their hopes dissolved as the hearing unfolded. Raiding the liquor stores and later the specimen alcohol had involved both crew and officers. Fingers pointed at one another. The half-mad carpenter Coffin stated that he had seen Hubbard Chester "under the influence of alcohol." Evidence emerged that Emil Schuman made a key in his engine room workshop to open the lock to Bessel's alcohol locker.

Schuman attempted to deflect the blame onto George Tyson. "I saw Captain Tyson drunk like old mischief," the engineer volunteered. "I saw Captain Tyson when he could scarcely move along."

When Bryan finally came before the board, he implicated everyone except Captain Hall. The chaplain told of how the crew discovered they could reach the locked alcohol by crawling along the space surrounding the engine shaft. Of the officers, he said, "Of course when the officers did go and take the liquor and did get drunk, all that could be done was to accept the fact, and keep them quiet and get them to bed as soon as possible."

No easy answers came from the second inquiry. Events following the terrible night of October 15 remained frustratingly out of focus, even when seen from the other point of view. How diligently had Buddington and the crew aboard the *Polaris* really looked for their companions? For every question the board asked, it got an ambiguous answer.

Chester insisted he had spent most of the day up the mast looking for his shipmates. Hobby also claimed to have looked. "I was up twice to look for the separated party," he testified. But he admitted that "there was no one looking from the masthead about 4 P.M.," the exact time Tyson's party saw the ship tie up to the iceberg.

Noah Hayes added more: "After the separation, when morning came, I do not think we looked for our comrades right away."

Only Coffin thought he saw the abandoned party. Unsure and confused about reality, he told Chester. "In regard to the ice floe party, I had an idea—whether it was imagination or not I do not know—but I thought I saw a large number of men on the piece of ice that was nearly like a berg, and a number sufficiently great to indicate that it was our party."

Chester spoke of seeing dark objects on the ice that he took to be provisions, but Coffin disagreed. "I saw no provisions, or anything else." What he saw were men, he thought. "They were near enough to me to take in the whole outline of them; they were on a piece of ice that was floating—moving with the current very rapidly. The time I thought I saw these men on the ice was just before dark."

Of all those left aboard the *Polaris*, the paranoid carpenter was the last person anyone would believe. In the end the carpenter doubted his own eyes.

One of the doubts that plagued Bryan emerged under questioning. "The separation of the ice floe party was entirely accidental," he said. But then his concern slipped out. "Unless some person maliciously cut the rope." Shaking his head, he corrected his lapse. "Which I have no idea was the case," he added.

Finally the board turned to the last—and most disturbing—part of its examination: the death of Charles Francis Hall. Since Bessel had treated Hall, Robeson enlisted the help of W. K. Barnes, surgeon general of the army, and J. Beale, surgeon general of the navy, to evaluate the treatment. After all, the patient had died. The testimony by Noah Hayes of Bessel's laughing and lighthearted quip that "Captain Hall's death was the best thing that could happen for the expedition" raised serious questions that the doctor might have murdered his commander. The blue vapors and poisonous odors that Mauch (who had some training in pharmacology) smelled further fueled the fires of suspicion.

Bessel faced the two surgeons and his three interrogators with his usual haughty disdain. While everyone else managed to lose their scientific records and logbooks, Bessel had saved his notes, especially the ones made during Captain Hall's final days.

Apoplexy, Bessel answered without hesitation. Captain Hall had suffered a stroke.

"What might have been the immediate cause of the seizure?" Surgeon General Barnes asked.

"My idea of the cause of the first attack is that he had been exposed to very low temperature during the time that he was on the sledge journey," Bessel surmised. "He came back and entered a warm cabin without taking off his heavy fur clothing, and then took a warm cup of coffee." The "little German dancing master" paused for effect. "And anyone knows what the consequences of that would be."

A hot cup of coffee will not cause a stroke—not even in a hypothermic person, and Hall was not hypothermic. He had just mushed back to camp, so he was, if anything, overheated.

Incredibly the two surgeons general of the military swallowed Bessel's explanation. Perhaps the two officers had not practiced medicine for some time and had forgotten their clinical training. Rising to the rank of a surgeon general in the army or navy, a medical officer trades in his stethoscope and becomes an administrator. In all likelihood the two physicians cross-examining Bessel had not laid hands on a patient for years. That would be the kindest interpretation for their lack of medical knowledge. Sadly the admiral and general fell victim to their pride and refused to admit to their ignorance of clinical medicine.

A far darker possibility exists. Perhaps the two examining doctors refrained from criticizing Bessel's treatment under orders. Hall was dead. Nothing could bring him back. Accusing Bessel of poisoning Hall or even mismanaging his care would have opened grave questions that would lead directly to those who had chosen the doctor. After all, the reputations of the Smithsonian and the National Academy of Sciences rode on the line with Bessel's competence. Not a shard of evidence exists to support this, however. But the blind acceptance of Bessel's strange antics by his medical peers is very troubling.

When Bessel saw the two doctors' heads nod sagely in agreement, the Prussian must have known after that they would believe whatever he told them, especially since he had it written down.

Using his notes as reference, Bessel continued, glossing over the fact that stomach pains, of a burning nature, and vomiting do not usually precede a cerebrovascular accident. "While he was in this comatose state I applied a mustard poultice to his legs and breast. Besides that, I made cold water applications to his head and put blisters on his neck."

Slapping cold compresses and mustard plasters on his body did nothing to help Hall but is consistent with medical treatment of the time. Having nothing useful to offer, a doctor would fall back on poultices. When President Abraham Lincoln was dying after a bullet had destroyed his brain, his doctors applied mustard plasters for want of something else to do.

"In about twenty-five minutes he recovered consciousness. I found that he was taken by hemiplegia. His left arm and left side were paralyzed, including the face and tongue, the point of which was deflected to the left. I made him take purgatives. I gave him a cathartic consisting of castor oil and three or four drops of croton oil."

Purging would not help a patient with an acute stroke. In fact, the dehydration and shift in electrolytes it might cause could prove harmful. But here again, Bessel's treatment was within the scope of current practice. Certainly paralysis of one side of the body is consistent with a finding of cerebrovascular accident, but certain types of poison can produce the same effect. Yet Hall's paralysis is confirmed only by Meyer's testimony. As the others stated, Hall was up and about before his fatal relapse. Herman Sieman wrote in his journal on November 1: "The captain appeared to grow better, as he spoke as sensibly as any of us."

The next day Bessel found Hall's temperature to fluctuate between 83°F and 111°F. To correct the elevated temperature, the doctor told the committee he injected one and a half grains of quinine under the skin of the explorer's leg. It is hard to imagine the two surgeons' accepting this. Quinine was used at the time to reduce fevers, but no human can survive with a temperature as low as 83°F or as high as 111°F. As mentioned before, the readings are unbelievable.

No one on the panel questioned why Bessel had continued injecting Hall with his white powder long after the man's temperature returned to normal. And no one wondered why Hall got better when he refused to let Bessel near him. When the suspicious leader permitted only Tookoolito to make his food, he recovered miraculously. When Hall refused to take Bessel's medicines, why did the doctor not allow Bryan to take the drink to prove to Hall it was not poisoned? Maybe it was. Perhaps the fact that it was the chaplain who eventually convinced Hall to resume the Prussian's injections later tormented Mr. Bryan.

> The doctor at one time wanted to administer a dose of quinine, and the captain would not take it. The doctor came to me and wanted me to persuade Captain Hall to take it. I did so, and saw him prepare the medicine; he had little white crystals, and he heated them in a little glass bowl; heated the water apparently to dissolve the crystals. That is all I know about any medicine. It was given in the form of an injection under the skin in his leg.

Immediately after that, Hall suddenly reversed his recovery and died.

In the end the surgeons found no reason to suspect foul play or criticize Emil Bessel's conduct. It was easier to turn a blind eye. Questioning the good doctor's actions would besmirch the National Academy of Sciences and the Smithsonian. Their select committee had, after all, chosen Bessel. It was bad enough that the expedition had failed to reach the Pole and lost the bulk of its scientific observations. Finding a killer in their midst was too unthinkable, especially one who had been chosen by the country's preeminent scientists.

At Secretary Robeson's request, the two surgeons general affixed their conclusions to the report:

We, the undersigned, were present by request of the Honorable Secretary of the Navy, at the examination of Dr. Emil Bessel, in regard to the cruise of the *Polaris* and the circumstances connected with the illness and death of Captain Hall. We listened to his testimony with great care and put to him such questions as we deemed necessary.

From the circumstances and symptoms detailed by him, and comparing them with the medical testimony of all the witnesses, we are conclusively of the opinion that Captain Hall died from natural causes, viz., apoplexy; and that the treatment of the case by Dr. Bessel was the best practicable under the circumstances.

That was it. Bessel, the chosen one, was above reproach. Buddington, for all his faults, was a civilian and could not be court-martialed by the navy. Tyson and his complaints were dismissed as the ramblings of a malcontent. The poor performance of the crew? Well, they had suffered enough.

The board recommended that no action be taken against any of the members of the expedition. No further investigations ought to be undertaken, they wrote. To the relief of all the bureaucrats, the case was closed.

All the dirt was swept under the rug. But it made a sizable bump, one that refused to flatten out of view.

The public's taste for Arctic discovery, for the brave men who risked their lives in that region, and especially for more details of what had happened to the *Polaris* remained unsatisfied. Already books about the disaster were in the works. The specter of the doomed ship continued to loom over the whole affair. Instead of being called the United States polar expedition, everyone referred to the exploration as the *Polaris* expedition.

Charles Francis Hall was elevated to the status of a martyr. His only known photograph was copied and transposed onto various lithographs. In the first book published about the *Polaris*, Hall's image appears as the frontispiece, sharing a page with a photograph of the saintly Dr. Elisha Kent Kane.

The first book to hit the bookstalls tried its best to put a good face on the fiasco. William H. Cunnington appended *The Polar*

Exploration onto Epes Sargent's *The Wonders of the Arctic World*, published by the Philadelphia Book Company in 1873, just months after the rescue and hearings.

"From Official and Trustworthy Sources," the subtitle said. But no mention was made of the divisiveness that had rocked the expedition. Little was said of Hall's ranting about poison and nothing about Buddington's attraction to liquor. One example demonstrates the book's tone:

> It is known to our readers that when news of Captain Hall's death was first received in this country the grief and consternation in the public mind was intensified by rumors that he had been poisoned. As ill reports like ill news travel apace, it was soon in everybody's mouth that malice, engendered by jealousy or by distaste of his rule, had destroyed the daring and enterprising navigator. Secretary Robeson, with his characteristic promptness, determined to sift these vague charges, and fearlessly to bring the foul deed home to its perpetrator, or to prove their falsity and relieve the absent from their taint. He saw that a thorough investigation alone could effect this. . . .

The cover-up had begun.

The authors quoted from the official report: "We reach the unanimous opinion that the death of Captain Hall resulted naturally, from disease, without fault on the part of any one." Grandly Sargent and Cunnington followed that with a sweeping paragraph:

> Thus, the vague rumors, and the more positive charges built on them, were swept away, and the people of the country, while sincerely mourning their eminent fellow American and heartily deploring his death, were relieved from the state of excitement that his supposed murder had naturally induced.

The next book out was not so kind. *Arctic Experiences, Containing Capt. George E. Tyson's Wonderful Drift on the Ice-Floe*, edited by E. Vale Blake, was published in 1874 by Harper & Brothers in New York. The publisher that had caught the first photographic image of the Tyson party saw the need for a more informative treatment.

Relying heavily on George Tyson's journal, the book widely disseminated the navigator's bitter accusations against Buddington, Meyer, and Bessel. Unlike Cunnington's work, Blake included testimony from the hearing, notes, and Tyson's journals. On December 22, 1873, two days before testifying, Chaplain Bryan had answered a letter from Blake requesting his thoughts on the number of people who had climbed the mast to look for Tyson's group. Sadly, Bryan answered with candor: "During the winter I greatly regretted that I did not go up the masthead myself, but I never had an idea that I would have seen them."

Blake's book fanned the embers of the persistent stories, causing them to burst into flames. The fact that the Geographic Society of Paris awarded the Gold Medal of the Roquette Foundation posthumously to Charles Francis Hall did little to dispel the rumors. Finally the U.S. government moved to quash the whole affair. It commissioned Rear Adm. C. H. Davis of the Naval Observatory to write the official version of the event. Published by the Government Printing Office, the *Narrative of the North Polar Expedition, U.S. Ship* Polaris appeared in 1876 and sought to be the definitive work on what had happened. To those alert enough to read the title page, the words "edited under the direction of the Hon. G. M. Robeson, Secretary of the Navy" must have proved troubling.

Davis's 686-page book, bound with a gilt cover, amounted to a massive whitewash. Mesmerizing the reader with day-by-day minutiae, the admiral glosses over the conflicts and shortcomings of the expedition. Testimony, journals, and even the official inquiries are edited to present the most favorable picture. Viewed through Davis's rose-colored glasses, the *Polaris* expedition consisted of happy, singing comrades who had suffered bad luck yet went on in the best possible tradition of the navy.

Nothing could have been further from the truth. But the "official report" achieved its desired goal. The disaster of the *Polaris* expedition gradually faded from people's minds.

Chapter Seventeen

1968

Nowhere along the coast of Greenland have I seen such a desolate strip of shore as the site of Polaris House and its neighborhood, and the first glance shows that the selection of the site was not a matter of choice, but of the direst necessity.

—ROBERT EDWIN PEARY, 1898

Beneath a threatening sky, four men stood beside the pile of dirt and willow-laced stones that marked the grave of Charles Francis Hall. The time was August 1968, three years and three months shy of a century since the coffin of the commander of the *Polaris* expedition had been lowered into the frozen ground. Their presence was no mere coincidence. To stand on that desolate strip of rocky scree had taken months of hard work, research, and perseverance. The leader of this tiny group was Charles C. Loomis, professor of English at Dartmouth College and a renowned Arctic scholar with four previous explorations to the frozen North under his belt. His love of photography had led him to the Arctic, prompted by his filming of musk oxen on Alaska's Nunivak Island. Loomis was preparing a biography of Charles Francis Hall under a Smithsonian postdoctoral fellowship.

On their arrival the previous morning, a windless day and clear blue sky had greeted the group. The single-engine Otter leaped over the foothills ringing the plain and descended in widening arcs over the ice-free blue waters of Hall Basin. Following the scalloped shoreline of Thank God Harbor, the aircraft touched down on a relatively level site a mile below the wreckage of Emil Bessel's observatory. The large tundra tires bounced and scrunched over the rough shale, and the radial engine sputtered to a halt.

Time and clear flying weather are especially precious to every bush pilot. A storm might loom over the horizon at any moment, flipping the plane or forcing an unwanted stay. Hurriedly the passengers unloaded their gear and stepped back. The plane's engine coughed to life, belching a cloud of oily smoke. Revving the engine, the pilot, W. W. Phipps, spun the nose into the light wind and took off, trailing a cloud of glacial silt and pebbles. Phipps would return in two weeks, weather permitting. The men were on their own.

As Loomis watched their link to civilization vanish into a silver speck, the utter and terrible isolation of this place struck him. One minute they had been flying bumpily along, encased in a marvel of modern aeronautical engineering, and the next instant the four of them were standing alone on a desolate plain. Stretching as far as their eyes could see was a steely ocean and a brooding umber land that killed humans with total indifference.

Half-dazed, the four men pitched camp and wandered about the plain. They walked to the ruins of Bessel's observatory. The four wooden walls built by Chester and Coffin lay shattered and blown down as if ripped apart by a bomb blast. The Arctic winds had flattened the unwanted building, but ice and snow had not destroyed the traces of that fateful party. Instead, the cold had preserved things that would have vanished long ago in warmer climates.

Wandering about the wreck of the observatory, the four stepped back a century in time. The same brass nails, ice saw, cast-iron stoves, shards of glass, and scraps of sailcloth abandoned by the original *Polaris* expedition lay at their feet. In their hands they held objects that men long dead had touched. One of Loomis's companions, ex-marine Tom Gignoux, recently back from a tour of duty in Vietnam, uncovered a wooden board on which Sgt. William Cross of the doomed Greely expedition had carved his name before the land killed him. Gignoux recognized the round ice balls scattered about the ruins for what they were—ice grenades, balls of ice packed with gunpowder, constructed long ago by the crew of the

Polaris in their futile attempt to blast the ship free of the ice. The black powder retained its explosive properties in the cold climate.

Upon their arrival, the Arctic looked benign. Overnight its mood changed. Pewter clouds scudded overhead, so low that they appeared touchable. The sea took its cue from the darkened sky and turned leaden.

Unlike the sparse numbers of explorers who had passed Hall's grave, these modern visitors came to open it. After nearly one hundred years of questions, these men sought answers. During his research for Hall's biography, Loomis was troubled by the hasty judgment by the Navy Department's board of inquiry and its disregard of conflicting testimony. Studying the journals and transcripts gave Loomis no strong feeling that Hall had been murdered. He would later write in his book, *Weird and Tragic Shores*:

> My conclusion was, not that Hall certainly had been murdered, not even that he probably had been murdered, but only that murder was at least possible and plausible. The conclusion of the Board of Inquiry that he died of "natural causes, viz, apoplexy," also was possible and plausible, but it had been reached hastily and only by ignoring much of the evidence that the Board itself had wheedled out of the witnesses. Secretary Robeson had been under considerable pressure to end the investigation; scandal was in the making.

The unanswered questions prompted Loomis to seek an autopsy.

Reaching this point had not been easy. Flying to the remote site aboard a single-engine Otter, they quickly crossed the straits that had baffled so many before them. But surmounting the miles of red tape that had blocked their travel took months of dealing with the Danish Ministry for Greenland. Putting forth the argument that an autopsy would rightly have been ordered if Hall had died under suspicious circumstances in modern times, Loomis requested permission to visit the grave and disinter Hall's body.

The Danes referred Loomis to Count Eigel Knuth, an archaeologist and Arctic explorer who advised Denmark's Ministry for Greenland on proposed projects in its northern region. Knuth found the idea of digging up Hall's grave, which he had visited and considered "a hallowed place," totally repugnant. Only after flying to Copenhagen to meet with Knuth could Loomis change the old explorer's mind. Loomis promised to return the grave to exactly the condition in which he found it.

Now he stood beside the grave with William Barrett, Tom Gignoux, and Dr. Franklin Paddock, a pathologist. Paddock would perform the autopsy.

Things change slowly in the Arctic, and they hoped Captain Hall's body would speak from his grave. The recent studies on lead poisoning of Sir John Franklin's party gave reason to be optimistic. The frozen and well-preserved bodies of Royal Marine W. Braine and seamen John Hartnell and John Torrington, unearthed on Beechey Island in Lancaster Sound, provided useful information as to their deaths. Those men had died in 1846, long before Hall.

With some trepidation Loomis watched as Gignoux unroofed the shallow grave. Encased in ice, the Arctic retained its grip on the dead man. With luck the body would be perfectly preserved. The pine coffin appeared intact, even though the top was almost level with the ground. As the professor watched, he recalled the men of Hall's command laboring in the long night to carve the shallow grave out of frozen soil. Gignoux's task proved just as daunting. The layers of ice forced him to dig and shovel hunched over the coffin.

Suddenly the fetid odor of decay rose from the coffin. Loomis felt his heart sink. The mound of dirt had protected the pine wood, but the summer sun had melted the permafrost above the lid. Would the shallow nature of the grave defeat them? Was their quest in vain? Had Hall rotted in his tomb until only his bones remained? Loomis worried.

Gignoux's shovel caught a corner of the lid, splintering off a portion. Light fell upon white stars sewn on a field of blue. For the first time in almost a century, sunlight played upon an American flag that had flown when Ulysses Grant was president.

Loomis pried off the rest of the lid. The American flag covered Hall's face and the upper half of his body. Milky ice, melted and refrozen countless times over the century, encased the lower part of the body and held the back in its firm grip. Incongruously two stocking-covered feet poked through the sheet of ice.

Folding back the flag, Loomis studied Hall's face. Exposure to thawing and decay had altered the once-strong features. The robust beard and dark hair were gone, replaced by token wisps of brittle hair. Caught between the processes of mummification and decay, empty eye sockets and a sardonic grin greeted them. Minerals in the water had tanned what skin remained into a rich mahogany. In addition the dye from the flag had stained portions of the explorer's face blue, while the weave of the cloth textured the skin. To Loomis the face reminded him of a "Rouault portrait."

Performing the autopsy proved next to impossible. Frozen into the land he loved, Hall's coffin and body resisted all inspection. In a way his body had become an inseparable part of the land, as his spirit had. Wisely the men decided not to totally exhume the body. Working bent over the grave, Paddock found the internal organs totally dissolved into a frozen soup of ice. Unlike the bodies examined from Franklin's expedition, no viscera could be studied or tested. No stomach or intestines could be sampled for traces of poison or infection. No lungs could be examined for pneumonia or tuberculosis. And certainly nothing remained of the brain to tell whether it had suffered the stroke that Emil Bessel diagnosed. In despair the pathologist collected scraps of hair and a single fingernail.

With infinite care born of respect, the men restored the grave to its original state. It bothered Loomis that they could not avoid stripping away the ground willow that Hayes and Sieman had planted so long ago. Loomis himself replaced Noah Hayes's crowbar at its crooked angle.

During the two-week wait for their pilot, the specter of Captain Hall seemed to haunt them. In long walks they found themselves avoiding the grave site. The patterned face lingered in their thoughts. During that time the Arctic teased them with its changing weather, just as it had the men of the *Polaris*. The clear Hall Basin abruptly filled with ice and icebergs. Ghostly fogs came and went.

On the group's return home, the fingernail and hair were sent to the Toronto Center of Forensic Sciences for neutron-activation testing. No mention was made of the specifics of the sample, so the center had no idea who "C. F. Hall" was or the circumstances surrounding his death. Using neutrons to bombard the atoms in a test specimen causes that material's nuclei to become unstable. In the process those unstable nuclei decay, emitting electrons and protons. The half-life of that decay and the type of particles emitted are specific for different atomic elements. Iron, silver, gold, and arsenic all give off unique patterns.

The hair and fingernails of living subjects readily take up arsenic, making those tissues accurate markers of arsenic poisoning. The problem used to be the need for large quantities of tissue for analysis. Neutron-activation testing of minute quantities changed all that. Using neutron-activation analysis to search for arsenic received much publicity in the 1960s, when Sten Forshufvud used it to prove that Napoléon Bonaparte had been systematically poisoned with arsenic. By the mid-1960s the timing of the poisoning could also be determined by analyzing the deposits of the poison along a single strand of human hair. Each 5 millimeters of hair length represents fifteen days in the subject's life, while fingernails grow at 0.7 millimeter per week.

The report from the Toronto Center shocked everyone. It read, *"an intake of considerable amounts of arsenic by C. F. Hall in the last two weeks of life."*

Hall's fingernail told the story. The tip contained 24.6 parts per million of arsenic, while the base of the nail contained 76.7 parts per million, an enormous amount. Arsenic was commonly used in the nineteenth century in various medicines. Fowler's Solution (potassium arsenate) was a common remedy for skin eruptions and fevers, and arsphenamine was the drug of choice for syphilis. Loomis notes, " 'Arsenious acid,' comments the *Dispensatory of the United States* of 1875 in one of its longest entries, 'has been exhibited in a variety of diseases.' " Certainly arsenic compounds were among the medical supplies aboard the *Polaris*. But there is no record of the pious Hall's ever having been treated for syphilis, and the only documented medications and injections he received in the last two weeks of his life came from the hand of Emil Bessel. The doctor, for all his careful records, never mentioned using any arsenicals.

Also arsenic was found in high concentrations of 22.0 parts per million in the soil surrounding the grave site. Some might have migrated into the body over the years. Prior treatments and the soil might account for the high levels at the end of the fingernail, but nothing other than ingestion or injection could have produced the extremely high levels found at the base of the nail. And such high levels would have to produce distressing symptoms.

After nearly one hundred years, Charles Francis Hall had cried out from his grave. He had been poisoned.

Suddenly all the signs and symptoms at odds with a stroke fall into place. The too-sweet taste of the coffee, the intense burning of Hall's stomach, the vomiting, difficulty swallowing, dementia, and paralysis are all consistent with acute arsenic poisoning. Even the curious blisters about Hall's mouth are late signs.

But who would have poisoned Hall? And for what reason? The cook and steward initially handled the coffee cup, but they had no reason to poison their commander. Certainly Buddington and Meyer had their differences with Captain Hall and might have handed him the poisoned coffee. However, those two men did not constantly attend Hall during his illness. No one could seriously suspect Tookoolito. Her loyalty to Hall was well demonstrated by her pledge to preserve his writing desk. Despite her efforts to save the contents of the desk, nothing emerged from Hall's papers to shed any new light on his murder. The faithful Morton also is above suspicion.

That leaves only one person with the knowledge and the ready access to arsenic. That same person was frequently by the stricken man's side, administering potions and injecting solutions of his white powder. What better way to poison a person than openly, under the guise of treating him as a patient? With all his prestigious degrees, no one would doubt Emil Bessel's treatment plan. Bessel must have used arsenic from the ship's supplies. Clever criminals commonly used arsenious oxide, which is odorless and tasteless. That substance would definitely not be in the medical supplies. The sweet, metallic taste in the coffee suggests that another arsenic compound was used.

Now, too, Emil Bessel's early prognosis that Hall would never recover makes more sense. The Prussian physician was less a skilled diagnostician than a clever murderer. He made sure his nemesis would not survive, but it took him a second try. The hearty nature of Hall's physique required finishing the job by lethal injections. With all the attention drawn to the strange-tasting coffee and the sudden onset of symptoms after Hall drank it, Bessel probably decided to switch to injecting the arsenic to reduce the incidence of stomach symptoms.

Emil Bessel's inconsistent actions point toward his guilt. When the first cup of coffee had been served to Hall, Bessel insisted he was in the observatory, but Morton and Mauch thought Bessel was present when Hall drank his coffee. The fact that the doctor refused to perform an initial emetic suggests he wanted the poisonous contents of the coffee to remain in Hall's stomach. The later purgatives ensured that the poison would travel the length of the man's digestive tract and would be maximally absorbed rather than vomited out. When Hall rejected his medicine, Bessel's refusal to allow either Buddington or Bryan to sample the potion raises the question of whether the mixture was harmful. What reason had Bessel for continuing his injections of "quinine," which he said were to lower the wildly high temperature, once Hall's temperature had returned to normal? Hall rapidly recovered when he rejected Bessel's treatment. Only after Bryan convinced the captain to place himself under the doctor's care once again did the fatal relapse occur.

For a physician who had hovered over his patient, why did Bessel suddenly race to his observatory when Morton notified him that Hall had taken a severe turn for the worse? Was he trying to establish an alibi?

Bessel's actions surely troubled the examiners. Yet they refused to believe the evidence. Skirting the obvious, they couched their questions so as to get their fears refuted.

"Did you not think there was any difficulty between Captain Hall and any of the scientific party, that would be an inducement for them to do anything toward injuring him?" the board of inquiry had asked George Tyson.

"No, sir," Tyson answered quickly. But then he reflected and replied, "unless a man were a monster he could not do any such thing as that."

What were Bessel's motives? Surely his intense dislike for Hall was enough. As Noah Hayes noted, "the one long night" went far to destroy "moral responsibility." A grain of hatred grows in the

Arctic darkness to monstrous proportions. Jealousy, envy, a desire to lead the expedition—all add to the possible reasons. In France arsenic was known as "the inheritance powder," and Emil Bessel's actions prove that he felt himself best suited to inherit overall command of the expedition. But first he had to create the vacancy. There is no doubt that Bessel underestimated the physical requirements and stamina needed to reach the North Pole by sled. Most members of the expedition did. Since Bessel already considered himself superior to Hall as a scientist, it is easy to surmise that the German doctor felt he would also be a better explorer. The glory of reaching the North Pole would be added to his scientific achievements. Only Charles Francis Hall stood in his way.

Possibly Bessel was working under orders from Bismarck to sabotage the American effort. Did Germany feel threatened by the prospect of an American presence at the North Pole and by closer ties between Denmark and the United States? A strong ally like the United States backing Denmark would not suit Bismarck's goals. Killing Hall guaranteed failure of the expedition and weakened the American presence in the Arctic. In those days an American flag planted at the North Pole would have laid claim to the area for the United States. Looking across the globe, one sees that the North Pole is dangerously close to Germany's North Sea. No documents could be found to substantiate a Prussian plot. But Germany had sought to alter America's actions before this and would attempt to do so in the years to come. The use of Hessian soldiers during the American Revolution and the Zimmerman telegram promising Mexico the return of Texas, Arizona, and New Mexico are two examples, along with two world wars.

Nevertheless, Bessel's ongoing loyalty to Germany demonstrated that he had not transferred his allegiance to the United States. His first telegrams on being saved were to Germany. His first publication of his scientific findings from the *Polaris* expedition was also in German, and he was in no hurry to produce an English version. Eventually he would return to die in the fatherland. Clearly Bessel's allegiance lay somewhere other than the United States—but that alone is not enough to convict a man. However, given the presence of motive, opportunity, and in all likelihood access to the substance that killed Hall, Bessel is the most logical choice.

Was Buddington a willing or unknowing accomplice? His actions after Hall's death suggest that he knew or suspected more than he let on. In E. Vale Blake's *Arctic Experiences*, George Tyson's diary alludes to "an astonishing proposition" made to him by Buddington. Tyson told this to Captain Bartlett while aboard the *Tigress*. Tyson accused Buddington of proposing that the two men take the *Polaris* south into heavily traveled whaling waters and scuttle the ship. According to Buddington, they could then winter on land in relative safety until spring. After being rescued by whalers, the two could collect their pay and avoid any risks. When the *Tigress*'s owner passed this information on to the American Consulate in Scotland, he was advised to keep it secret. Fifty years after the rescue, the family of the owner of the *Tigress* repeated the story.

One other event raises the question of Buddington's complicity with Bessel. On June 4, 1873, when prospects of his two boats' being rescued by sealing ships grew certain, Captain Buddington became deathly ill after eating supper. Davis notes, "Captain Buddington suddenly became very sick, and for a time there was doubt of his recovery. . . ." No one else got sick, and they had all eaten the same hot soup made from captured auks. Buddington's abrupt, severe illness to the point that he was expected to die, followed by an equally rapid recovery, raises the question of another poisoning attempt.

Was Emil Bessel trying to tie up loose ends? Had he tried to poison Buddington because he knew too much? Both men took that answer to their graves.

What we do know is that what came to be called the *Polaris* expedition was beset by problems from its inception. Polar exploration is a daunting task, and the toll that the natural elements exact on human beings is heavy. Charles Francis Hall and the men of the *Polaris* not only had to face the worst that the implacable Arctic had to offer—biting winds, fierce cold, and spirit-numbing darkness. They also engaged in a battle with the darker parts of their own fragile human nature as they explored the other side of heroism. That all but one of them returned from that journey is a remarkable testament both to the whims of fate and to the raw power of human will.

AFTERMATH

In 1874, a year after the *Polaris* inquiry closed, a British admiral wrote, "The navy needs some action to wake it up from the sloth of routine and save it from the canker of prolonged peace." In a direct reference to Charles Francis Hall's grave, he continued, "The rude wooden monument to the intrepid American, standing lone in the Polar solitude, is at the same time a grand memorial, a trophy, *and a challenge.*"

Accordingly the Royal Navy launched the *Alert* and the *Discovery* under Capt. George Nares, with Captain H. F. Stephenson second in command, to assault the North Pole. In the spirit of co-operation, Secretary Robeson offered the British expedition the use of the American stores of coal and supplies stockpiled at Disko and Thank God Harbor. The British gratefully accepted.

While cohesion of their party was far superior to that of the *Polaris*, the Nares expedition fared little better. To guide them, they enlisted the services of Hans, the Inuit, by now a legend in his own time. Retracing Hall's path, Captain Nares stopped at Buddington's winter camp, where "some boxes of books, instruments, etc. were found." Making no attempt to bring them back, the British pushed on. The *Discovery*, under Stephenson, wintered at Lady Franklin Sound, opposite Thank God Harbor, while Nares, in the *Alert*, beat northward.

On their way north, the British passed through Polaris Bay. The ruined remains of Bessel's observatory greeted them in mute testimony. A coil of wire, an ice saw, and the tattered remnants of a canvas tent littered the field. The weathered piece of door marking the head of Hall's grave rose some distance away. Noah Hayes's crowbar maintained its lonely vigil about a foot from the headboard. The ground willow that Sieman had planted covered the mound.

On May 13 Captain Stephenson raised an American flag over the grave and erected a brass plaque at the head of the mound. Brought from England, the tablet read:

Sacred to the Memory of
CAPTAIN C. F. HALL
Of the U.S. ship 'Polaris'
Who sacrificed his life
in the advancement of Science
on Nov. 8, 1871
This tablet has been erected by the British Polar Expedition
of 1875, which, following in his footsteps, has profited
by his experience.

Within weeks disaster would strike the Nares expedition. In a fateful preview of things to come, the British elected to explore northward using manpower instead of dogs to pull their sleds. One group used fifteen men to pull three sledges loaded with two whaleboats and sixty-three days of provisions. With every sled weighing more than two thousand pounds, each crewman pulled four hundred pounds. To cross the hummocks and *sastrugi*, they were forced to cut a road with picks and shovels. Men died of exposure, scurvy, and frostbite before they turned back. For all their sacrifice, they reached 83°71' N, not much farther than Hall had got.

Stumbling back, the party returned to Polaris Promontory. There James Hand, one of their crew, died of scurvy. On June 8, 1875, they buried Hand near Captain Hall's grave. After the turn of the century, Scott would repeat the same fatal mistake of substituting men and ponies for dogs when he attempted to reach the South Pole.

Six years later Adolphus Greely with members of his expedition crossed the straits to visit the site. The lonely, windswept spot had acquired the name of Hall's Rest by now. While Greely searched for cached supplies amid the ruins, a bored Sgt. William Cross carved his name on a broken board at Bessel's observatory. Scarcely one year later the Arctic would claim the life of Sergeant Cross along with eighteen other members of the ill-fated Greely expedition. On that score Greely's group fared far worse than the *Polaris* expedition. Forced to eat their leather clothing to stay alive as George Tyson's party had done, only Greely and six of his men survived.

Ironically among the dead was Dr. Octave Pavy. In a bizarre twist of fate, Dr. Pavy had listened to Charles Francis Hall give his impassioned speech to the American Geographical Society before the *Polaris* sailed. Pavy would accompany Greely as his chief scientist. The European-educated Pavy would hamper Greely's efforts just as Emil Bessel had Hall's. The soldier Greely found Pavy insubordinate and disobedient, while Pavy condescended to deal with his uneducated commander. History repeated itself with fatal results.

The quest to reach the North Pole would continue. Germany, Sweden, Great Britain, and the United States mounted further explorations. Most amassed mountains of scientific data but scarcely passed the highest point reached by Captain Hall. Thirty-eight years after Hall's death, Robert E. Peary reached the top of the world by dogsled with his companion Matthew Henson. Even now controversy swirls about this claim. Richard E. Byrd did land at the North Pole using an airplane in 1926, followed in that same year by Roald Amundsen and Lincoln Ellsworth in a dirigible flown by the Italian Umberto Nobile.

In regard to the survivors of the *Polaris*, some fared better than others. The Inuit Hans almost lost his life when a fit of depression caused him to desert the Nares party. What caused his despair is not mentioned, but it may have been alcohol. British ships even now are not "dry," as the U.S. Navy ships are. Perhaps some infirmity convinced him his useful life was done, and he chose the time-honored Inuit way of removing an unnecessary mouth to feed. Tracking the despondent native down, the British found him huddled in a hole in the snow, prepared to die. They brought him back to camp, and eventually he recovered.

Ebierbing and Tookoolito bought a piece of land with a small house near New London, Connecticut. With their adopted daughter Puney, they lived the life of celebrities while Ebierbing fished the warmer waters.

Tragedy touched the valiant *Tigress*. After she was sold back to the sealing enterprise of Harvey & Company, of St. John's, Newfoundland, her boilers exploded while she was sailing amid the ice. Coming one month shy of a year after the ship had rescued George Tyson and his men, the explosion killed ten of the *Tigress*'s crew outright and burned another eleven so badly that they died the next day. Captain Bartlett emerged unscathed and brought the ruined ship safely home.

Sidney O. Buddington's reputation and career were ruined. He never captained another whaling vessel. In fact, he never returned to sea at the head of any sailing vessel.

Capt. George Tyson returned to the Arctic as the sailing master of another Arctic exploration, headed by Capt. Henry Howgate.

As the only one to salvage his scientific records, Emil Bessel published the findings of his studies in German. Over a period of ten years, he represented a thorn in the side of the Smithsonian. Despite letters from Spencer Baird urging him to accelerate his efforts, Bessel dragged out his work to compile an English version. Ensconced in a small room at the Smithsonian, Bessel grew more acerbic and eccentric with each passing year. A *New York Herald* reporter described Bessel's strange office: "When the portals are entered, passing under the heavy folds of green drapery which nearly hide the entrance, the visitor would suppose he had been suddenly translated into the retreat of Faustus."

Interviewed while the United States prepared for the International Polar Year of 1882, Bessel criticized a failed Arctic exploration under the command of Capt. Henry Howgate, the same Signal Corps officer who had served on the *Polaris* board of inquiry. In discussing Howgate's adventure, Bessel slipped into blending it with his own experience with Captain Hall. Referring to the scientists aboard, he snapped, "They had to submit to the orders of an incompetent, harsh skipper, who most seriously interfered with their duties." However, this time the "incompetent, harsh skipper" was George Tyson.

By 1883 Spencer Baird had had enough. Bessel's salary was cut off, and he received a pithy note from William Rhees, Baird's secretary:

Dear Doctor:

We need immediate possession of the room now occupied by you near the north entrance, as we find it necessary to make improved toilet arrangements for visitors. Please therefore remove your property and greatly oblige.

Yours truly,

WM. J. RHEES

Displaced by a toilet, Bessel returned to Germany. In another twist of fate, in 1888 he died from apoplexy.

Select Bibliography

Blake, E. Vale, ed. *Arctic Experiences, Containing Capt. George E. Tyson's Wonderful Drift on the Ice-Floe, a History of the Po-laris Expedition.* New York: Harper & Brothers, 1874.

Davis, C. H. *Narrative of the North Polar Expedition, U.S. Ship Polaris, Captain Charles Francis Hall Commanding.* Washington, D.C.: Government Printing Office, 1876.

Government Printing Office. *Examination of the Party Separated on the Ice from the United States Steamer Polaris Expedition toward the North Pole.* Washington, D.C.: Government Printing Office, 1873.

Hyde, A., A. C. Baldwin, and W. L. Gage. *The Frozen Zone and Its Explorers: A Comprehensive History of Voyages, Travels, Adventures, Disasters, and Discoveries in the Arctic Regions.* Hartford, Conn.: R. W. Bliss & Company, 1880.

Loomis, Chauncey C. *Weird and Tragic Shores: The Story of Charles Francis Hall, Explorer.* New York: Knopf, 1971.

Sargent, Epes, and W. H. Cunnington. *Wonders of the Arctic World: Together with a Complete and Reliable History of the Polaris Expedition.* Philadelphia: Philadelphia Book Company, 1873.

INDEX

aakkarniq, 22
Advance, 65, 72
Agassiz, Louis, 41
Akasofu, Sun, 130
Albert, 35
Alert, 306
Allen, Captain, 282
American Geographical Society, 14, 46, 47
Amundsen, Roald, 308
Antarctic, 10
Anthing, Frederick, 40, 157, 272–273
Arctic, 280–281, 282
Arctic
  animals of, 65, 69, 84–85, 88, 92, 147, 150–152, 248–249
  British exploration of, 7, 9–13, 16–23
  darkness of winter, 138
  German exploration of, 38
  ice, varieties of, 22–23, 24–25
  lost settlements, 11, 15
  Peary expedition reaches North Pole, 308
  plants of, 154
  post-*Polaris* explorations, 306–308
  and protective clothing, 10, 55, 90
  seasons, 28, 138, 140, 150–151, 154, 172, 182, 237
  U.S. government support of expedition, 6–9
  See also North Pole
Arctic Experiences, Containing Capt. George E. Tyson's Wonderful

Drift on the Ice-Floe (Vale), 294–295, 305
Arctic Ocean, early explorations of, 18, 21
Arctic Research and Life among the Esquimaux (Hall), 34
Arctic Resolution, 8, 23–24
Arctic Voyage of 1635 (Fox), 27
Arrowtah, 239
arsenic poisoning, 301–303
artifacts
  collected on expedition, 91–92
  preparation of animal remains, 93
Augustina, 200
aurora borealis, 4, 126, 223
  creation of, 130
Awahtah, 237
Awahtok, 230–232, 237

Baffin Bay, 18, 185
  opening of, 56, 67
Baffin, William, 18, 21
Baird, Spencer, 35, 36, 41, 265, 266, 276, 283, 309
Barnes, W. K., 289–290
Barrett, William, 299
Barrow Strait, 11, 21
Bartlett, Captain, 262, 309
Bay Roberts, 262
Bayne, Peter, 53, 54
Beale, J., 289
Beaufort Gyral Stream, 70
Beaufort Sea, 12, 18
Beechey Island, and Franklin disaster, 11, 299

Belcher, Sir Edward, 32, 84
Bering Sea, 7, 12
Bessel, Emil
    ambition of, 124, 140–141, 177,
        238, 304
    background information, 35–37
    in Buddington camp, 231, 234,
        238, 239–241, 245
    and death of Hall, 107–118, 269,
        303–305
    disagreements with Buddington,
        136–137, 141–145, 148–149,
        238
    Hall's dislike of, 46, 231
    insubordination of, 53, 55, 58–59,
        74
    persona/behavior of, 83, 103, 112,
        114, 145, 176–177, 204, 309
    photo taking, 148
    plans to reach North Pole, 141–144
    position after Hall's death, 124–125
    reaction to Hall's death, 122,
        123–124
    release from German army, 38–39
    after rescue, 282–283, 304,
        309–310
    selection as chief scientist, 35–39,
        60
    snow blindness, 148, 161, 177, 231
    testimony at investigation, 290–292
    trapped in storm, 127, 135
    work on expedition, 91–92, 167,
        177–178
Bilroth, Theodor, 37
Bismarck, Otto von, 37–38, 39, 304
Booth, John, 79, 168, 205
Braine, D. L., 276
Braine, W., 299
Brevoort, J. Carson, 101
Brooklyn Navy Yard, 28, 32, 44, 48,
    277
Bryan, E. D., 59
Bryan, R. W. D.
    background information, 39–40
    and Buddington camp, 242–245
    and Hall's funeral, 4, 119
    and Hall's illness, 115
    on land expeditions, 88–91

persona of, 87, 137, 204
snow blindness/frostbite, 243–244
special prayers and expedition, 4,
    57, 100
testimony at investigation, 288–289
Buddington, James, 32, 59, 276
Buddington, Sidney O.
    abandons ship with crew, 207,
        210–212, 230–245
    as accomplice to Bessel, 305
    actions after storm, 204–212
    actions during storm, 190–195
    alcohol problem of, 60, 92, 123,
        133, 139, 144–145, 168, 178,
        266, 269, 285
    background information, 30, 122
    disagreements with Bessel,
        136–137, 141–145, 148–149
    disagreements with Hall, 73–74,
        83–84, 98–100, 266
    fears of, 83–84, 120–121, 122–123,
        149, 180
    and Hall's illness, 108, 111–116,
        118, 267
    past feud with Hall, 30–32
    past feud with Tyson, 32–33
    as Polaris commander, 123,
        124–125
    reaction to Hall's death, 120–121,
        122, 267
    after rescue, 309
    rescued, 275–281
    selection as skipper, 30, 32
    testimony at investigation, 283–288
Bull, John, 7
Byrd, Richard E., 308

Cabot, 280
Cabot, John, 17
Cabot, Sebastian, 17
Campbell, Walter, 79, 105, 168, 188,
    205
Canada, exploration for trade route,
    18–19
Canada Basin, 70
cannibalism, 224–225
Cape Brevoort, 101
Cape Constitution, 147, 178

Cape Disaster, 159
Cape Farewell, 38
Cape Folly, 159, 160
Cape Frazer, 178
Cape Grinnell, 185
Cape Horn, 7
    dangers of, 18
Cape Lupton, 92, 155, 160
Cape York, 276, 278
Carin Point, 206
Catalpa, 283
celestial navigation, 72
Chase, Salmon P., 13
Chester, Hubbard, 204, 206
    background information, 39
    and Buddington camp, 231–233,
        237, 241, 244–245
    and Hall's funeral, 118–119
    and Hall's grave, 170–171
    and Hall's illness, 111–118
    land expedition with Hall, 97,
        100–106
    look-out for survivors, 208
    testimony at investigation, 289
    and whaleboat expeditions,
        149–150, 156–166
Christian, Hans, 56, 65–66, 88, 119
    end of mission, 277
    on Nares expedition, 306, 308
    son born to, 174–175
    and survival on floe, 218, 220–221,
        223–224, 226, 227, 248
    wife of, 200
chronometer, 71–72
Civil War, 7, 15, 30
clothing, protective, 10, 55, 90
Coffin, Nathan, 48, 49, 211
    and Buddington camp, 231, 241,
        244
    and Hall's funeral, 118–119
    mental problems of, 125, 134
    testimony at investigation, 289
Coleman, Patrick, shooting by Hall,
        52–54
Colfax, Vice President, 23–24
Colfax, Schuyler, 8
Commagere, Frank Y., 277
compass, uselessness of, 70, 143

Congress, 48, 49, 56–59
Coppermine River, 23
Countess of Warwick Sound, 15
Cox, Joseph, 41
crew of Polaris
    division during expedition, 51–52,
        76, 247
    German, 35–39, 40, 51
    muster roll, xiii
    scientific contingent, 33–41
    selection of, 29–43
Cross, William, 297, 307
Crozier, Francis R. M., 209–210
Crozier Island, 178
Cunnington, William H., 293–294

Daily Press, 12
Davenport, Captain, 59–61, 121
Davis, C. H., 136, 155, 295
Davis Strait, 7, 18, 68, 229
DeLange, Captain, 262
Delano, Mr., 44, 46
DeLong, George Washington, 276
Devon Island, 56
diet. See food
Discovery, 306
Disko, 56–57, 77, 228–229
dovekies, 248

Ebierbing (Joe), 15, 30–31, 49, 88,
        109, 193
    after rescue, 308
    on rescue mission, 277, 278
    and survival on floe, 215–218, 220,
        222, 223–224, 227, 228, 246,
        248, 251, 258
    testimony at investigation, 271
Elberg, Lowertz, 67
Elisha Kent Kane Society, 46
Ellesmere Island, 56, 69, 70, 92,
        100–101, 234
Ellsworth, Lincoln, 308
Enterprise, 21
Erebus, 9, 11, 14, 16, 209
Erik the Red, 64
Eskimo. See Inuit
Etah, 230, 232, 234
Etookejeu, 234

Evallu, 234–235
evu, 157–158
Ewinokshua, 240
exploration versus academic
    knowledge, 20–21, 33–34
eyes
    light sensitivity of, 146–147
    snow blindness, 22, 148, 152, 161

Folly Bay, 159
food
    of Buddington camp, 233, 234,
        237, 238, 243, 244
    cannibalism, 224–225
    food poisoning, 107, 249
    fresh meat, 92, 147–148, 150–152,
        222, 226, 227–228, 249
    hunger, effects of, 224, 227, 228,
        250, 251–252, 256
    hunting for, 150–152, 216–217,
        220, 222, 224, 226–228, 233,
        237, 244, 248–249
    Inuit and sharing, 201, 209–210
    lead poisoning from, 11
    nutritional deficiencies, 126, 148,
        228, 235, 262
    of officers versus crew, 93–94
    after starvation, effects of, 250,
        262–263
    of survivors on floe, 201, 216, 219,
        220–222, 224–228, 248
    typical meal, 92
Forshufvud, Sten, 301
Fox, 14, 35
Fox, Luke, 27
Foxe Channel, 54
Franklin, Lady Jane, 11–12, 42, 49
Franklin, Sir John, 9–12
    British search for, 11–12
    disappearance of, 9–10, 11
    Hall's search for, 12–14, 15–16,
        209–210
Frobisher, Sir Martin, 15, 17
Frolic, 263, 264, 265
frostbite
    mechanism in, 10–11
    protection against, 10
    treatment of, 11

fur trade, 18
Fury, 22

Gannett, Henry, 55
Geographic Society of Paris, 295
George Henry, 14, 29, 30, 52
George M. Robeson, 149, 160–161
Georgiana, 29
Germania, 38
Germans
    problems as crew members, 51–52,
        58–59, 66, 121
    selection as crew members, 35–39,
        40
    survivors on floe, 223, 226
Germany
    and involvement in Arctic
        expedition, 37–39
    possible hidden agenda of, 304
Gignoux, Tom, 297, 299
glaciers, Greenland, 64
Godhavn, Disko, 56
gold, and Arctic explorations, 17
Goldsborough, Admiral, 265, 283
Grady Harbor, 261
Grand Banks of Newfoundland, 50
Grant Land, 92
Grant, Ulysses S., 4, 6, 8, 24, 44
    and *Polaris* inquiry, 263–264
    and rescue mission, 276–277
Great Britain
    lost Franklin expedition, 9–12
    North Pole expeditions of, 7, 9–13,
        17–23
Great Fish River, 23
Greely, Adolphus, 307–308
Greenland
    and Arctic expeditions, 19, 20
    geographical landscape of, 63–65
    German interest in, 37–38
    icebergs of, 67–68
    Polaris anchoring, 55–59
Greenwich meridian, 70
Greer, Commander, 277–280
Grinnel, Henry, 13–14, 47, 49, 54
Grinnell Land, 92
Griper, 21
guns, arming crew, 134–135, 223

Hall, Anna (daughter), 49
Hall Basin, 73, 296, 300
Hall, Charles Francis
  as authority, 45, 51–52, 60, 109
  background information on, 9, 13,
    49
  and death of Coleman, 52–54
  death of, 107–119
  first exploration of Arctic, 12–15
  forensic studies of, 296–303
  funeral of, 1–5, 119
  gravesite tended by crew, 170–171
  illustration of, 13
  investigation of death, 266–272,
    288–293
  last dispatch of, 103–104
  last expedition north, 100–107
  and lost Franklin expedition,
    12–14, 15–16, 209–210
  maps of, 15
  motives for murder of, 303–305
  northernmost point reached by,
    103–104, 165, 167, 307, 308
  posthumous recognition, 293, 295
  pre-expedition misgivings, 41–43,
    77–78
  and preparation of *Periwinkle*,
    24–27
  and selection of crew, 29–43
Hall, Charles (son), 49, 50
Hall, Mary (wife), 49–50
Hall's Rest, 307
Halsted, William Stewart, 37
Hand, James, 307
Hansa, 38, 226
Harper's Illustrated Weekly, 264
Harrison, John, 71
Hartnell, John, 299
Hartstene Bay, 72
Hayes, Dr. Isaac, 13, 14, 31, 34–35,
  47, 65, 72
Hayes, Noah, 40, 204
  and Hall's funeral, 4, 119
  job on ship, 137
Hayes Sound, 238
Hecla, 21–23
Heggleman, 26, 160–165, 169
Henry, Joseph, 35, 36, 41, 276

Henry VIII, 17
Henson, Matthew, 308
Herron, John, 49, 58, 86, 148
  diary entries of, 273
  with survivors on floe, 196, 225,
    246, 248–250
  testimony at investigation, 271–272
Hobby, Henry, 112–113, 120–121,
  124, 204, 241
Holsteinsborg, Greenland, 55
Howgate, Henry, 265, 309
Hudson Bay, 17
Hudson Bay Trading Company, 12,
  18, 23
Hudson, Henry, 17–18, 19, 138
Humboldt Glacier, 56, 69, 181, 238
hunting
  and Buddington's camp, 233, 237,
    244
  expeditions, 88, 150–152
  and survivors on floe, 216–217,
    220, 222, 224, 226–228,
    248–249
hypothermia
  mechanism of, 69–70, 89–90
  mental effects of, 90, 91, 201
  treatment of, 90–91

ice
  dangers of, 22–23, 24–25, 80–84
  floating islands, 156–158
  of Greenland, 64
  hypothermia, 69–70, 89–90
  Inuit words for, 22
  movement at North Pole, 70
  pack ice attack *(evu)*, 157–158
  slush *(qinuq)*, 205
  variations in, 22–23
ice grenades, 297–298
icebergs, 67–68, 79, 85, 157–159,
  166–167
  for shelter. *See* Providence Berg
Iceland, 38
igloos, 102, 218
imarnirsaq, 22, 250
International Polar Year (1882), 309
Intrepid, 281
Inui, 175

Inuit
    attire for cold, 10, 55, 90
    beliefs/customs of, 5, 31, 131, 174
    birthing method, 174
    boats of, 26–27
    with Buddington's camp, 230–231,
        234–235, 237, 239–242
    burial of dead, 241–242
    children of, 200
    Hall's interaction with, 15
    as hunters, 216–217, 220, 222, 224,
        226–228, 237, 244, 248–249
    hypothermia treatment of, 91
    ice, terms for, 22
    igloo building, 218
    on Polaris expedition, 49, 56–57,
        65–66
    after rescue, 264, 307, 308
    seal oil lamps of, 192, 218
    sharing of provisions, behavior
        related to, 201, 209–210
    snow blindness goggles, 161
    tattoos of, 234
    testimony at investigation, 270–271
    with Tyson's group, 191–193,
        196–197, 200, 201, 216–217,
        220, 222, 224, 226–228
    white man's attitude toward,
        30–31, 174, 225
investigation of Polaris disaster,
        263–276
    Bessel's testimony, 290–292
    Bryan's testimony, 288
    Buddington's testimony, 283–288
    Chester's testimony, 289
    conclusions of, 274–275, 293
    foreign crew testimony, 272–273
    of Hall's death, 266–272, 288–293
    Herron's testimony, 271–272
    Inuit testimony, 270–271
    journals of crew in, 273–274,
        279–280
    Meyer's testimony, 267–270
    and missing Hall documents,
        266–267, 269–270, 271, 280,
        287
    Tyson's testimony, 265–267
Investigator, 21

Jackson, William, 86, 93–94, 106,
        111, 214, 246
    testimony at investigation, 273
Jakobshavn Glacier, 64
Jamka, Frederick, 40, 201, 272
Jim, 242
Johnson, Peter, 190, 223, 272–273
Jones Sound, 56
Juniata, 275–276, 278

Kane Basin, 56, 69
Kane, Dr. Elisha Kent, 39, 41, 46,
        47, 65–66, 72–73, 234–235,
        242
Kennedy Channel, 56, 69, 72, 152,
        172, 178
King, John, 17
King William Island, 16, 209
Knuth, Eigel, 298–299
Kocher, Emil Theodor, 37
Kodlunarn Island, 15
Koldewey, Captain, 38
Kruger, J. W., 40, 164–165, 222,
        246–247, 272
    on rescue mission, 277

Labrador Current, 68
Lady Franklin Sound, 306
Lancaster Sound, early explorations
        of, 11, 12, 18, 21
land expeditions
    distances, deception related to, 88
    Halls's last, 100–107
    hunting, 88, 150–152
    igloos, use of, 102
    treacherous conditions, 88–91
    See also sled trips
Lapland, 17, 180
Le Vesconte, H. T. D., 16
lead poisoning, from tinned food,
        11
Lifeboat Cove, 206, 212, 230, 234
light deprivation, effects of, 138,
        146–147
Lincoln Sea, 69, 101
Lind, James, 126
Lindermann, William, 129
    on rescue mission, 277

Lingquist, Gustavus, 190
  on rescue mission, 277
  with survivors on floe, 194–196,
    223
  testimony at investigation, 272–273
Little Juniata, 276, 278
Littleton Island, 206, 220, 278
Lomonosov Ridge, 70
longitude, measurement of, 70–71
Loomis, Charles C., 296–300

McClintock, Francis, 14, 42
McGary Island, 278
Mackenzie River, 12, 23
Makarov Basin, 70
maniillat, 22
maps, Hall as cartographer, 15
Mauch, Joseph, 40, 204
  after Hall's death, 137, 140
  and Hall's illness, 112–113, 115
  as log-keeper, 61, 66, 105–106, 115
  lost in cold, 89–91
measurement instruments
  ineffectiveness in Arctic, 70–71
  thermometers, 85
melatonin, and light deprivation, 138
Melville, Herman, 48
Melville Island, 21
Merkut (Christiana), 200
  birth of son, 174–175
Meyer, Frederick
  background information, 40
  diary entries of, 273
  insubordination of, 53, 58–59, 61
  reaction to Hall's death, 121
  scientific expeditions, 88–90, 140
  with survivors on floe, 195–196,
    219–220, 223, 247, 254–255,
    256
  testimony at investigation, 267–270
Miouk, 230–232, 241
Molloy, Mr., 262–263
Monticello, 39
Morton, William, 106–107, 204
  background information, 39, 65–66
  diary entries of, 273–274
  frostbite injury, 125–126
  and Hall's funeral, 118–119

  and Hall's illness, 108, 111, 112,
    116–118
mukluks, 90
Muscovy Company, 17, 180
musk ox, 150–152
muster roll of *Polaris,* xiii

Nansen Basin, 70
Nares, George, 306–307
*Narrative of the North Pole
    Expedition* (Davis), 136, 295
narwhals, 248–249
National Academy of Sciences, 33, 35,
    276
Neafles & Levy, 25
New London, Connecticut, 49, 50
New York Herald, 277, 282
Newfoundland, and Arctic
    explorations, 17
Newman Bay, 73, 101, 139, 144, 160
Newman, John Philip, 4, 44, 49, 57,
    61, 100
Newton, Dr. Robert, 41
Nobile, Umberto, 308
North Pole
  basins of, 70
  latitude of, 19–20
  measurement instruments,
      ineffectiveness of, 70–71
  moving ice of, 70
  See also Arctic
Northumberland Island, 220, 278
Northwest Passage, 9
  advantages of, 7
  search for, 17–23
nunataks, 63
Nunivak Island, 296

Observatory Bluff, 2, 173
Odell, Alvin, 96, 168, 173, 192, 205
  background information, 49
Oelrichs & Company, 39
oogjook, 249
oomiak, 26, 69, 234, 235
Open Polar Sea, 65
Open Polar Sea, The (Hayes), 34
optical illusions, paraselene, 131
Owwer, 209

Paddock, Franklin, 299
pancake ice, dangers of, 22–23
paraselene, 131
Parry, William Edward, explorations
    of, 9–10, 21–23
Pavy, Octave, 308
Peary, Robert E., 72, 308
Periwinkle, 7–8
    preparation for Arctic voyage,
        24–27
    See also Polaris
Petermann, August, 35, 38, 283
Phipps, W. W., 297
polar bear, 147, 184, 237, 251
Polar Exploration, The (Cunnington),
    293–294
Polaris
    effects of cold on, 81–82, 85–87,
        96, 135–136, 145–146
    effects of storms on, 126–132, 145,
        189–197
    exploratory boats of, 26
    illustrations of, xii, 45, 132, 195
    limitations of, 27
    preparation for Arctic voyage,
        24–27
    special boilers of, 26, 61
    wreck of, 232–233, 236–237, 244
Polaris disaster
    abandoning ship, 207, 210–212
    crew abandons ship (Buddington's
        group), 207, 210–212,
        230–245
    crew on ice floe (Tyson's group),
        213–229, 246–261
    crew remaining on ship
        (Buddington's group), 204–212
    crew separated from ship (Tyson's
        group), 189–204, 208
    inquiry. *See* investigation of *Polaris*
        disaster
    official report on, 136, 155, 295
    rescue of (Buddington's group),
        275–281
    rescue of (Tyson's group), 258–264
Polaris expedition
    artifacts collected, 91–92, 93
    attempt to sail home, 176–180

books published about, 293–295
coal usage, 139–140, 160, 162,
    173, 182, 183, 207, 232, 236
crew of. *See* crew of *Polaris*
damage to ship, 136, 145–146,
    153–154, 159, 162, 164,
    205–206, 210–211
disorder after Hall's death,
    133–134, 136–139, 169
flaws of expedition, 33, 40–43, 48,
    59–61
freed from iceberg, 175–176
by land. *See* land expeditions; sled
    trips
pre-sail events, 44–49
progress reports (floating bottles),
    45
saboteur aboard, 61, 168
science versus exploration
    confusion, 40–43, 46, 55,
    58–59
trapped in ice, 1–2, 80–84,
    179–189
trapped/lifted by iceberg, 131–132,
    145–146, 150, 159, 163–164,
    172–173
whaleboat expeditions, 149–151,
    155–166
winter home of, 84–88, 132–147
Polaris (star), and navigation, 72
Polaris Bay, 73, 84
Polaris, Charles, 174–175, 192, 200,
    228
Port Foulke, 72, 73, 139
Prince of Wales, 9
Providence Berg, 85, 128, 159, 162,
    166–167
    capsize/splitting of, 172–173, 175,
        179–180
    effects of storm on, 129–132, 135
    illustration of, 132
Pugh, George, 13
Puney, 49, 200, 308

qinuq, 205
Quayle, John, 14, 31
quinine, 111
quppaq, 22

Ravenscraig, 280–281
Reid, William, 282
reindeer hide clothing, 55
Rensselaer Harbor, 72
Repulse Bay, 53
Repulse Harbor, 81
Rescue, 29
Resolute, 32
Reynolds, Commodore, 265
Rhees, William, 309–310
Robeson Channel, 73, 79, 100, 101, 104
Robeson, George, 35, 44, 45, 47, 124–125
   and *Polaris* inquiry, 264–267, 271, 274–277
   and rescue mission, 277
Robeson Straits, 160, 172
Ross, James, 21
Ross, Sir John, 12, 18
Royal Society, 20
Russian Trading Company, 18

Saint Brendan, 67
St. John's, Newfoundland, 50–51, 262
Sargent, Epes, 294
sastrugi, 22, 70, 75, 189, 220, 239, 240, 307
Schoonmaker, Commander, 265
Schuman, Emil
   background information, 40
   and Hall's illness, 113
   problems of, 48
   work during expedition, 80, 96, 168, 182, 183, 189–190, 193–194, 205, 206
Schurz, Carl, 37
Scoresby, William, expeditions of, 19–21
Scott, Robert, 66, 138
scow, destruction by ice, 171
scurvy, 126, 148, 227, 235, 262
   prevention of, 126
seal oil lamps, 192, 218
sealskin clothing, 10
shamanism, 31
Sherman, John, 8

Sherman, William Tecumseh, 8
Sieman, Herman, 40, 82, 126–127, 164–165, 204
   diary entries of, 274, 291
   and Hall's illness, 108–109, 112
sikurluk, 22
Sisimiut, 55
sled dogs
   aboard *Polaris,* 65, 66, 86, 113, 176
   used as food, 221, 234
sled trips
   of early explorers, 21–22
   experienced crew, 75–76
   hunting trips, 88, 92, 93
   inexperienced crew, 140
   led by Bessel, 147, 238–241
   powered by men, 142, 145
Smith, Karrup, 57
Smith Organ Company, 27
Smith Passage, 220
Smith Sound, 56, 67, 69, 181, 184
Smithsonian Institution, 33, 35
snow blindness, 22, 148, 152, 161
   Inuit goggles for, 161
Somerset Island, early explorations of, 12, 18, 21
Sonntag, August, 244
Southhampton Island, 17
starvation, effects of, 224, 227, 228, 250, 251–252, 256
Stephenson, H. F., 306–307
Succi, 200
Sultana, 80
Sumner Headlands, 73
sunlight, light deprivation, 138

Tallapoosa, 265, 283
Tamerlane, 16
Tasiussaq, 63, 66
Terror, 9, 11, 14, 209
Thank God Harbor, 85, 101, 123, 128, 241, 296
thermometers, 85, 110
thrumming, 183
Tigress, 260–262, 277–278, 280, 305, 309
Tobias, 200

Tookoolito (Hannah), 15, 30–31, 49, 119, 192–193
  and birth of infant, 174
  and Hall's illness, 109, 115
  and Hall's letters, 193
  after rescue, 308
  separated from ship, 192–193, 196–197
  survival provisions of, 192
  testimony at investigation, 270–271
Torrington, John, 299
Trent affair, 7
Tutkeeta, 209
Tyson, George
  background information, 29–30
  with crew on ice floe, 189–204, 208, 213–229, 246–261
  disapproval of Buddington/Bessel, 137, 150
  as explorer, 75–76
  and Hall's funeral, 4, 119
  and Hall's illness, 108, 113–114
  official commission for, 57
  past feud with Buddington, 32–33
  after rescue, 309
  on rescue mission, 277–280
  rescued, 258–264
  support of Hall, 74–75, 83–84
  testimony at investigation, 265–267
  and whaleboat expeditions, 149–150, 156, 159–166

United States, 72
Upernavik, 56, 63, 276
U.S. government
  investigation of Polaris expedition, 263–276
  rescue mission for Buddington party, 275–281
  support of Arctic expedition, 6–9, 23–24, 33–35
U.S. Grant, 149, 156, 157, 158

Vale, E. Blake, 51, 294–295, 305
Vancouver, Sir George, 18–19
Victory, 23
Von Otto, Frederick, 56

Walker, Dr. David, 35
walrus, 69
Walrus, 262
Washington Navy Yard, 24, 28, 44, 264
Weird and Tragic Shores (Loomis), 298
Wellington Channel, 11
West Greenland Current, 55
whaleboats
  destruction of, 157–159
  expeditions, 149–151, 155–166
  of survivors on floe, 197, 199, 202, 214–215, 217, 219, 253
Whaleman's Chapel, 74
whaling
  products of, 7
  profits of, 7, 16
  voyages to north, 122
whiteouts, 2
Wilkes, Charles, 47–48
Willoughby, Sir Hugh, 17, 180
witches gold, 17
Wonders of the Arctic World, The (Sergent), 294

ABOUT THE AUTHOR

RICHARD PARRY is a retired surgeon whose practice was based in Fairbanks, Alaska. He now lives in Sun City, Arizona. He is the author of three acclaimed novels about Wyatt Earp, as well as *That Fateful Lightning: A Novel of Ulysses S. Grant*.